LESSONS FROM ABROAD

LESSONS FROM ABROAD

How Other Countries Educate Their Children

Richard P. McAdams, Ed.D.

TECHNOMIC
PUBLISHING CO., INC.
LANCASTER · BASEL

Lessons from Abroad
a **TECHNOMIC**® publication

Published in the Western Hemisphere by
Technomic Publishing Company, Inc.
851 New Holland Avenue, Box 3535
Lancaster, Pennsylvania 17604 U.S.A.

Distributed in the Rest of the World by
Technomic Publishing AG
Missionsstrasse 44
CH-4055 Basel, Switzerland

Cover Design by Patricia McAdams

Printed in the United States of America
10 9 8 7 6 5 4 3 2

Main entry under title:
    Lessons from Abroad: How Other Countries Educate Their Children

A Technomic Publishing Company book
Bibliography: p. 329
Includes index p. 335

Library of Congress Catalog Card No. 93-60192
ISBN No. 0-87762-986-2

To My Parents
Richard P. and Julia E. McAdams
My First and Best Teachers

CONTENTS

Chapter 7: Japan—A Culture Shapes Its Schools   193

Chapter 8: Comparing Schools in Six Cultures   229

Chapter 9: Cultural and Societal Influences on the Schools   271

Chapter 10: Lessons for America's Schools   295

THIS IS A book that will shake the educational reform establishment to its roots. It is a book that boldly challenges some of the major assumptions of how to go about improving schools in America. It is a book that practitioners, professors, and policy leaders will have to read and confront. I hope it is not too late to be able to recast educational reform to include some of McAdams' findings.

Richard McAdams was curious. Were America's schools all *that bad?* Smart enough to know that many of the reformers have their own axes to grind, and many, too many, have never had much real experience in running schools, McAdams decided to ask a unique group of people who had worked in American schools what was right and wrong about them. He decided to query the foreign teaching corps that came to America as Fulbright exchange teachers. These talented foreign pedagogues brought experienced professional training and fresh eyes to what U.S. schools were all about. McAdams went to learn from them directly in Washington, D.C. He got to know them. This book is about what he learned.

It ought to be remembered that on most international comparisons of educational achievement, the U.S. fares very poorly. The Fulbright exchange teachers from abroad represent many countries that are ahead of the U.S. in academic achievement. What are they doing that we are not? What McAdams learned was that some of our ideas of reforms have very little to do with improving education, and a lot to do with changing governance patterns that may have little or nothing to do with really upgrading American schools to *world class standards.*

Here is what awaits the reader of this book:

- Foreign exchange teachers noted that their American colleagues worked a longer day than they did, and performed menial duties such as bus and bathroom duties, among others.

- Foreign teachers in American schools saw that American parents have a greater say in their children's education than foreign parents, and are chiefly responsible for grade inflation in American schools.
- American teachers are very vulnerable to parental pressure and American parents view teachers with considerably less respect than foreign parents view their teachers.
- The American concept of local control accounts for two things foreign teachers found hard to accept: a potpourri curriculum and terrible discrepancies in the funding base between school districts in the U.S. Foreign teachers found the fiscal discrepancies in American education very disconcerting.
- Because of the presence of a national exam in their countries, foreign parents want their teachers to be as hard as possible on their students, preparing them to take and pass the exam. Because there is no national exam in the U.S., American parents want high grades and want easier teachers. American teachers are viewed as antagonists and impediments by parents instead of as friends, as they are more apt to be viewed abroad.
- The presence of the automobile in American culture and the desire by American students to acquire one, result in less emphasis on developing a full intellectual life and high academic standards. Some foreign countries severely limit the extent to which their students can hold jobs outside of their schools.
- American students expect more tests and quizzes than the foreign exchange teachers gave their own students back home.

McAdams has been able to capture these foreign pedagogues' perspectives with a minimum of defensiveness. After all, he has been a U.S. teacher and superintendent of schools. I'm sure at times he must have had to swallow hard, and I'm sure he must have winced at some of the Fulbright exchange teachers' fresh insights into practices American educators have long taken for granted.

The one lesson that McAdams' book teaches forcefully is that *a nation's schools are inevitably linked to its culture,* and the dominant values of that culture. To that extent, American schools are in trouble because American society is in trouble.

The second lesson that McAdams' book brings home is that we will never be able to attain *world class standards* until we better understand other nations' educational systems and their cultures as well. *World class standards* cannot be divorced from the world and its cultures. To truly understand the nature of such benchmarks, we must bring to the discussion more than a knowledge of psychometrics.

I wish I had read this book sooner. I wish it had been written sooner. If it had been, I'm sure some of the reform package would have been different in Kentucky, as I suspect it would have been elsewhere.

McAdams' *Lessons from Abroad* is for us, about us, and involves us. What he has done is hold up the world's cultures as a mirror to our schooling practices. I am sure the reader will see old landscape with new eyes as I did. You will never look at American education the same way again.

Betty E. Steffy

Associate Professor of Educational Administration, College of Education, University of Kentucky and former Deputy Superintendent of Instruction, Kentucky Department of Education

A BOOK SUCH as this, by its nature, requires the cooperation and assistance of many individuals. First and foremost, I would like to acknowledge the assistance and encouragement of Dr. Jochen Hoffmann, Chief of the Teacher Exchange Branch of the United States Information Agency, for helping me to contact the Fulbright Exchange teachers visiting the United States during the 1991 – 1992 school year. My thanks also to Senior Program Officers Ilo-Mai Harding and Charles Raisner of the Fulbright Exchange for their efforts in my behalf. Winifred Flanagan of the Fulbright Program and Maurice Feldman of the International Visitors Center of Maryland were also of great assistance in helping me to meet and interact with the Fulbright Exchange teachers.

Stephanie Sisle of the Fulbright Program was helpful in providing me with publications directed toward exchange teachers in the countries included in my study. Judith Cantley of the Central Bureau in Scotland provided much useful material on education in the United Kingdom. My thanks also to Beth Davis, an American teacher and friend of the author, for sharing her experiences as a Fulbright Exchange teacher in Canada.

My special thanks are extended to the following Fulbright Exchange teachers who spoke with me at length about the schools in their home countries: Knud Kolbaek, Annette Priskorn, and Annelise Brondsted of Denmark; Ulrike Kolling, Ursula Nold, Sibylle Riel-Kermann, Renate Korte, Susanne Baeuml, and Dagmar Pohl of Germany; Angela Potter, Anthony Cox, Vicki Coalter, Stephen Hale, and Pamela Simpson of England; and Florence Graham, Elaine Friend, Dale McKinnon, and Lila Korol of Canada.

My appreciation also to Chieko Yamada, a Japanese juku teacher, and Yumiko Ito, a foreign exchange student from Japan, who shared their knowledge of the Japanese educational system with me. A special debt of gratitude is acknowledged to Florence Graham, Knud Kolbaek,

Angela Potter, Ursula Nold, and Chieko Yamada, who provided a written critique of the initial draft of the chapter on the home country of each.

The information reported on daily life in the schools of the survey countries is based upon extensive interviews with the Fulbright teachers about the schools in their native countries. I assume full responsibility for any errors of fact or interpretation regarding day-to-day school life in these countries. I would also like to thank my editor, Joe Eckenrode, and his able assistants, Susan Farmer and Leo Motter, for their insight and encouragement at every stage of the publishing process.

TEN YEARS HAVE passed since a clarion call for educational reform was sounded from the White House Rose Garden with the release of the Presidential Commission's report, *A Nation at Risk*. Countless initiatives in thousands of locations have been tried in the name of school reform. Many such attempts have been quietly abandoned while others, such as school choice in Minnesota and site-based management in Chicago, exhibit the staying power of an idea whose time has come.

A perceived strength of America's schools, the autonomy and power implicit in local control, actually impedes the adoption of successful reforms beyond their initial experimental site. Reform efforts usually attack educational problems in a piecemeal fashion, failing to address many elements that, collectively, could produce significant school improvement. Regrettably, political infighting among various educational interest groups often hinders innovation and creates a policymaking gridlock.

There are countries abroad that provide a nationwide laboratory for many of the educational innovations proposed for America's schools. A closer look at how several of these countries educate their children, as well as the political process for setting educational policies, suggests a multitude of initiatives that could be profitably adapted to the American scene. A survey of foreign schools also permits an objectivity in examining the relationship between a nation's culture and its schools that is difficult to obtain when examining our own American schools. This cultural dimension highlights the general societal influences that impact on the relative success or failure of a nation's schools.

Since real life rarely conforms to policy guidelines, I have conducted interviews with foreign teachers to discover how educational policies and practices abroad are given expression at the local school level. Except for the Japanese interviewees, the teachers were Fulbright Exchange teachers in the United States during the 1991 – 1992 school year.

These educators, having taught both in the United States and in their native countries, offered valuable insights regarding educational practices both at home and in the United States.

Throughout this book I have attempted to bring a researcher's objectivity to a subject that has been my life's work for twenty-five years, twenty of them as a school principal and district superintendent. A local school district superintendent represents the interface, or even a buffer, between the daily realities of school life, and the expectations of the general society regarding its schools. This perspective allows me to understand the frustrations of opinion leaders regarding the intractable problems of our schools, as well as the justifiable resentment of teachers to the unreasonable criticisms of misinformed critics.

Such critics of public education, most often speaking from the Olympian heights of major think tanks, newspaper editorial offices, and universities, do bring a certain detachment and objectivity to identifying our educational deficiencies. Their ignorance of the daily realities and constraints faced by American educators, however, leads them to propose inadequate and often naive solutions to our educational crisis.

The unrelenting barrage of criticism directed toward educators, a constant in the American culture throughout my twenty-five years in public education, has created a siege mentality within the education profession. This defensiveness leaves us unreasonably resistant to reforms such as statewide curricula and student assessments, the development of rigorous standards of academic performance, and various school choice proposals.

My hope is that both public educators and their critics will, through this book, stand shoulder to shoulder to look at how other countries educate their children. All concerned will learn much that confirms their current thinking about the problems in our schools. They will also learn of successful practices abroad that should lead them to reevaluate some of their previous assumptions. This exercise will allow all concerned to identify practical strategies to significantly improve public education in a systematic fashion.

CHAPTER 1

Schooling Across Cultures

BALTIMORE, MARYLAND, SEPTEMBER 26, 1991 — The moonlit night in Baltimore's Inner Harbor illuminated the sailing ships gliding slowly out to sea. The tall masts of the *U.S.S. Constellation,* moored along the harbor walkway, and the pungent aroma of fish and the bay, created a memorable setting for the visiting tourists. Gathered around outdoor tables at Phillips' restaurant, hungry tourists sipped their drinks and enjoyed the local delicacy, Maryland crabcakes. Five other visitors were engaged in animated conversation as they leisurely strolled along the waterfront on this balmy early autumn night.

All five were visiting teachers from foreign countries who were taking part in the Fulbright Teacher Exchange Program. All were in their late twenties to early thirties, and filled with anticipation and excitement as they began their year as exchange teachers. Along with fifteen other foreign teachers assigned to schools in the Middle Atlantic States, they were attending a regional meeting sponsored by the Fulbright Exchange Program. During the two-day meeting they would share their initial impressions of American schools and society.

On this first evening, however, their conversation was both informal and varied, covering the whole spectrum of their experiences in America. Two of the teachers were women from Germany. One, with brown hair and brown eyes, exhibited a serious and reserved demeanor. The other one, a blue-eyed blonde, used self-deprecating humor and a tone of wry amusement in relaying her attempt to "grapple with the blizzard of paperwork" that confronted her during her first weeks teaching in an American high school.

The young woman from Cyprus had the dark hair, piercing eyes, and olive complexion characteristic of people from the Mediterranean region. She told of her disbelief when a student asked her for a wooden lavatory pass to visit the bathroom. "I told the student to stop trying to fool her new teacher," she said, "and the entire class broke out in

1

laughter." Pierre, with black wavy hair atop a six-foot-two-inch athletic frame, fit the mold of the dashing young Frenchman. Exuding an air of confidence, he marveled at "the informality of American students, the open and friendly way that they greeted their new teacher from France."

The teacher from Colombia, a young man of medium height, solid physique, and dark hair, interspersed his comments on American education with more personal concerns. He had just finished a phone call to the girl that he was engaged to marry back in Colombia. He was beginning to worry about the logistics of this long-distance romance, and his fiancee's unenthusiastic response to his decision to spend a year in the United States.

As the five teachers continued their walk they shared their wonder, amusement, and consternation regarding many aspects of American schools. One commented upon the docility of the students. Another spoke with bemusement of the apparently universal practice of reciting the Pledge of Allegiance at the beginning of each school day. A third found the easy access to higher education in America quite impressive. Several noted the surprisingly heavy work load of American teachers. Heda from Germany ruefully remarked that "Americans seem to live for work."

FIRST IMPRESSIONS OF THE FULBRIGHT TEACHERS

These teachers, and 100 others, first met at the Fulbright Program's general orientation program held at American University in Washington D.C. in early August. There they learned what to expect from American schools, American culture, and Americans themselves. Six weeks later these foreign visitors were eager to compare notes.

Almost everyone found the cultural adjustment to be far more difficult than expected. Everyday activities such as driving and shopping were surprisingly different in America. Assumptions, teaching techniques, and practices that had worked for years in their home country were often ineffective or irrelevant in the United States. American practices regarding homework assignments and frequency of testing were two instructional issues that the exchange teachers found particularly perplexing. The Baltimore meeting provided a welcome opportunity for them to share their initial experiences with other Fulbright Exchange teachers. They soon found that what they had felt and seen during their first few weeks in America also formed the common experiences of their Fulbright colleagues.

The formal meeting for these exchange teachers occurred the next day at the Radisson Hotel in downtown Baltimore. Most of the teachers attended the meeting with an administrator from their American school, usually the principal. The ornate and polished decor of this hotel provided an elegant setting for discussing "life in the trenches" of American schools. The teachers and administrators each met separately in morning sessions conducted by Fulbright Exchange staff members, under the leadership of Senior Program Officer Ilo-Mai Harding. Each group developed a list of experiences, insights, and problems common to its group.

Jean Hudder, a Fulbright Exchange staff member, conducted the meeting of the Fulbright Exchange teachers. Although some remarks reflected experiences unique to a particular teacher, the following comments received common assent.

(*1*) The student population in the United States is amazingly diverse.

(*2*) Easy access to higher education is a major advantage.

(*3*) The daily Pledge of Allegiance to the flag seemed strange to the exchange teachers.

(*4*) Students are generally docile and unresponsive.

(*5*) American teachers must complete a burdensome amount of paperwork.

(*6*) The relationship between teachers and students is more casual than is customary in most of the countries represented by the exchange teachers.

(*7*) School political control and financing are at a local level, rather than at a national level as is true in most countries.

(*8*) There are great differences in the financial resources available to the different school districts.

(*9*) The American teacher works a very long day with few breaks or other opportunities to interact with colleagues.

(*10*) Students in American schools are more closely supervised than are students in foreign schools. Most exchange teachers were unfamiliar with hall passes, bathroom patrol, and cafeteria supervision.

(*11*) There is a heavy emphasis on sports in American schools and society.

(*12*) While American schools have more professional support staff such as counselors and administrators, there are fewer support staff members such as teacher aides.

A second meeting for administrators was taking place simultaneously in an adjoining room. At this meeting principals and other supervisors shared impressions of their respective Fulbright teacher's initial encounters with an American school. This discussion was led by another Fulbright staffer, Janet Reid. Many of the observations reported by the teachers were reiterated by the administrators. As American educators, however, the administrators saw the exchange process from a different perspective. Some of the observations that seemed to strike a familiar chord among the administrators present were as follows.

(1) American students expected more frequent tests and quizzes than the exchange teachers typically provided in their home countries.

(2) The exchange teachers considered American students to be too concerned with grades and to expect higher grades than they had earned.

(3) The exchange teachers seemed to rely primarily on lecturing as a teaching technique and were less likely than American teachers to employ student activities and class participation as instructional tools.

(4) Many exchange teachers had difficulty adjusting to the lack of respect for teachers displayed by some students. Conversely, many teachers seemed to enjoy the willingness of students to approach their teachers and engage them in conversation outside the classroom.

(5) The exchange teachers seemed to be accustomed to a lighter teaching load than they were assigned in the United States. Foreign teachers expressed amazement that they were expected to patrol bathrooms, monitor study halls, and perform bus supervisory duties.

(6) Many exchange teachers indicated surprise at the high level of parental contact with teachers and general involvement of parents with the education of their children.

(7) Exchange teachers missed having teaching aides to help them with setting up labs or the supervision of students.

How accurate were these first impressions of American schools by foreign educators, who at this point had spent one month in American classrooms? Many of their comments echoed the criticisms of American schools that have been familiar staples of educational discussions in the United States since the release of *A Nation at Risk* in 1983. Comments about grade inflation, student passivity, lack of respect for authority, and the heavy emphasis on sports in the schools were especially familiar criticisms.

Many of their other comments, however, would strike the average American as somewhat surprising. Do American teachers have a heavier work load and longer workday than their counterparts in other industrialized nations? Are American students more directly supervised in a school setting than is common elsewhere? Do American teachers employ more varied and stimulating teaching techniques than are typically used by teachers abroad? And, if so, why are our students so passive and indifferent? Is there actually more parental involvement in American schools than is the practice in foreign countries? Is it true that American principals observe classes and formally evaluate our teachers more extensively than do supervisors of teachers from the other countries?

Many of these observations by foreign teachers correspond to those which, when made by American educators, are greeted with great skepticism by the American public. Several examples follow of such observations, also commonly made by American educators, that are largely ignored by the public. The exchange teachers view the heavy reliance on local funding, and the accompanying great diversity in student expenditures among districts, as a serious weakness of the American system. The requirement that American teachers perform supervisory duties such as lunch duty and bathroom patrol are seen as demeaning by most visiting teachers. The relatively low social status accorded the American teacher is quickly apparent to the Fulbright Exchange teachers. The great diversity of the American student population utterly amazed the visiting teachers.

The following chapters explore these issues, and many others, concerning international schooling at the close of the twentieth century. Topics explored include comparisons of international student achievement data, educational funding levels, and other standard educational indicators. These data are interpreted in light of supplemental data from actual schools and classrooms in the countries reviewed. Individual interviews by the author with classroom teachers from the survey countries provided a major source of current information about these foreign school systems.

The comprehensiveness of the discussion illuminates the cultural component of schooling in each country, a factor that partially explains the differences in educational quality among the countries under consideration. Except for the Japanese interviewees, the foreign teachers interviewed in the researching of this book were all Fulbright Exchange teachers during the 1991 – 1992 academic year. As such, they were in a unique position to consider the operation of schools in their home country from the perspective of their American experiences. In addition to describing the official educational practices and policies unique to their individual countries, these astute educators also identified major cultural factors affecting school performance in their home country.

The schools of six nations, including the United States, are visited and discussed in separate chapters of the book. A discussion of this scope, of necessity, produces many generalizations that will not be valid in every school and classroom. Nevertheless, these generalizations can form a useful basis for identifying practical changes in our American schools that will lead to better educational results. These international comparisons highlight many cultural factors in the United States which, were they addressed and modified, would have a significant positive impact on the achievement of American students.

The educational systems selected for comparison are the United States, England, Canada, Germany, Japan, and Denmark. Each country is a modern industrial democracy with a high standard of living and a well-developed educational system. Figure 1.1 provides a comparison of educational expenditures in these six countries, as well as others, in terms of gross domestic product per capita, public spending on education per capita, and public spending on education per pupil. These data indicate that all six countries to be studied devote substantial resources to the educational enterprise, and therefore it is reasonable to make comparisons on the quality and quantity of educational opportunities that these countries provide to their citizens.

England and Canada are included because their culture, history, language, and governmental structures most closely resemble those of the United States. Germany and Japan were chosen because they are often cited as having educational systems that are far superior to that of the United States. Both of them, but particularly Japan, have cultural traditions and practices that differ greatly from those of America. Denmark was selected as a representative of a democratic modern state with a governmental and economic system significantly different from that of the United States. Denmark has a socialistic governmental structure featuring high taxation and a highly developed welfare state. The educational system of the country is a major component of this welfare state. In considering the educational system of each country, special

Gross Domestic Product per Capita

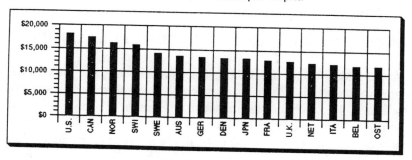

Public Spending on Education per Capita

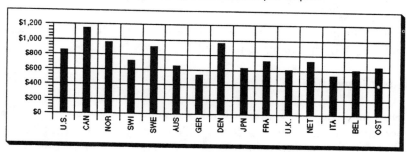

Public Spending on Education per Pupil

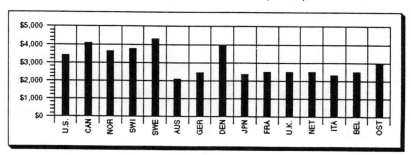

Note: All figures in U.S. dollars using purchasing power parities for currency conversion.

Figure 1.1 *International comparisons of public spending on education (with permission from Nelson, F. H. 1991.* International Comparisons of Public Spending on Education. *Washington, DC: American Federation of Teachers, p. 16).*

attention is given to the manner in which the general culture impacts upon the quality of the educational system.

TOPICS INCLUDED IN CROSS-CULTURAL COMPARISONS

A multitude of factors could be selected in comparing schooling across cultures. Five major dimensions, or perspectives, have been chosen for this study. The student, as the central concern of the educational enterprise, offers the most obvious basis for educational comparison. Teachers, also, play a direct and critical role in determining educational quality. The role of the school principal, school governance practices, and the impact of social and cultural influences on the schools are also compared. All of these factors play a critical role in determining educational success or failure.

Following is a full description of the issues addressed on each dimension for each of the countries profiled.

Student Dimension

How many days each year do students attend school, how long is the school day, and what subjects do the students study? What is the practice in each country regarding high school students holding part-time jobs, driving and/or owning cars, and boy-girl dating relationships? What is the status of student behavior and discipline in the schools of each country and what options are available to teachers to deal effectively with student discipline problems? How are students grouped for instruction? What assessment methods do schools employ to evaluate students and what becomes of students who fail to meet academic standards? What post-high school educational opportunities are available to students in each country? Must students attain certain scores on standardized tests or achieve specific cumulative grade point averages as a condition of admission to a university? What are the practices in each country regarding student tuition at the college level?

Teacher Dimension

What are the length and content of a typical workday for a teacher in each country? How many days each year are teachers employed and to what extent do teachers hold second part-time jobs during the school year or during vacation periods? How do teachers allocate their work schedules among various activities such as providing direct instruction, planning for classes, supervising students in cafeterias or study halls, meeting with the school faculty or department members, and becoming involved with students in after-school activities? How do salaries, working conditions, and the general status of teachers compare with those of other occupations in each country? How does each country determine teacher salaries? Is there a standard salary schedule for all teachers or do teachers of different grade levels and subjects earn different salaries? What is the role of teacher unions or teacher organizations in each country?

What are the educational requirements for becoming a teacher in each country? Are experienced teachers required to participate in additional training or educational experiences? How is teaching performance formally evaluated? Does the principal visit classes to observe and evaluate teachers? Is there any provision for merit pay? What type of relationships do teachers typically have with students, colleagues, supervisors, and parents in each country? How are teaching vacancies filled in each country? How many students are in a typical class and how many different students does a teacher typically instruct on a given day? What teaching styles or techniques do teachers employ most frequently in each country?

Principal Dimension

How are principals or head teachers selected in each country? What other support personnel (such as assistant principals, guidance counselors, reading specialists, etc.) are generally available at the school level in each country? What role do principals or head teachers fulfill in the areas of teacher selection, staff evaluation, budget development, school schedule and organization, curriculum development and implementation, and student discipline? How do the salary, work schedule, and status of principals or head teachers compare with those of teachers in each country? What special education, training, or experience, is required for a person to be appointed a principal or head teacher in each country?

Governance Dimension

What are the respective roles of the local, regional, and national governments in each country with reference to education? Are there local school boards in other countries as there are in the United States and, if so, what roles do they play in the governance of the schools? How is education financed in each country? Are there national goals or national curricula in each country? How are private schools financed in each country? Do parents have significant choices or decision-making power regarding the schools their children will attend? What are some of the current educational issues, concerns, and trends in each country?

Societal Dimension

Are families with children eligible for special financial or other social supports in each country? What is the status of families with children in each country regarding economic security, the divorce rate, and the incidence of single-parent families? What connections and interactions exist in each country to relate the schools to the workplace? How do members of the general public view education and educators in each country?

SOURCES AND REFERENCES FOR COMPARISON STUDY

Interest in schooling practices in the industrialized West has increased markedly in recent years, and comparison of the achievement of American students with their peers in other nations has received special attention. The major basis for this comparison has been the international testing data that has been collected and analyzed by the International Association for the Evaluation of Educational Achievement (IEA). For more than twenty years these data have consistently portrayed American students as performing very poorly in comparison to most other countries included in the comparison studies.

The school reform movement in the United States continues to rely heavily upon these data as the rationale for advocating revolutionary changes in the operation of American schools. Defenders of the current American educational system counter that the international testing data are not comparable from country to country, since the cultural and social milieus in which the schools function make direct comparisons invalid. Such critics of the IEA studies further assert that the tests themselves, as well as the conditions under which they are taken, may vary sufficiently from country to country so as to make direct comparisons invalid. Translating the test into different languages, for example, can affect the level of difficulty of the questions from one nation to another. Also, some countries may emphasize the importance of the tests to their students while other countries, such as the United States, may administer the tests under conditions that minimize their importance, and thus negatively affect student performance.[1]

The analysis that follows goes beyond simple comparisons of international test scores and provides descriptive information regarding the actual daily operation of representative schools across six cultures, including the United States. By exploring topics such as class size, performance standards, curriculum, teaching methods, and school culture, significant similarities and differences among the six nations become evident. Formal school practices are analyzed in terms of the social and cultural settings in which the schools function.

The comparison of actual schooling practices in typical schools across six cultures provides usable information for making more valid comparisons of educational systems. Such a cross-cultural study serves as an antidote to the tendency by statisticians and researchers to over-interpret the testing data and arrive at rather simplistic judgments regarding the quality of American schools. Likewise, such an examination of actual international schooling practices should help to dispel some of the myths regarding foreign schools that allow American educators simply to reject attempts to draw meaningful international comparisons.

In completing the research for this book, I consulted sources such as current books, periodicals, journal articles, and research studies concerning education in each of the countries profiled in the book. In addition, significant weight was given to the testimony and judgments of experienced classroom teachers in the countries studied. As Fulbright Exchange teachers, the teachers interviewed for this book had the advantage of personal knowledge of the schools both in their home countries and in the United States. This perspective contributed immensely to the insights that they were able to offer regarding the relative strengths and weaknesses of American schools versus schools in their native countries.

Personnel from the Fulbright Teacher Exchange Program, administered by the United States Information Agency, also provided valuable insights into the educational systems of the countries included in the study. Many of these Fulbright Program officials have for many years interacted both with Americans teaching abroad and with foreign exchange teachers working in the United States. They have had the opportunity to consider the testimony and experiences of a multitude of classroom teachers over a period of many years.

This book is essentially descriptive in nature and does not attempt to provide a rigorous and scholarly analysis of public education in the countries studied. This descriptive analysis, however, warrants the formulation of some generalizations about the educational system in each country studied. These generalizations then form the basis for the broad generalizations regarding the educational systems and cultures of the six nations. The comparisons drawn, however tentative, will be of general interest to educators in the United States and abroad, and should provide a starting point for more rigorous analysis and consideration by qualified educational researchers.

The balance of this chapter summarizes the findings from existing international comparisons of educational achievement by students from the countries profiled in this book. The available data regarding the performance of current American students relative to their older siblings and parents are also presented. These data provide the context for considering the perceived shortcomings of current American students relative to those in earlier eras. The data further allow comparison of the current performance of American students relative to the performance by students from other countries and cultures.

Subsequent chapters describe the public schools in each of the six nations. Each chapter begins with a brief history of public education in the country under discussion and is followed by descriptions of typical schools and the characteristics of students, teachers, and building administrators. Each chapter includes a discussion of the cultural and societal factors affecting the schools in that country. This approach provides a broader context for understanding factors beyond the school setting that may significantly impact on student performance. In Chapters 8 and 9 the schools in each country are compared on the major dimensions detailed in the chapter on each country. The final chapter contains recommendations for American educational policymakers based on successful practices in foreign countries and schools, which should be both politically and culturally acceptable to American citizens.

WHY DOESN'T AMERICA HAVE BETTER SCHOOLS?

Criticism of America's public schools is a constant in public policy discussions. A more detailed history of such criticisms will be found in Chapter 2 on American education. Such criticism reached a crescendo following the *A Nation at Risk* report to the President in 1983. We will first consider the primary evidence advanced by the critics of American public education, and introduce some of the counterarguments offered by defenders of our educational system. While the existing evidence strongly suggests serious problems with America's schools, developing workable strategies to correct our deficiencies requires that we extend our comparative analysis to issues beyond relative student performance on international achievement tests.

Scholastic Aptitude Test Scores

The first evidence of educational decline to be considered involves the decline in the scores on the Scholastic Aptitude Test. The phenomenon of the decline in SAT scores is probably the most cited and the least meaningful of any of the indicators of educational achievement. The SAT was first administered to about 10,000 students in 1941 in an attempt to measure the *aptitude* of high school seniors to succeed at college level academic work.[2] To this day, the SAT does not measure academic achievement, but rather academic aptitude. Furthermore, only about half of high school seniors take the test, making it a poor measure of the performance of the entire population of students.

In spite of its total unsuitability as a broad measure of student achievement, the September announcement each year of average SAT scores is the subject of front page newspaper coverage. The news stories are frequently followed by hand-wringing editorials pointing to this further evidence of academic decline in the United States. In 1977 the Educational Testing Service (ETS), publishers of the SAT, appointed a commission to determine the reasons for the then-existing fourteen year decline in SAT scores. Although the commission offered many possible explanations, the most compelling reason advanced for the declining scores was the fact that the population of students being tested had changed radically.

There had been a significant increase in the absolute number of students taking the test, thereby guaranteeing that the SAT data would include more students with lower academic ability and achievement. There was also a dramatic increase in the number of minority students, often from culturally deprived backgrounds and inferior schools, who were taking the tests to meet application requirements for colleges and universities that were aggressively recruiting minority students. Finally, the proportion of female students taking the SAT increased dramatically. This negatively affected average scores since women, for unknown reasons, earn lower scores than males on the test.[3]

During the past decade the number of potential college freshmen has declined and colleges have tried to maintain enrollment levels by recruiting ever deeper into the pool of graduating high school seniors. Even though more students are required to take the SAT, these students know that a low score will not be a barrier to entrance into college. Thus most students make little attempt to prepare for the test and they attach little importance to it. A less prepared pool of test takers, with little incentive to perform well, offers an additional explanation for the relatively low scores that continue to be reported each year. For all of the previous reasons, SAT scores provide a very weak basis for generalizing about the quality of America's schools.

National Standardized Achievement Tests

A second source of information regarding the academic achievement of American students is the nationally standardized achievement tests administered to students in individual school districts and by many states. These commercially prepared achievement tests allow individual schools and districts to compare the achievement of their students against that of a carefully selected sample of students, chosen by the testing company to represent the entire school population. In many school districts the annual release of results from these tests provides reassurance that the students in a given district are performing well relative to national average performance. Most laymen do not understand that these tests merely compare one student's level of performance with that of other students, and that the achievement scores do not represent achievement as measured against objective performance standards.

America's trust in standardized test scores was severely shaken in 1987 by a brief report published by Dr. John Cannell, a physician from West Virginia. Dr. Cannell provided data from all fifty states that indicated that, according to the standardized test results, 90 percent of local school districts claimed that their students were performing above the national average on such tests.[4] This phenomenon gained much national attention and was dubbed the "Lake Wobegon Effect," after the mythical town featured on humorist Garrison Keillor's radio program where "all the children are above average."

The uproar following these revelations made future references to standardized testing results suspect at best. Reports that certain school districts were doing quite well by national norms were increasingly greeted with skepticism if not outright disbelief. There is, however, a rather straightforward explanation for the phenomenon of the Lake Wobegon Effect. Over the past decade there has been an increasing interest in standardized testing as a method for assessing the quality of the schools. Administrators in school districts throughout the country naturally took steps to align their curricula more closely with the material found on the tests. Many schools also coached students on the best test-taking strategies to maximize scores on standardized tests. Teachers impressed upon students the importance of the tests to their future academic success. Extra care was taken in individual schools to optimize the conditions under which the tests were given.

As students took the same type of test in succeeding years, a practice effect also had a positive influence on test scores. And yes, in some instances, teachers and principals cheated to produce superior test results.[5] These predictable reactions to an overemphasis on standardized test results produced an improved performance by students relative to the norming, or comparison, group of students who took the original test. The group of students that are selected by the test publishers as the norming group typically have none of the above advantages. They are not coached on the importance of the test, they have no opportunity for a practice effect, and no attempt is made by the school district to align the curriculum to the test that is being "normed." Thus it is not at all remarkable that subsequent students tested, who have the experiences outlined previously, will perform better than the original norming group.

The fact that most school districts report above average performance is not the result of a conspiracy, or of a desire on the part of administrators intentionally to mislead the public. It is simply the natural result of a situation where increasing importance is placed upon test results in assessing the performance of a school district and its administrators and teachers. Nonetheless, the debate over the Lake Wobegon Effect has damaged whatever limited utility such testing has enjoyed in the past. It should be noted, nonetheless, that "after falling in the 1960s and early 1970s, scores on standardized tests began rising in the mid-1970s – and, by 1986, some stood at a thirty-year high."[6]

National Assessment of Educational Progress

A third source of information on the achievement levels of American students is the twenty-year-old National Assessment of Educational Progress (NAEP). Administered by the National Center for Education

Statistics, this project measures academic achievement of American students at the elementary, middle, and high school levels. NAEP has produced more than 200 reports covering eleven instructional areas. It is the only continuous, comparable, and representative assessment of what American students know and can do. These reports represent a unique resource to monitor student achievement in the United States.[7]

A recent report produced by the Educational Testing Service, *America's Challenge: Accelerating Academic Achievement,* summarizes the data from the last twenty years on the various subject areas and reaches conclusions regarding American students' performance over time on these measures. The first chapter of this publication, titled "What is the Current Level of Student Achievement?" contains the following summary:

> When the NAEP results are taken as a whole . . . the result is a bleak portrait of the status of student achievement in the United States. Large proportions, perhaps more than half, of our elementary, middle school, and high school students are unable to demonstrate competence in challenging subject matter in English, mathematics, science, history, and geography. . . . Fewer than 10 percent appear to have both an understanding of the specialized material and ideas comprising that curriculum area and the ability to work with these data to interpret, integrate, infer, draw generalizations, and articulate conclusions.
>
> Because the definitions of "competence" and "challenging subject matter" are open to debate, it is difficult to estimate exactly how much our nation needs to improve to reach our education achievement goal. We are far from attaining it, however, regardless of any reasonable definition. The current levels of student achievement are unacceptably low for our country's needs and aspirations and for the personal goals of its citizens.[8]

A subsequent chapter in this publication addresses the issue of changes in student performance over the twenty-year period and identifies overall trends in student performance for each of the major areas tested. Following are excerpts of these trend summaries as reported in *America's Challenge: Accelerating Academic Achievement:*

> In general the achievement trends are not heartening. There have been various declines and improvements from assessment to assessment; but over the long term, achievement levels are quite stable.
>
> *Reading.* Across all age groups assessed, overall reading performance in

1988 was as good as, if not slightly better than, it was nearly two decades earlier. Nine-year-olds participating in the most recent assessment were reading significantly better than their counterparts in 1971, although their average proficiency did not improve in the 1980s and may actually have declined somewhat during that period. The reading proficiency of thirteen-year-olds has shown little change, while seventeen-year-olds were reading better than in 1971, reflecting gains made during the 1980s.

Mathematics. In 1986, mathematics performance had changed very little from the levels achieved in 1973. However, at all three ages, and at age seventeen in particular, the results suggested a pattern of dips in performance followed by recovery. Therefore, recent performance may be gradually improving, albeit somewhat unevenly. The question remains, however, whether the recent upturn in performance represents the beginning of a positive trend back to and even beyond previous levels or only an abatement of previous declines.

Science. Viewed as a whole, science achievement in 1986 remained below levels attained in 1969. Trends at ages nine and thirteen are characterized by a decline in the early 1970s, stable performance at that lower level of achievement through the 1970s, and improvement in the 1980s. With these gains, average proficiency at age nine returned to that of the first science assessment in 1970, but average proficiency at age thirteen still remained slightly below the 1970 level. At age seventeen, science performance dropped steadily from 1969 to 1982, but improved significantly from 1982 to 1986. Although the recent gains are encouraging, performance in 1986 remained well below that of seventeen-year-olds in 1969.

Civics. In general, students' achievement in civics was not as high in 1988 as it was in 1976. Although thirteen-year-olds tended to perform as well as, if not better than, their predecessors, seventeen-year-olds performed significantly worse than their counterparts in either 1976 or 1982.

Writing. Writing achievement appears to have been relatively stable across the 1970s and 1980s. Trend assessments conducted in 1974, 1979, and 1984 indicated mixed results at age nine, and the trend assessments from 1984 to 1988 indicated little overall change in the writing of elementary school students, although they improved on some tasks and did not decline in any. For middle school students, the net effect is also one of relative stability. Mixed results between 1974 and 1979 were followed by improved performance in 1984. However, between 1984 and 1988, eighth graders showed more declines than gains. Despite evidence of a dip in performance in 1979, performance for high school students also has been quite stable.

In summarizing achievement trends in various subject ares over the past twenty years or so, we see little evidence to suggest that achievement levels are much higher as we proceed into the 1990s than they were when we entered the decade of the 1970s.[9]

Figure 1.2 presents the previous summary information in graphic form. Note that the vertical axis on each graph represents proficiency levels of student achievement. The numerical value for scores on the reading test, for example, can be converted to the following proficiency statements.

- 350 – Can synthesize and learn from specialized reading materials.
- 300 – Can find, understand, summarize, and explain relatively complicated information.
- 250 – Can search for specific information, interrelate ideas, and make generalizations.
- 200 – Can comprehend specific or sequentially related information.
- 150 – Can carry out simple, discrete reading tasks.[10]

As is readily apparent by reviewing the graph in Figure 1.2 regarding reading achievement, the sophistication of American students as readers, even as seventeen-year-olds, is not impressive. The same story of relatively stable, but low levels of achievement, holds true across all other subject areas. The best that can be said for the performance of American students on comparable tests of basic skills over a twenty-year period is that student achievement has been relatively stable, but that performance has plateaued at a relatively low level. This uninspiring result has occurred during a time of unrelenting criticism of America's schools. During this same period we experienced a host of educational, sociological, and political initiatives to improve student performance. There is little evidence that either the criticisms or the initiatives has brought about the desired improvements.

International Comparisons of Student Achievement

We now consider the types of student achievement data that are most germane to the subject of this book. How does the performance of U.S. students compare with similar students in other industrialized nations? The International Association for the Evaluation of Educational

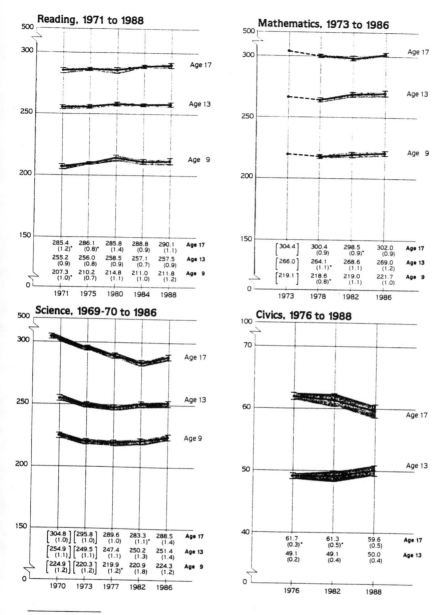

Standard errors are presented in parentheses. It can be said with 95 percent confidence that the average proficiency of the population of interest is within ± 2 standard errors of the estimated value.

[- - -] Extrapolations based on previous NAEP analyses.
*Statistically significant difference from the most recent assessment at the .05 level.

95% confidence interval

Figure 1.2 *National trends in average proficiency in various subject areas: ages nine, thirteen, and seventeen. Source: Mullins, I. V. S. et al. 1990.* America's Challenge: Accelerating Academic Achievement. *Princeton, NJ: Educational Testing Service, p. 32.*

Achievement (IEA) has been the main source for international comparisons of student achievement.[11]

Members of this organization first began planning for these studies in the late 1950s. The first international comparison in mathematics occurred in the early 1960s. A more ambitious survey of six subjects (reading, literature, science, civics, and English and French as foreign languages) followed shortly thereafter. In more recent years the IEA has conducted second studies in mathematics and science, and a study of written composition.[12]

The methodologies employed by these international achievement studies are often criticized by those who wish to question the validity of the comparisons. It is certainly true that making valid comparisons across cultures and languages is a formidable undertaking. It is also true that education officials in different countries place varying degrees of importance on the tests, and the attitudes of these officials are communicated to both teachers and students. Finally, some of the content being tested might not be taught at a given grade level in certain countries, thus offering a virtual assurance that students from these countries will not perform well on these materials.

The statisticians and researchers who have designed these comparative studies for many years, however, have a high degree of confidence that the results they report do reflect real differences in student performance levels. Alan Purves, 1989 Chairman of the International Association for the Evaluation of Educational Achievement, summarizes the approach to these studies as follows:

> In general, IEA's methodology is one of survey research, with an emphasis on careful test construction combined with a set of questionnaires for students, teachers, and school heads, as well as "national" curriculum questionnaires and supplementary histories and interviews. Over the course of its history, IEA has used various approaches to the analysis of data and has been among the pioneers of various sorts of modeling and analysis.[13]

Perhaps the school subject that is least affected by language and cultural differences is mathematics, and international comparisons in this area may therefore be the most valid of any subject tested. The 1991 edition of the *Digest of Education Statistics 1990* summarizes international achievement in mathematics in the following manner:

> U.S. students ranked well below average in a 1981 – 82 international test of mathematical skills of eighth grade students. Only six of the nineteen

other nations and Canadian provinces scored below the United States. U.S. students scored above the international average on arithmetic and statistics, but they scored below the international average on algebra, geometry, and measurement tests. (see Figure 1.3)

In an analysis of international mathematics testing for the most advanced twelfth grade mathematics students, U.S. students ranked next to last among the thirteen participating nations. The best scores were made by Japanese students, who had the highest average scores on each of the three parts of the test: algebra, geometry, and calculus. Japanese schools were also among the most likely to cover the material that was tested on the exam. American schools covered the smallest portion of the material, with the exception of schools in British Columbia. (see Figure 1.4)

In the 1988 International Assessment of Educational Progress, the U.S. thirteen-year-olds scored among the lowest in mathematics . . . among a group of countries and Canadian provinces. (see Figure 1.5)[14]

Science offers another subject area for international comparisons in which the difficulties of language and translation are minimal. The *Digest of Education Statistics 1990* provides the following summaries of U.S. student comparative performances on international science tests:

In the 1988 International Assessment of Educational Progress, the U.S. thirteen-year-olds scored . . . in the bottom third in science achievement among a group of countries and Canadian provinces. (see Figure 1.6)

In a series of science tests administered to a selected group of countries between 1983 and 1986, the U.S. fourteen-year-olds scored somewhat lower than their peers in twelve other countries, better than one other country, and about the same as Hong Kong, Singapore, and Thailand. (see Figure 1.7)[15]

In 1988 the Gallup Organization, Inc. conducted an international survey to assess knowledge of geography by residents of different countries and by different age groups within those countries. The survey directed respondents to identify sixteen countries or bodies of water on a world map: Canada, Central America, Egypt, France, Italy, Japan, Mexico, Pacific Ocean, Persian Gulf, South Africa, Sweden, United Kingdom, U.S.A., the then-existing U.S.S.R., West Germany, and Vietnam (see Figure 1.8).[16]

This survey was rather straightforward in design and provided little opportunity for misinterpretation or mistranslation of the survey questions from country to country. The information solicited is certainly quite basic and clearly should be a part of the school curriculum in every

Country or province	Mean percent correct, all items [1]	Arithmetic	Algebra	Geometry	Measurement	Statistics
1	2	3	4	5	6	7
Average	**47.4**	**50.5**	**43.1**	**41.4**	**50.8**	**54.7**
Belgium						
Flemish	53.2	58.0	52.9	42.5	58.2	58.2
French	51.4	57.0	49.1	42.8	56.8	52.0
Canada						
British Columbia	51.6	58.0	47.9	42.3	51.9	61.3
Ontario	49.0	54.5	42.0	43.2	50.8	57.0
England and Wales	47.2	48.2	40.1	44.8	48.6	60.2
Finland	46.8	45.5	43.6	43.2	51.3	57.6
France	52.5	57.7	55.0	38.0	59.5	57.4
Hong Kong [2]	48.4	55.1	43.2	42.5	52.6	55.9
Hungary	56.0	56.8	50.4	53.4	62.1	60.4
Israel	45.0	49.9	44.0	35.9	46.4	51.9
Japan [2]	62.1	60.3	60.3	57.6	68.6	70.9
Luxembourg	37.5	45.4	31.2	25.3	50.1	37.3
Netherlands	57.1	59.3	51.3	52.0	61.9	65.9
New Zealand	45.5	45.6	39.4	44.8	45.1	57.3
Nigeria	33.6	40.8	32.4	26.2	30.7	37.0
Scotland	48.4	50.2	42.9	45.5	48.4	59.3
Swaziland	31.5	32.3	25.1	31.1	35.2	36.0
Sweden	41.8	40.6	32.3	39.4	48.7	56.3
Thailand	42.2	43.1	37.7	39.3	48.3	45.3
United States	45.3	51.4	42.1	37.8	40.8	57.7

[1] Weighted average determined by the number of items in each test component.
[2] Students in Japan and Hong Kong were attending the seventh grade.

Livingston. This table was based on the "Second International Mathematics Study" conducted by the International Association for the Evaluation of Educational Achievement. (This table was prepared October 1986.)

SOURCE: U.S. Department of Education, National Center for Education Statistics, contractor report, *Perceptions of the Intended and Implemented Curriculums*, by Ian

Figure 1.3 Average percentage of items answered correctly on an international mathematics test of eighth grade students: selected countries 1981–1982. Source: National Center for Education Statistics. 1991. Digest of Education Statistics 1990. Washington, DC: U.S. Government Printing Office, p. 383.

Figure 1.4 International mathematics test scores and percentage of age group taking tests in the twelfth grade[1]: selected countries, 1981–1982.

Country or province	Average age of students	Percent of age group taking test	Percent of analysis items students had been taught	Achievement scores for top 5 percent of age group			
				Average score[2]	Algebra	Geometry	Analysis (calculus)
1	2	3	4	5	6	7	8
Average	**17**	**16**	**76**	**57.1**	**57.6**	**57.2**	**56.4**
Belgium							
Flemish	17	10	88	56.3	57.5	55.9	55.5
French	17	10	—	54.2	55.3	53.6	53.7
Canada							
British Columbia	17	30	32	57.3	60.9	59.2	51.8
Ontario	18	19	83	59.4	59.6	59.3	59.4
England and Wales	17	6	85	55.5	54.9	55.5	56.1
Finland	18	15	87	60.5	60.7	59.8	61.0
Hungary	17	50	67	59.9	60.9	61.1	57.7
Israel	17	6	78	50.0	51.5	47.7	50.9
Japan	17	12	92	65.0	63.7	64.9	66.5
New Zealand	17	11	93	57.2	56.8	57.0	57.7
Scotland	16	18	—	55.7	56.2	58.0	52.9
Sweden	18	12	86	58.9	58.5	59.0	59.2
Thailand	—	—	63	—	—	—	—
United States	17	13	54	52.2	52.8	53.0	50.9

[1] For all countries, this table includes students attending precollege mathematics classes at the highest level of secondary school. In some countries, the students had been in school longer than 12 years.

[2] Average of scores on algebra, geometry, and analysis tests with 98 items. This score is based on a standardized distribution of data from all 15 participating countries, then adjusted to a mean of 50 and a standard deviation of 10.

—Data not available.

SOURCE: U.S. Department of Education, National Center for Education Statistics, unpublished contractor report based on the "Second International Mathematics Study" conducted by the International Association for the Evaluation of Educational Achievement. (This table was prepared October 1986.)

Source: National Center for Education Statistics. 1991. Digest of Education Statistics 1990. Washington, DC: U.S. Government Printing Office, p. 383.

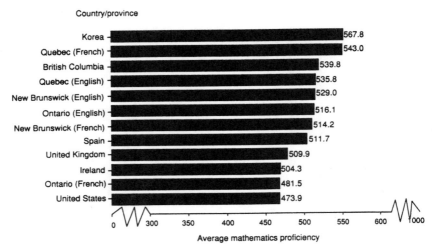

Figure 1.5 *Mathematics proficiency at age thirteen by country/province: 1988. Source: National Center for Education Statistics. 1991.* Digest of Education Statistics 1990. *Washington, DC: U.S. Government Printing Office, p. 377.*

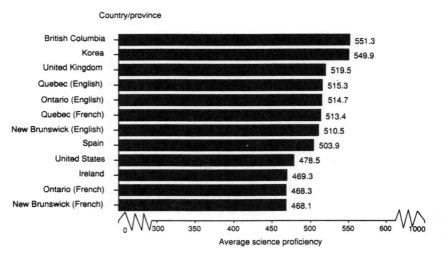

Figure 1.6 *Science proficiency at age thirteen by country/province: 1988. Source: U.S. National Center for Education Statistics. 1991.* Digest of Education Statistics 1990. *Washington, DC: U.S. Government Printing Office, p. 377.*

24

| Country | Grade tested | 14-year-olds | | | |
| | | Average test scores | Percent of age group in school | Mean age, in years and months | Standard deviation of age, in months |
1	7	8	9	10	11
Australia	8, 9, 10	17.8	98	14:5	3.3
Canada (English)	9	18.6	99	15:0	6.1
England	9	16.7	98	14:2	3.6
Finland	8	18.5	99	14:10	4.1
Hong Kong	8	16.4	99	14:7	10.9
Hungary	8	21.7	98	14:3	4.7
Italy	8, 9	16.7	99	14:7	5.4
Japan	9	20.2	99	14:7	3.5
Korea (South)	9	18.1	99	15:0	7.2
Netherlands	9	19.8	99	15:6	12.5
Norway	9	17.9	99	15:10	4.0
Philippines	9	11.5	60	16:1	18.9
Poland	8	18.1	91	15:0	5.8
Singapore	9	16.5	91	15:3	9.0
Sweden	8	18.4	99	14:9	3.8
Thailand	9	16.5	32	15:4	8.9
United States	9	16.5	99	15:4	9.1

[1]Tests were conducted between 1983 and 1986.
—Data not available.

SOURCE: International Association for the Evaluation of Educational Achievement, *Science Achievement in Seventeen Countries, A Preliminary Report.* Copyright © 1988 by Pergamon Press. (This table was prepared January 1989.)

Figure 1.7 Science test scores for fourteen-year-olds, percentage of age groups in school, and mean ages of students tested in selected countries: 1983 to 1986[1]. Source: National Center for Education Statistics. 1991. Digest of Education Statistics 1990. Washington, DC: U.S. Government Printing Office, p. 384.

Figure 1.8 *Mean number of areas[1] correctly identified in a test of geography knowledge, by country and age: 1988. Source: National Center for Education Statistics. 1991. Digest of Education Statistics 1990. Washington, DC: U.S. Government Printing Office, p. 385.*

Country	Age				
	18 to 24	25 to 34	35 to 44	45 to 54	55 and over
1	2	3	4	5	6
Canada	9.3	9.2	10.5	8.3	8.7
France	9.2	9.6	10.1	9.0	8.8
Germany, West	11.2	11.2	11.0	11.8	10.9
Italy	9.3	9.3	8.4	7.8	5.5
Japan	9.5	10.8	10.5	9.7	7.9
Mexico	8.2	6.9	7.6	6.4	5.7
Sweden	11.9	12.3	12.5	11.5	10.3
United Kingdom	9.0	8.4	9.2	8.9	7.8
United States	6.9	8.8	9.6	8.8	8.4

[1] Individuals were asked to identify 16 countries or bodies of water on a world map: Canada, Central America, Egypt, France, Italy, Japan, Mexico, Pacific Ocean, Persian Gulf, South Africa, Sweden, United Kingdom, U.S.A., U.S.S.R., West Germany, and Vietnam.

SOURCE: The Gallup Organization, Inc., *Geography: An International Gallup Survey, 1988.* (This table was prepared March 1989.)

country. In the eighteen- to twenty-four-year-old age bracket the perfor-mance of U.S. citizens was the worst of all nations tested. Among older adults, the performance of U.S. citizens moved toward the middle of the range.

Of particular interest is the fact that geographic knowledge among middle-aged Americans, ages thirty-five to forty-four, is roughly com-parable with that of similar citizens in most other countries. The perfor-mance of younger Americans, however, is significantly lower than that of similar young people in other countries. This one study provides a graphic picture of decline in geographic knowledge of younger Americans whether compared with other countries or against older generations of Americans.

In his book, *We Must Take Charge,* Chester Finn quotes from the Gallup study as follows: "The United States is the only one of the nine countries whose youngest respondents did not do better than the oldest. . . . Thus, while other countries that did not do well overall . . . seem to be making strides in the right direction, the U.S. seems to be heading the opposite way all by itself." [17] (Reprinted with permission, © 1991 by Chester E. Finn, Jr.)

The figures contained in this chapter comparing U.S. to foreign schools include most of the countries to be explored in this book. In most cases, these other countries show student achievement results that are superior to those of U.S. students. In the following chapter we begin to look beyond this raw data to examine the daily life in schools in six cultures. In this way we can escape from our cultural provincialism and objectively consider the way that other countries, several of them with great success, organize their educational systems. We must escape our own limited experiences to appreciate the perceptions of others regard-ing their own schools, and to better recognize the successes and failures of our own schooling practices. [18]

In this book we will consider some of the societal and cultural factors external to the schools that might influence educational performance. Models used in the IEA and other studies typically consider only educa-tional inputs, processes, outputs, and outcomes. They ignore political, cultural, social, and economic realities that might offer more powerful explanations for academic success or failure than the more limited school-related factors contained in their models. [19]

As we follow our itinerary across several cultures we will encounter many practices and attitudes that may strike Americans as quite strange. The Fulbright Exchange teachers that we will be meeting throughout the book have a comparable reaction to many practices in American schools. Since these same practices are familiar to us, we find them to be perfectly reasonable and necessary. Kifer, in his paper on the IEA studies, makes a similar point about the variety of different practices that are uncovered when we study schools in different cultures:

> French schools are closed on Wednesday afternoons. New Zealand students begin school on the day of their sixth birthday; not on the first day of school that year. Japanese mathematics teachers have comparably large numbers of students to teach, but they teach just three of the six days of the school week. All children in Sweden are introduced to a second foreign language. Elementary students in the United States recite a Pledge of Allegiance each morning.[20] (Reprinted with permission, © 1989 by ASCD.)

Our study of the educational systems in six countries will begin with the United States. A good understanding of our own educational heritage and experience is critical to the comparisons that will be drawn with the systems in other nations. Particular attention is given to the history of public education in the United States, especially the criticisms and calls for reform that have been a major feature of the educational dialogue for the past generation. The final chapters of the book provide comparisons of the state of education in each country and culture, as well as recommendations for further study. We will find many lessons to be learned from these other cultures that could bolster the performance of our own educational system.

REFERENCES

1. Bracey, G. W. 1991. "Why Can't They Be Like We Were?" *Phi Delta Kappan*, 73(October):104–117.
2. Bracey, G. W., pp. 108–109.
3. Bracey, G. W., pp. 108–109.
4. Cannell, J. 1987. *Nationally Normed Elementary Achievement Testing in America's Public Schools: How All Fifty States Are Above the National Average*. Daniels, WV: Friends for Education, pp. 1–2.
5. 1992. "Schools for Scandal," *U.S. News and World Report* (April 27):66–72.
6. Bracey, G. W., p. 107.
7. Mullins, I. V. S. et al. 1990. *America's Challenge: Accelerating Academic Achievement*. Princeton, NJ: Educational Testing Service, p. 3.
8. *America's Challenge: Accelerating Academic Achievement*, p. 29.
9. *America's Challenge: Accelerating Academic Achievement*, pp. 31–33.

10. *America's Challenge: Accelerating Academic Achievement*, p. 14.
11. Purves, A. C., ed. 1989. *International Comparisons and Educational Reform.* Washington, DC: Association for Supervision and Curriculum Development, p. vii.
12. Purves, A. C., ed., p. viii.
13. Purves, A. C., ed., p. viii.
14. National Center for Education Statistics. 1991. *Digest of Education Statistics 1990.* Washington, DC: U.S. Government Printing Office, pp. 373–374.
15. National Center for Education Statistics, p. 374.
16. National Center for Education Statistics, p. 385.
17. Finn, C. E., Jr. 1991. *We Must Take Charge: Our Schools and Our Future.* New York, NY: The Free Press, p. 18.
18. Westbury, I. 1989. "The Problems of Comparing Curriculums Across Educational Systems," in *International Comparisons and Educational Reform*, A. Purves, ed., Washington, DC: Association for Supervision and Curriculum Development, p. 33.
19. Spaulding, S. 1989. "Comparing Educational Phenomena: Promises, Prospects, and Problems," in *International Comparisons and Educational Reform*, A. Purves, ed., Washington, DC: Association for Supervision and Curriculum Development, pp. 7–8.
20. Kifer, E. 1989. "What IEA Studies Say About Curriculum and School Organization," in *International Comparisons and Educational Reform*, A. Purves, ed., Washington, DC: Association for Supervision and Curriculum Development, p. 51.

CHAPTER 2

The American Educational System

HISTORY AND DEVELOPMENT OF AMERICAN SCHOOLS

LONG BEFORE JEFFERSON'S dictum connecting education and freedom, the emerging new American nation placed a value on education and schooling that was uncommon in the world of the seventeenth century. In 1647 the Massachusetts Bay Colony passed a law known as The Old Deluder Satan Act.[1] This act required that every town in the colony establish a school to teach the rudiments of reading. In addition to serving a civil purpose, such schooling would enable young people to read the Bible and thus resist the blandishments of that Old Deluder Satan.

Schools in the early colonies were strongly religious in character and were largely private. Limited public funds provided at least a minimal education to paupers and others who could not pay directly for services. During the colonial period, schools were in session for only several months each year, student attendance was often sporadic, teachers were often itinerant, and the typical student attended for only a few years.

This general model applied for almost two centuries and was carried with the settlers as they formed new communities on their march toward the West Coast. Basic knowledge of reading, writing, and arithmetic was sufficient to the needs of the era, and represented the limits of education for all but the wealthiest citizens. By the time of the Revolution, the wealthier classes had established private elementary and secondary schools for their sons and daughters. The secondary schools emphasized classical learning from Greece and Rome. Monied young gentlemen could attend colleges such as Harvard and Yale in New England and William and Mary in the Virginia Colony.

The first mention of education in the documents of the new American nation was in the Northwest Ordinance of 1792. This federal law, designed to govern the procedures for establishing new states, provided that each new local community set aside a portion of its land for the establishment of a school. This marked the limit of federal government involvement in education at that time, however, since education was viewed as one of the powers reserved to the states under the Tenth Amendment to the Constitution.

This localized and rather informal approach to schooling continued from the early years of the Republic through the middle of the nineteenth century. By the 1840s, state constitutions were beginning to incorporate requirements and guarantees for the education of children. Typical wording from several of these constitutions declared that the state should provide for a *thorough and efficient* system of public education. Horace Mann, the first Commissioner of Education in the Commonwealth of Massachusetts, was the nineteenth century's most influential figure in developing the concept and practice of public funding and public control of education.[2] Throughout the second half of the nineteenth century, state after state enacted constitutional requirements for public education and passed supplementary laws dealing with compulsory attendance and compulsory education.

Education thus became a major function of state government and the state legislature. Most states established minimal curriculum guidelines as well as primitive funding mechanisms for distributing the meager funds available from state sources. Since they were unable to directly control local schools at the state level, legislatures established local school boards as the local enforcement and oversight bodies to ensure that the mandates of the state were fulfilled.

Local school boards were already familiar fixtures in American communities, since schools from the colonial period onward had been governed by local citizens. The adoption of constitutional provisions and state laws regarding education, however, marked a major shift in educational policymaking from the local to the state level. The general public was unaware of the significance of this monumental change since the previous instrument of local control, the school board, remained as a visible governing body in each community. Over time these local school boards would become ever more circumscribed in their decision-making powers by a host of outside forces and pressures.

Nevertheless, the American commitment to lay boards of education is the most extensive in the world. Canada has a somewhat parallel system of local control of school governance. England also has elements of local lay control of schools, although the actual patterns of control differ from those in the United States.[3] For over 100 years, local school boards in America have exercised grass-roots level control of public education.

Early in the twentieth century it was still possible for most local school boards to effectively oversee the school budget, hire the teachers, faithfully execute state educational requirements, and monitor the simple curriculum of the time. By the dawn of this century, however, an ever larger proportion of the population was attending school for an ever increasing number of years. The courts consistently upheld the concept of public support for secondary schools. Succeeding waves of immigrants used this free and public education system to become assimilated into the language and culture of the United States.

The rapid industrialization of the United States required a work force with a higher level of literacy and, of equal importance, the ability to adhere to rigid time schedules and to accept a highly regimented work life. Society viewed the schools, with their bells, clocks, and the lockstep progression of students through the grades, as the major instrument for preparing children for the requirements of industrial life. Education began to be perceived as a public as well as a private good, and schooling increasingly came under governmental control and direction.

Early in this century, states began to consolidate schooling requirements in elaborate school codes that specified what was to be taught, the requirements for construction of schools, certification requirements for teachers, ages of attendance for students, formulas for allocating money to schools, and a host of other matters that had previously been left to local discretion. First in the major cities, but eventually throughout the nation, school districts created bureaucracies to enforce these state mandates and to administer the schools on a daily basis.

School superintendents and other district level administrators became necessary to implement the ever increasing state requirements regarding the operation of the schools. Real control of education passed from locally elected lay board members to a professional cadre of administrators at both the local and state level. Federal government involvement with the schools remained minimal. William T. Harris, who served as superintendent in the St. Louis public schools (1868–1880), became the prototype of the modern day school superintendent. He addressed the problem of a burgeoning school population by creating the graded school, a system that assigned students to classes by age and monitored their progress from grade to grade according to their academic progress.[4]

As the twentieth century progressed, the schools moved away from their emphasis on classical learning and strict academic instruction. John Dewey in his seminal works *School and Society* and *Democracy in Education* advocated new purposes and methods for public education. He criticized existing schooling for its passivity in methods and the uniformity of its curriculum. He proposed schools that would reflect the life of the larger society and improve society by serving as an instrument of social change.[5] The theories of Dewey and others steadily influenced the purposes, methods, and content of public education and led to a radical change in the nature of the schools.

By the Second World War, progressive education was a dominant influence in the education of teachers and on policy development by education officials and professors. The movement evolved into "life adjustment education," with its emphasis on promoting educational experiences that would help children adjust to their society and environment. The endorsement of these goals by public school teachers and leaders further separated American public education from the traditional viewpoint of education as mastery of a discrete body of content and skills.

The baby boom of the 1950s led to an unprecedented expansion of the public schools. This increase in students, coupled with a desire for all students to complete high school, created an unquenchable demand for teachers, classrooms, and money. Major cities throughout the country experienced a migration of their young adults to surrounding suburbs, featuring tract housing and instant communities. New schools opened at a feverish pace and the typical public school district as we know it today began to take form (see Figure 2.1).

Meanwhile, school districts in the major cities experienced a growth in enrollment of minority black children, whose families had migrated from the South to the ghettos of the large cities. These cities experienced a flight of their middle-class white citizens to the suburbs. This caused a serious erosion of the local tax base, and deprived the urban schools of the financial resources necessary to meet the challenges of their changing school clientele. Subsequent waves of Hispanic and Asian students overwhelmed these systems and created educational disaster areas that persist to the present day.

The 1950s saw a reaction against progressive education and life adjustment through the publication of scathing attacks on the public schools such as Arthur Bestor's *Educational Wastelands,* Rudolf Flesch's *Why Johnny Can't Read,* and Hyman Rickover's *Education and Freedom.* These critics, and many others, preached a return to the more traditional goals and content of education to better serve the desires and

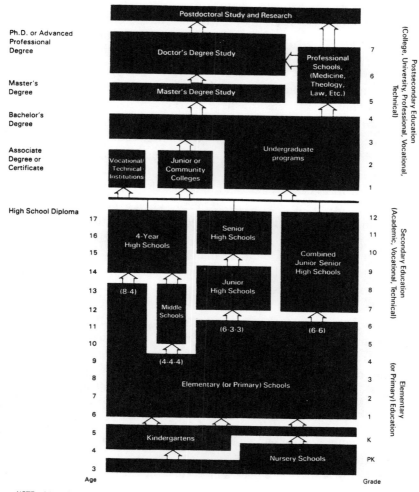

Figure 2.1 *The structure of education in the United States. Source: National Center for Education Statistics. 1991.* Digest of Education Statistics 1990. *Washington, DC: U.S. Government Printing Office, p. 7.*

needs of America's students. The launching of Sputnik in 1956 contributed to the outcry for change by highlighting a perceived Soviet superiority in science and technology, compared with the repeated failures in the space program of the United States. For many critics, the blame for this sorry state of affairs rested squarely at the feet of a public school system devoid of rigor and standards.

The 1960s brought a variety of curriculum initiatives in the area of science and mathematics. These new curricula were designed to improve public school deficiencies in these subjects, which were considered critical to the predominant position of the United States both militarily and economically. This thrust for curriculum reform, however, was overshadowed by the quest for equity as defined through the civil rights movement. The educational manifestation of this initiative was the national effort to desegregate and integrate the public schools. Policymakers perceived the schools to be the principal avenue through which major shifts in racial attitudes and behavior could be rapidly achieved.

A second major social force affecting the schools in the 1960s was the student protests relating to the Vietnam War. This anti-authoritarian and anti-establishment mind-set led to student protests and sit-ins at local high schools. The courts consistently overturned restrictions on student hairstyles, dress, and student expression in school publications. Teachers, principals, and parents all experienced a radical change in the power and control relationships between adults and students. It became ever more critical to entice and interest students in their subjects, since appeals to adult authority as a reason for study were increasingly ineffective. This effort to provide *relevancy* in education led to the introduction of courses and programs that were far removed from the content and methods of traditional schooling. The parents of today's students were themselves students during this period of unrest and change in the 1960s and 1970s.

The 1970s witnessed a backlash against the decline in standards and student achievement that seemed to accompany the emphasis on equity, the loosening of student disciplinary practices, and the excesses of the quest for relevancy. This backlash expressed itself in the back-to-basics movement. The same criticisms raised in the 1950s were reintroduced, along with statistical data indicating that there were real declines in student performance relative to past years. The first wave of international educational achievement data also became available. This information reinforced the portrait of an American educational system in need of reform.

As the next decade arrived, there seemed to be some indication that progress was being made in the achievement of rudimentary skills in reading and mathematics. A growing track record of data from the National Assessment of Educational Progress (NAEP) began to reflect improvement in basic skills, particularly among minority students. These positive signs were meager, however, when compared with other compelling evidence that the academic achievement of the great mass of American students was far from adequate.

Publication of the Presidential Commission on Education report *A Nation at Risk* in 1983 provided the clarion call for the reform movement of the past decade. It is this report that contains the following oft-quoted statement:

> If an unfriendly foreign power had attempted to impose on America the mediocre educational performance that exists today, we might well have viewed it as an act of war. As it stands, we have allowed this to happen to ourselves. . . . We have, in effect, been committing an act of unthinking, unilateral educational disarmament.

The response to this report in the public media and among policymakers at the state and federal levels was electric. Within a year many similar reports were issued, each of which reiterated the negative conclusions of *A Nation at Risk,* and reported on additional aspects of American educational failure in areas such as teacher education and vocational training.

These prestigious reports during the 1983 – 1984 period gave rise to a plethora of educational reform initiatives throughout the nation. Activist governors such as Lamar Alexander and Bill Clinton spearheaded far-reaching reforms in their home states that raised graduation requirements, imposed standardized testing of students, instituted rigorous teacher assessment systems along with career ladders for teachers, and infused large amounts of additional state funding to local school systems. These new funds often supported higher teacher salaries, which were at a very low ebb in the early 1980s. Significant increases in teacher salaries were fairly common by the latter part of the decade, but these gains became jeopardized by the recession-related cutbacks that would shortly be imposed.

During the 1980s the emphasis of the reform movement changed from top-down initiatives such as higher graduation requirements and statewide testing, to local school initiatives such as teacher empowerment, site-based management, and greater parental involvement. The

1990 – 1992 recession caused retrenchments in state educational funding and greater pressure on the property-tax resources of schools at the local level. Many state legislatures found it necessary to withdraw the additional resources that supported school improvement efforts.

Although educational reform was a major concern of national and state opinion leaders and the media, local superintendents and school board members heard few calls for school reform by either community members or staff members.

> We display the symptoms of a curious national schizophrenia. Nearly everyone now acknowledges that the United States has lapsed into a grave state of educational and social decay from which it urgently needs to extricate itself. Most Americans are satisfied with their own immediate situation, the education of their children and the performance of the schools that they know best. As a result, few of us feel a strong impulse to alter our own behavior or educational circumstances. Other people should definitely change theirs.[6]

Recent polling data provide additional insight regarding the prevailing attitudes of the American public toward its schools. For years there has been "a recurrent pattern in the annual Gallup education survey questions that ask people to grade U.S. public schools in general and then, separately, to assess the schools of their community and those attended by their own children. Year in and year out, the parents of public school students give higher ratings in all categories than does the general public. Year in and year out, parents award better grades to local schools than to public schools in general and higher marks still to the schools their own youngsters attend." [7]

This general satisfaction with the status quo extends to teachers, administrators, and the students themselves. A Harris poll in 1989 revealed that fully 92 percent of teachers stated that their school was providing their students with a good to excellent education. An Allstate survey of school administrators in 1990 found that 91 percent of them believed that American public education was doing a good, very good, or excellent job of producing an educated populace. A 1990 survey of 2,600 Minnesota high school students found that 63 percent were satisfied or very satisfied with their education and an additional 25 percent considered their education to be okay.[8]

The American public school system is a behemoth engaging the daily energies of more than 4 million adults and 40 million students. About 2.4 million staff members are classroom teachers while an additional

200,000 fulfill administrative roles. Remaining personnel include clerical, custodial, food service, and transportation workers. Thus, present-
day public school education in over 15,000 public school districts
involves almost one in every six Americans.[9]

The previous review details the development and evolution of a system
that enjoys a fairly high level of support from its clients and staff
participants. At the same time, we have a system that fares badly in
international achievement comparisons and that has been found seriously deficient by a large number of prestigious commissions and
individual critics. In the following pages we will closely explore the daily
operation of public schools in the United States, including the cultural
and social factors that impact upon them. Such a review will help to
explain how a system that is performing poorly by objective standards
can at the same time be held in relatively high esteem by the general
public, particularly the patrons of the public schools.

THE TEACHER IN AMERICAN SCHOOLS

There are more than 2.4 million elementary and secondary school
teachers in America's public schools. Seventy percent of these teachers
are women and 90 percent are Caucasian. Nearly all are college
graduates, with more than 50 percent holding advanced academic
degrees. The median age of the teaching force is forty-one years and the
median years of teaching experience is fifteen. The average teacher
salary in 1990 was approximately $31,000.[10] Average salaries con-
tinued to increase by about 5 percent each year in the early 1990s.

Many members of the current teaching cadre represent the first
generation of college graduates from their families. They viewed teaching as an avenue to move from a blue-collar to a white-collar occupation.
Salary levels for teachers have generally improved over the past decade
so that today average salaries are within the range considered as middle
income. When teacher salaries are compared to other occupations on a
per diem basis, compensation matches or exceeds that of other college
graduates in the U.S. economy.

The typical school year consists of 180 student instructional days. An
additional five or six days are allocated for staff training, orientation, or
administrative requirements. A teacher's formal workday at school is
just over seven hours.[11] He or she will spend an additional hour or two
at home or school in lesson preparation and the grading of student tests,
reports, and homework.

The time devoted to such out-of-class work varies greatly among teachers. A physical education teacher, for example, may need to spend relatively little time preparing lesson plans. The high school teacher of English, on the other hand, might spend several hours each day grading student papers. The first grade teacher might invest several hours preparing the many lessons that he/she teaches each day and grading or otherwise responding to the daily student seatwork assignments that have been completed. The industrial arts teacher in a secondary school, however, typically has few out-of-class assignments to grade, and relatively little material to prepare for a given class period.

This great variance in the level of effort required of different teachers leads to a continuous debate among supporters and critics of teachers. Strong supporters of American teachers have a mental image of the English teacher or elementary teacher toiling mightily to meet his/her responsibilities. Teacher critics, on the other hand, think of the physical education or industrial arts teacher whose time commitment to the job seems somewhat limited. Teachers working at second jobs in the afternoons and evenings during the school year only reinforce this perception by the critics.

The phenomenon known as the single salary schedule is also a source of contention among the critics of American education. Virtually all school districts in the United States have a salary schedule for teachers that is based solely upon earned academic degrees and years of teaching experience. Thus, every teacher in the school district with a master's degree and ten years of teaching experience will earn exactly the same salary. This will be true regardless of whether the teacher spends several hours per day preparing for classes or only a few minutes. A high school teacher of physics earns exactly the same amount as a teacher of second grade. There is also no attempt made to distinguish, for compensation purposes, between the teacher who is merely adequate and the teacher who is truly outstanding.

A general criticism of American teachers is that they are not well or broadly educated, and that they often do not have sufficient knowledge of their teaching field. A recent book titled *Ed School Follies*, by Rita Kramer, provides a nationwide tour of current teaching practices at representative schools of education. She offers compelling testimony that undergraduate teacher education programs are shockingly inadequate. Studies have repeatedly shown that teachers are not themselves good students, and that most teachers are drawn from the bottom half of their college classes. SAT scores of college freshmen who chose an education major are among the lowest of incoming students.[12] Relatively few of the advanced degrees earned by teachers are in academic fields. Teachers usually earn advanced degrees in various educational majors, which are all-too-often lacking in academic rigor.

In spite of comparatively easy entry into the profession, and the improving salaries relative to other occupations, the United States continues to experience a shortage of qualified teachers. As salaries have risen in recent years there has been a slight increase in the proportion of college students who have entered the education major. As many as 25 percent of college graduates will need to enter education over the next decade, however, if enough qualified teachers are to be available. Today fewer than 10 percent of college graduates earn degrees in education.[13]

There are several explanations for this limited interest in teaching as a career. Strikes and other labor strife have somewhat tarnished the image of the American teacher. Colleges of education are often held in low esteem on college campuses, and teacher candidates are often viewed as less able intellectually than their college peers. Until recently, teaching was one of the few professions available to bright young women. This is no longer the case. Members of this formerly reliable source of new, intelligent, and well-educated teachers are increasingly pursuing alternative career options.

American society does not accord true professional status to its teachers. The fact that many teachers belong to militant labor unions is a further detriment to professionalism. Teachers typically have very little control over their work schedules, have little influence on policymaking within their school or district, and frequently work under the traditional industrial model of management-labor relations.

There is little recognition of teachers for outstanding performance, and there is little differentiation among teachers in their work assignments as a result of special skills and experience. Teachers must leave the classroom and assume an administrative role to experience an increase in status or compensation. Teachers also have relatively few opportunities for professional development, or for sharing their experiences and concerns with colleagues.

Many teachers do not have a private place to work, ready access to a telephone, or the availability of any secretarial services. During the workday the American teacher spends the vast majority of his or her time directly interacting with students and has little opportunity to talk with colleagues or to engage in quiet study and reflection.

THE AMERICAN ELEMENTARY TEACHER

The workday schedules for elementary teachers across the United States are remarkably similar. Kathy Noble, a teacher of third grade whom we will meet shortly, has primary responsibility for twenty-five to thirty eight-year-old children. She will spend at least five hours of a six-and-one-half hour teaching day in an 850 square foot classroom with her students. Students will leave the classroom for a thirty- to forty-five-minute lunch period, as well as for one or two short recess periods during the day.

The teacher provides instruction to her children in all the basic school subjects. These subjects include reading, language arts (including English, spelling, and writing), mathematics, social studies, science, and health. The teacher might also provide instruction in subjects such as music, art, physical education, and computers. More typically, however, these courses are taught by special teachers certified in these subjects. When such additional teachers are available, they replace the regular teacher for the forty-five-minute period that the special subject is taught, thus providing the teacher with an opportunity for some private planning time.

Elementary teachers typically, but not always, have one such brief planning period per day. During this time, teachers will plan future lessons, prepare materials and worksheets for later classes, telephone or meet parents, and conduct necessary business with the principal, counselor, or other members of the support staff. A teacher might also use part of this time to have a cup of coffee and talk with colleagues in the faculty room.[14] Besides this planning period, the teacher will have a thirty- to forty-five-minute lunch period, when he or she generally will be free of direct responsibility for students.

A brief homeroom period marks the beginning of the school day. Students and teachers use this time to socialize and conduct minor administrative tasks. The teacher records student attendance while administrative announcements are made over the school loudspeaker. A similar brief period will occur at the end of the day during which time students will be called to their buses or dismissed directly by their teacher.

From beginning to end, the formal teacher day in the United States is from seven to seven-and-one-half hours in length. Since insufficient time is available during this official day for planning and required paperwork, a teacher will usually spend an additional two to three hours before school, after school, and at home in lesson preparation and the evaluation of student homework, classwork, and tests. The teacher records grades for most of these activities in a roll book, which becomes the principal document used to assign grades to students. Teachers often maintain portfolios with examples of student work to share with parents at Back-to-School Night or at parent conferences. Detailed documentation of student progress by the classroom teacher is an important requirement in the typical public school.

THE AMERICAN SECONDARY SCHOOL TEACHER

The daily work schedule of an American secondary school teacher is similar to, although somewhat lighter than, his or her elementary school colleague. The workday of the public high school teacher may start as early as 7:30 A.M. Students arrive at school by bus, car, and on foot during the first thirty minutes of the day. Most teachers will supervise a homeroom group of about thirty students during this time. After homeroom the school will begin its regular academic schedule of seven class periods, each about forty-five minutes in length.

We will look more closely at the daily schedule of Sam Cramer, a high school mathematics teacher. Sam instructs students for five teaching periods during the day. Three of the classes are ninth grade students studying algebra 1. Our teacher also teaches a class in tenth grade geometry, and a twelfth grade class in basic arithmetic for nonacademic students. Cafeteria supervision occupies one of his two nonteaching periods of the day. The remaining period is available to Sam for planning purposes or to meet with students, parents, or other teachers and administrators.

Thus Sam must prepare lessons for three different courses, as well as variations for the three algebra 1 classes of different ability. The average class size in American high schools is about twenty-five. Therefore, Sam will interact with about 125 different students each day, plus those students that he supervises in homeroom and in the cafeteria. The pace of such a day is frenetic, since Sam will meet with his classes in succession, with only three or four minutes between classes for students to move to their next class. It is also possible that he might need to move from one room to another for his classes, thus contributing to a feeling that his workday consists of a series of brief episodes of interaction with different groups of students.

Our math teacher is also the soccer coach. The end of the academic day at 2:30 P.M. marks the beginning time for the daily practice. The practice continues until 5:00 P.M., although it is 5:30 before the last student has left and the teacher can begin his trip home. During the evening Sam will spend an additional hour grading student papers and preparing for the next day's lessons. In all he can only devote about ten minutes each day to prepare each lesson, with an additional ten minutes per class to check homework and grade tests and quizzes. Since Sam is a coach, his typical workday extends for eleven hours. His colleagues who are not involved in extracurricular activities will find that their typical workday is about nine hours long.[15]

Both Kathy at the elementary school and Sam at the high school experience many of the same elements in their work life. They spend about twenty to twenty-three hours per week providing direct instruction to students, with an additional five to seven hours supervising the cafeteria, homeroom, study hall, and/or recess. Planning lessons and grading student work requires an additional ten to fifteen hours per week. Sam also spends about fifteen hours per week on his duties as a soccer coach. Conscientious teachers such as Kathy and Sam regularly devote fifty to sixty hours per week to their teaching duties.

Their limited time for proper planning causes them to rely heavily on the textbook and other prepackaged teaching materials. Instructional strategies tend toward direct instruction and question-and-answer formats, since these approaches require the least planning and are the easiest to control. The wide variation in the interests and abilities of students compounds the challenges facing the teacher. This is true even at the high school level, where there is most often an attempt to group students for instruction according to prior learning and ability.

The harried pace of the teacher's day leaves little time for interaction among teachers on instructional matters. Curriculum guides are usually available that can provide the teacher with help in planning daily lessons and with developing strategies for instruction and evaluating student progress. In practice, however, teachers seldom consult these curriculum guides. With the limited time available to them for planning, teachers typically prefer to rely on their own prior knowledge and experience, rather than to invest the energy necessary to significantly alter their program on the chance that instruction and learning might improve.

Public schools in the United States, unlike those of many other countries, do make some formal attempt to evaluate teachers and supervise the quality of instruction provided. This supervisory task falls primarily to the building principal, who often has neither the time nor the expertise to fulfill this supervisory function adequately. Most states require that new teachers be formally observed and evaluated once or twice per year during their first two or three years of teaching. School principals also typically observe and evaluate experienced teachers on an annual basis. These formal evaluation procedures are generally perfunctory at best, and do little to promote improvements in classroom instruction. They do serve as a monitoring device that can lead to the removal of particularly inept teachers from the classroom.

A few public school systems devote the necessary resources to support a systematic teacher evaluation and improvement program. These generally affluent school systems usually have a series of department heads or subject specialists who visit classrooms on a regular basis to coach teachers toward improving their performance. Building administrators also observe classes and work with teachers on instructional improvement. Effective programs of this type, however, exist in only a small number of school districts.

The portrait of the American teacher that emerges from the previous discussion is not encouraging. We see hardworking, conscientious people who are often ill-equipped for the instructional challenges they will face. They work at a frenetic pace to instruct large numbers of students of varying ability and motivation, while receiving little support and assistance from supervisors or colleagues. They usually work in virtual isolation and must rely upon their own limited resources in their struggle to educate their students.

THE ELEMENTARY SCHOOL STUDENT

The diversity among students attending public schools in the United States makes generalizations particularly difficult. Therefore, portraits of several students of different ages and circumstances will serve as a composite picture of the American public school student. There are more than 40 million students attending American public schools. Seventy percent of these students are white, 16 percent black, 10 percent Hispanic, and 4 percent other.[16]

Students in Kathy Noble's elementary school live in a working class suburb of a large city. They attend schools with the financial resources necessary to provide an adequate education by United States' standards.

There are twenty-seven students in Kathy Noble's third grade class. Twenty of the students are white, three are black, and the remaining four are Vietnamese immigrants. Fifteen of the students live in two parent households with their natural parents, four live with a parent and step-parent, and the remaining eight live in single parent households.

Only two of the students come from homes with a working father and a full-time mother at home. Two-thirds of the children enjoy a middle-class economic lifestyle as a result of the two incomes earned by their parents, who are employed in blue-collar, semiskilled occupations. Many of the children from female-headed single parent households live slightly above the poverty level while others qualify for public assistance.

Three of the children come from homes with at least one college-educated parent, most have parents who are high school graduates, and many, particularly the immigrant children, come from homes where the parents have little formal education. The typical parents of students in Kathy Noble's class display somewhat ambivalent attitudes toward education.

Such parents do not expect that their children will need to work hard to succeed at school. Parents typically attribute student failure to poor teaching or low student ability, rather than to a lack of student effort or parental indifference. Parents are frequently overextended in their own lives and are not eager to be active partners with the school in the education of their children. They appreciate the fact that their children are assigned little homework or other out-of-class projects, thus relieving them of the responsibility of supervising the work of their children.

Children at this age usually enjoy school and take satisfaction from learning to read and do simple arithmetic. The more culturally deprived among the students are, by the third grade, beginning to fall behind many of their classmates in reading and general school performance. The highlights of the school day from the students' perspective will be lunch, recess, and gym class.

During the morning hours their teacher will meet for about thirty minutes each with the four reading groups in the class. These teacher-led groups will read a story together from the basic reading text. The remaining students, meanwhile, will be completing worksheets and performing other seatwork at their desks. The teacher will grade and return all of these worksheets to the students within a day or two.

Math is generally taught to the entire group, although in some schools students will be grouped for math, and may even change classrooms and teachers for their math lesson. The teacher will work with the class as a whole for social studies, science, health, spelling, and geography. For these classes, students will read from a textbook, answer teacher questions regarding the subject, view a film or filmstrip, or complete worksheets on the topic.

Early in the afternoon the teacher leads the students down the hall, where they attend a forty-five-minute gym class taught by a physical education teacher. Once back in the classroom the students might work on a long-term assignment for science or social studies. They might use construction paper, crayons, pens, tape, and other such materials to create a project on a given theme or topic. A normal day might also include an opportunity for students to write in their journals or engage in silent reading of a book of their choice.

Many American elementary classrooms contain learning centers where students can work individually on special topics. Computers may also be available for students to perform remedial or advanced drill and practice exercises in math or other subjects. A businesslike, yet relaxed, atmosphere permeates the classroom. There is a low hum of purposeful talking among students and between the teacher and the students. Desks may be arranged in a myriad of configurations, and some students might be lying on a rug in a corner and reading a book. The teacher seeks to assert only the level of authority necessary to maintain a productive learning atmosphere in the classroom.

Student discipline at the elementary school is not a serious problem in most United States school districts. There are too many cases, however, where one or more seriously disturbed children can terrorize a classroom, or even an entire elementary school. Insufficient resources to work with the seriously disturbed child means that these children remain too long in a regular public school setting without benefit of special services. There are also urban school districts where even elementary schools can be physically dangerous to students and teachers, and where reasonable classroom discipline is difficult to maintain.[17] Such situations seriously undermine the efforts of the school to preserve a suitable learning environment for the rest of the student body. Although the number of such districts is small, the 100 largest school districts, mostly urban and serving minority poverty populations, enroll approximately 20 percent of all students in the United States.[18]

Tim and Andrea are classmates in Kathy Noble's third grade class. They take a thirty-minute bus ride each morning to go to school. They arrive home to an empty house each afternoon at 3:30. No parent will be present in either home until 5:30 P.M. Neither their school nor the community provides after-school day care or other activities to keep these children productively occupied. Also, their parents would not be able to afford the fee for such services even if they were available.

Both Tim and Andrea watch cartoons on television while waiting for their mother to come home from work. During the week, each child will spend thirty-five to forty hours watching television. They will enjoy a period of physical activity in the late afternoon when Tim will play soccer with his friends and Andrea and her friends will bike around their neighborhood. Tim will help his mother prepare for dinner while Andrea is responsible for washing the dishes after dinner in her home. Each child will spend about twenty minutes on simple homework assignments, and will spend the rest of the evening in front of the television. It may be 11:00 P.M. before either child is sent to bed for the night.

Tim and Andrea interact with few adults other than their teachers and parents. Their role models for adult behavior are influenced heavily by the characters in television sitcoms and movies. Their heroes tend to be sports stars and entertainment personalities. They both live in small nuclear families and seldom see grandparents, aunts, uncles, and cousins. Both Tim and Andrea are experiencing a rather pleasant childhood and they seldom give a thought to their future life and career. Thus they are not motivated to make the effort necessary to excel academically.

AMERICAN SECONDARY SCHOOL STUDENTS

We will next visit an American high school from the perspective of the high school students. The composite high school described is representative of schools in the United States in the 1990s. It is not one of the relatively wealthy and upper-middle-class schools found in the advantaged suburbs, nor is it a school plagued by the intractable problems of the inner city ghettos. It is the same school where we earlier met Sam, the math teacher.

The school facility is a rambling one-story brick and concrete block building constructed to meet the expanding school populations of the early 1960s. The school contains a large classroom wing in which 850-square-foot classrooms are found, one after the other, down both sides of a long corridor. This is the only wing of the building having a second floor, which follows the same floor plan as the first floor. Students attend classes in this wing for their academic subjects. The classroom walls along the corridors contain brightly colored student lockers.

Additional wings of the building contain the gymnasium and other athletic facilities, the auditorium, the industrial arts and home economics wing, the cafeteria and library, and the school office complex. The school occupies a forty-acre tract of land containing numerous athletic fields, a track complex, a parking lot for staff, and an even larger parking lot for students' cars. The general layout and functioning of the building will be familiar to most Americans under fifty.

The students we will meet are eleventh grade students at Roosevelt High School. Our first student, Bob, enters the school at 7:40 A.M., after stopping at McDonald's for breakfast. Bob drives a four-year-old red sports car to school, which he finances through his earnings at his twenty-hour-per-week job at a local grocery store. Bob is an indifferent student who expects to graduate from high school, perhaps join the Army, or even begin attending classes at the local community college. He is equally likely to graduate from high school only to drift into any available unskilled job that will meet his somewhat limited immediate financial needs.

Bob is taking seven courses this year to meet the minimum district requirements for graduation. He chose a noncollege-bound track for his major subjects, a decision that groups him with students who have similar low aspirations and indifference toward academics. Bob's math teacher, Sam, has learned to expect little from Bob's class and finds it difficult to maintain even minimal academic standards with them. Bob's other courses include general English, American history, earth science, woodworking, physical education, and health. By his senior year Bob will have met his math and science requirements and will fill his schedule with elective courses, or request to be part of an early dismissal work release program. In either case, his academic load as a senior will be even less demanding than the light load he is currently carrying.

Bob finds the uninspiring and undemanding nature of his forty-five-minute classes boring and meaningless, but considers this a necessary price to pay for his high school diploma. He enjoys seeing his friends at school and socializes with them at lunch, during study hall periods, and at odd moments during classes. Most of his teachers give few homework assignments since students simply fail to complete them. Instruction depends heavily on teacher talk and activity since students will not prepare for class and will seldom participate in class discussions, unless asked a direct question by the teacher.

The teachers employ a series of weekly quizzes and major tests every three or four weeks as a method of encouraging at least a minimal academic effort from the students. Bob and his classmates might spend ten minutes or so during a study hall to review the material that will be covered on a test or quiz. These students tend to view their courses merely as obstacles to graduation. They view teachers as adversaries who are trying to require a higher level of academic effort and commitment than they are willing to give.

The school day ends at 2:30 P.M. and Bob leaves quickly to begin his four-hour workshift that begins at 3:00 P.M. He arrives home after seven, reheats dinner in the microwave, engages in a brief two-minute conversation with his mother, and leaves home to spend an evening with his friends. On a week night Bob is likely to visit a friend's house to play cards or watch a video for a few hours. Perhaps they will go to the mall for an hour or two. In any event, it will be eleven or twelve o'clock before Bob returns home for six or seven hours of sleep before the next day begins.

Bob's routine on the weekends will include more hours of work, as well as parties featuring large amounts of alcohol consumption and casual sexual encounters. He will be unlikely to visit a church during the weekend, will do no schoolwork, and will not participate in any meaningful family activities. Bob does not make time in his life to participate in any of the athletic or other extracurricular activities offered at his high school.

When Bob enters his homeroom each school day he sits next to a bright and attractive girl by the name of Melissa. They nod good morning to each other but otherwise do not engage in conversation. In fact they will not encounter each other again during the day, since they inhabit quite different worlds within the confines of the high school. Melissa plans to attend a highly competitive college and is using her high school years to master rigorous academic courses that will help her to gain acceptance to a top quality school.

Melissa's day, like Bob's, starts with a homeroom period and is followed by seven forty-five-minute classes plus lunch. Her classes, however, are much more intellectually challenging than Bob's, since both the teacher and the students are well prepared for each lesson. Melissa selected advanced placement classes in American history and computer science. She will most likely earn college credit for these classes by taking national college-level year-end exams in both courses. She also enrolled in a high-level math class, a chemistry course with lab periods, an honors English class, French 3, as well as health and physical education. She will not have classes with students such as Bob, except perhaps for physical education and health.

Melissa is also very active in extracurricular activities. She and a relatively small group of friends hold leadership positions on the Student Council, school paper, and class offices.[19] She is also a member of the field hockey team and the National Honor Society. She knows that involvement in these school activities will enhance her chances of being admitted to the college of her choice.

Her life outside of school is characteristic of an ambitious teenage girl of her class and social status. She spends five or more hours a week shopping with friends at a nearby mall. She works as a sales clerk at one of the stores in the mall for ten hours a week and uses this income for spending money and to satisfy her compulsion to buy new blouses on a regular basis. Melissa spends about twenty hours per week on homework and she is active in her church as a Sunday School teacher. She attends dances, goes to the movies, and occasionally attends parties where alcohol is freely available. She is sexually active, but is far more selective and careful than her classmates who travel with Bob's group.

On most school nights she and her two siblings have dinner together. She has a good relationship with her parents, who are supportive of her academic aspirations. Melissa does not have a steady boyfriend, but instead dates several boys on an occasional basis. Teachers and other adults view Melissa as the ideal teenager of the 1990s.

THE SCHOOL PRINCIPAL IN THE UNITED STATES

The role and training of school administrators in the United States differ significantly from practices in other nations. In America, administrators are considered to be an entirely different class of professional than the classroom teacher. In the other countries surveyed in this book, school principals are often considered to be the *head teacher* rather than as management or administrative personnel. The emphasis on the management side of school administration in the United States encourages a greater professional distance between teachers and administrators than is found in other countries.

This perceived gap between teachers and administrators is exacerbated by a strong unionization mentality among teachers in many school districts. Such a situation breeds a disparity of allegiances and interests between the principal and his or her teachers. In spite of calls for collegial decision making and site-based management, schools in the United States are typically governed according to the factory model of a strong management-oriented principal and worker teachers, who are only minimally involved in decision making and goal setting.

The major tasks of the principal are to provide for the smooth operation of the school, to defend teachers against the current enthusiasms of central administration, and to provide a well-disciplined learning environment by minimizing student misbehavior. The principal is also expected to *back* his or her teachers in controversies involving parents and to successfully mediate disagreements among the various elements of the school community. The school board and central administration expect the principal to keep parents relatively satisfied and to successfully diffuse any budding controversies that threaten to cause community-wide problems for the superintendent or the school board.

Most school principals are appointed to their posts after serving for five to fifteen years as a classroom teacher. The entry level administrative position in secondary schools is typically an assistant principalship at a middle school, junior high school, or high school. Elementary principals generally move directly from the classroom to the principalship. A high percentage of new administrators, particularly at the secondary level, have had experience as athletic coaches. Coaching experience is considered a good background for the development of the leadership and interpersonal skills necessary for success as a school administrator.

A new administrator in the United States is almost always the product of a formal administrative training program offered through a graduate program at a nearby university. Such programs consist of a series of survey courses on general administration, with some specialized coursework in specific areas of administrative responsibilities such as staff supervision, instructional leadership, or school facilities management. The quality of such programs varies greatly.

Virtually all school administrators gain their initial certification through a series of such courses offered on a part-time basis in the evenings and during summers. Many of the programs require an internship experience of one semester or one year. During this time the administrative candidate performs administrative functions in a school under the direction of a university professor and an on-site practicing administrator. The administrative candidate usually earns a master's degree in education by the end of the certification program. The perceived lack of quality of many administrative preparation programs in the United States has been referenced in some of the school reform proposals of recent years.

Few would contest that a dramatic improvement in the performance of school administrators is highly desirable and would have a bracing effect on public school performance. Preparation programs aside, there are other compelling factors limiting the quality of public school administrators. The most serious limiting factor is the nature of the pool of candidates from which new administrators are drawn. Previously cited data indicates that the intellectual capacity and academic performance of our existing cadre of teachers places them near the bottom in comparison with their college classmates.

This is the same pool of candidates from which future administrators are drawn ten to fifteen years after the new teachers graduate from college. There is also no known correlation between a teacher's abilities in the classroom and his or her subsequent selection as a school principal. The limited intellectual and academic talents of the students, coupled with the part-time nature of graduate school preparation programs, mitigate against rigorous and challenging administrative preparation programs.

Social dynamics in recent years have further restricted the number of top quality candidates for administrative positions. Rather dramatic increases in teacher pay in most areas have all but removed the financial incentive for a teacher to aspire to an administrative career. Also, the prevailing two-income household lifestyle has limited the pool of administrative candidates in two ways.

The two-income lifestyle implies that both spouses will participate fully in the operation of the household and in child care responsibilities. Since school administrators typically work a significantly longer school day and school year than classroom teachers, many otherwise fine candidates are not willing or able to invest the necessary time and energy to school administration in view of their home responsibilities. The traditional scenario of the male school principal devoting sixty to seventy hours per week to his school, while his wife tends to the home responsibilities, is now the exception rather than the rule.

The second major impact on school administration, resulting from societal changes, is the relative lack of mobility of aspiring school administrators. It is not as easy as it once was for a wife and children to follow the father and husband to wherever his administrative career might lead. The career and family income of the other spouse must now be considered when an administrative candidate contemplates applying to a school district in a different locality. For any given administrative vacancy, this dynamic restricts the number of applicants for a particular position. The previous factors taken together provide little reason to hope that the quality of school administrators will improve, or even maintain its current level.[20]

Bill Johnson is a veteran high school principal with twelve years of experience in administration. He first served as an assistant principal before succeeding his boss as principal of Rosewood High School. Bill began his career as a biology teacher in a school about thirty miles distant from Rosewood. He was active in extracurricular activities, serving as a basketball coach and advisor to the school newspaper. In his years as a teacher, Bill also participated actively in the affairs of his teacher union.

Bill entered a graduate program in administration at a nearby public university. His belief in public education and the anticipated challenges of the job motivated Bill to seek a principalship. His own principal encouraged him to enter the principal certification program. This principal served as an informal mentor during the three-year period that Bill earned his master's degree and obtained certification. Impressed with his enthusiasm and his record as a classroom teacher and coach, Rosewood School District selected Bill to be the assistant principal at the high school.

Bill is forty-five years old, married, and the father of two preadolescent children. His wife is a manager in a branch bank, and together they share the responsibilities of parenting and caring for their home in suburban Rosewood. He experiences frequent conflicts between the time and energy required by his principalship and his obligations as a parent and spouse. He frequently wonders whether the limited psychic and financial rewards of the principalship adequately compensate for the frenetic pace of his life.

Bill begins his workday at 6:00 A.M. with a cup of coffee in his den. He mentally reviews the business of the coming day and attempts to anticipate the consequences of various courses of action that he might pursue. This will be his only opportunity for reflection until late in the evening. He arrives at school by 7:15 A.M., glances at his schedule of eight appointments for the day, and reviews the four telephone messages on his desk.

Within minutes a procession of teachers and students arrive at his door with brief questions, comments, or concerns. Once the buses start arriving, Bill leaves his office for his daily morning walk around the school. During this fifteen-minute period he will interact briefly with fifty different students and teachers. Such visibility by an American school administrator is important to the maintenance of good student discipline in the school. As a result of his early morning conversations, Bill has accumulated eight minor problems and concerns that he will need to address later in the day.

Upon returning to his office, an angry parent confronts Bill demanding that her son's suspension for drug possession be rescinded. She first pleads for leniency, then denies that her son is guilty, and finally threatens to complain to the school board about Bill's arbitrary and unfair discipline methods. Bill ends this meeting with his stomach churning and the certain knowledge that he will be spending several hours defending his action to the superintendent and perhaps to the school board. He also realizes that justice dictates his stance on this matter, and that his teachers and community expect him to implement the drug and alcohol policy aggressively.

By 9:00 A.M. Bill is visiting a science class to observe the teacher, the class, and the curriculum. Since this is one of the two formal evaluations of this veteran teacher that will take place during the school year, a follow-up conference will be scheduled with the teacher. The class proceeds smoothly and Bill enjoys this quiet interlude to observe the educational process in action. Although he is quite impressed with the performance of this teacher, his thoughts wander to the three other teachers on his staff whose performance is marginal at best. At least two of these teachers will require much time and effort on his part, and will probably need to be rated unsatisfactory for the year. In each case, Bill can anticipate heavy involvement by the teachers' union and resistance from the affected teachers themselves.

Bill spends the next several hours in his office meeting with teachers, students, and parents. He also meets with his secretary for fifteen minutes to review her schedule for the day and to dictate correspondence. An urgent call to come to the cafeteria disrupts the office routine. Bill rushes to the cafeteria in time to break up a hair-pulling, nose-bloodying fight between two girls. Bill consumes an hour of his time before his investigation of the incident is complete. He then calls the parents of both girls to tell them that their daughters will be suspended for three days. Bill manages to squeeze a fifteen-minute visit to the teacher cafeteria for lunch before his scheduled meeting with department heads at 1:00 P.M.

The tension is thick at the department head meeting. The department heads are arguing against the plans of the district curriculum director regarding the format and procedures for curriculum development. Bill again finds himself caught in a conflict between the desires of his teachers and the requirements of his superiors at the district office. He thinks of himself as a mediator between the day-to-day concrete concerns of his teachers, and the more abstract and long-term priorities of the district office. His own sympathies lie primarily with the teachers.

The wrangling and discussions continue for two hours. Bill ends the meeting at 3:00 P.M. and proceeds to hold a series of five-minute meetings with seven or eight staff members in succession. He also spends thirty minutes with his assistant principal to review discipline and attendance concerns. He makes a brief visit to football practice before leaving for home at 5:00 P.M. He will return to school again at 7:00 P.M. to preside at the annual Back-to-School Night for parents. It will be 10:30 P.M. before Bill pulls into his driveway at home to end his work day.

A high school principal in America typically works a fifty- to sixty-hour week. A typical day for a principal will consist of a series of brief encounters with staff, students, and parents.[21] At various times he or she will play the roles of counselor, cheerleader, coach, disciplinarian, judge, policeman, mediator, mentor, and educator. During the school year the principal will attend various school functions on fifty to sixty evenings. His/her schedule during the summer will be somewhat lighter, with forty-hour work weeks and no evening meetings.

The principalship in the United States is characterized by action rather than reflection. The principal is far more likely to be a manager than a leader. Interpersonal skills, common sense, and courage are the major attributes of a successful principal. Few principals have either the time, ability, or inclination to provide the leadership necessary to produce substantive improvements in the educational program. The high school principalship, in particular, is a difficult job that must be performed under difficult circumstances.

Jayne Weathers is a colleague of Bill's who serves as principal of the Grove Street Elementary School in the Rosewood School District. She worked in the same elementary school for fifteen years as a teacher of fourth grade, and was appointed principal at Grove Street three years ago. Jayne's general academic training for the principalship was similar to Bill's, but with an emphasis on elementary school administration.

Her work day features the same frenetic pace that we saw with Bill Johnson. At the elementary school level, however, there is far more interaction with parents than in the secondary school. The typical parent is interested in his or her student's school adjustment and academic progress. Most American parents seem to place a greater emphasis on their child's happiness at school rather than his or her academic performance. Jayne Weathers spends a major portion of her time mediating concerns that parents have with the treatment the child is receiving from the teacher.

An elementary principal usually works closely with an active PTO group. These parents generally raise money to buy extra resources for the school. They may also become somewhat involved in broader school issues of curriculum and daily schedules. Such organized involvement by parents can be a mixed blessing, at best, if the parent leadership attempts to play an overly assertive role vis-à-vis the principal. Conflicts with parent groups can be a major problem for an elementary school principal.

An elementary principal is in a better position to be an instructional leader of a school than is his or her secondary counterpart. The curriculum is more basic and less varied. Elementary teachers are also characteristically more willing to accept instructional leadership from their principal than are department- and subject-oriented teachers at the secondary level. Elementary principals usually are able to visit classrooms more frequently than are secondary principals. Since elementary schools commonly enroll only 300 to 400 students, principals are able to establish more personal relationships with both teachers and students.

Very few elementary schools will have an assistant principal. Thus administrators such as Jayne Weathers will spend an inordinate amount of time and energy on minor student behavioral problems that occur on the buses, in the cafeteria, and on the playground. It is possible, however, for many elementary principals to provide the educational leadership necessary to produce excellent schools for their students. Principals with the willingness to produce excellent schools will devote fifty to sixty hours per week to their job. Less ambitious elementary principals can effectively manage their schools on a forty- to fifty-hour work week.

Power and authority relationships in American public schools operate at both a formal and informal level. At the formal level, hierarchical arrangements with sharp status distinctions between management and labor are the rule. The union movement in public education in recent decades has reinforced the role of the principal as manager and the teacher as worker. Administrative training programs also tend to emphasize the management role of the principal. These formal role designations have been challenged by recent initiatives in school-based management and teacher empowerment. School board members and school administrators often resist these initiatives.

At the informal level, however, the operation of the typical school is more collegial than the formal model would suggest. Experienced and successful principals involve opinion leaders on their faculties in most of the major decisions that need to be made. An experienced principal will seldom institute a policy that is strongly opposed by a majority of his or her faculty members. Principals with long tenure in a given position will often adopt a symbiotic relationship with the faculty. Such relationships create a bias toward the status quo and incline the principal toward inaction, rather than toward confronting serious problems of teacher incompetence or organizational dysfunction. It is not unusual for a principal to regard teachers as the constituent group to which he or she has primary allegiance.

SOCIETAL DIMENSION OF AMERICAN SCHOOLING

The social milieu in which a nation's schools operate impacts significantly upon the quality of the schools and the achievement of the students. A major factor influencing school quality is the nature of the student body. About one-fourth, or 10 million students, attend schools in poverty-stricken areas of our large cities or in poor and neglected rural enclaves. Several million of our students attend schools in our affluent suburbs, schools that offer several times the money resources behind each student than are found in our poorest school districts. The fact that so many of our children attend schools in economically depressed districts reflects the sorry truth that children are more likely to live in poverty conditions than is any other age group in our society.

Several social conditions have conspired to create the conditions leading to childhood poverty. First among these has been the dramatic breakdown in the proportion of children living in stable families. Within the past thirty years divorce rates have more than doubled, accompanied by a dramatic increase in single parent households, headed almost exclusively by women. The proportion of children born to unwed mothers has also increased from 11 percent in 1970 to 26 percent in 1988. In 1988, 58 percent of children in poverty lived in female-headed families.[22] The proportion of children under the age of eighteen living with both parents declined from 85 percent in 1970 to 67 percent in 1989. Children are increasingly likely to be growing up in home environments that do not provide the material and emotional support associated with good academic performance by children.

In a recent newspaper opinion column David Myers explored further dimensions of family decline. "Family decline is compounded by other indicators of social recession. Since 1960, the known rape rate has quadrupled; the violent crime rate has quintupled; the teenage suicide rate has tripled; the delinquency rate has more than doubled. . . . Cool statistics, yet behind each are countless crushed lives." [23]

About two-thirds, or 25 million students, attend schools between these two extremes of wealth. Such schools are well financed compared to schools in the developed countries of the world, and yet the performance of their students does not reflect the level of financial support that they enjoy. We must look to other than financial reasons to explain the relatively poor academic performance of the average American student attending these schools.

A study of Gallup, Harris, and other polls on American attitudes toward education reveals that Americans consider education to be important. Nonetheless, we are not inclined to evaluate critically the performance of schools or students in our own communities. American parents want their children to enjoy school and to experience at least a modicum of academic success. Such parents expect their students to make some effort to succeed in school. They do not, however, want their children to experience frustration, or to be required to work too diligently at their learning tasks. Academic failure by students is more likely to be attributed to lack of ability or poor teaching, rather than to a lack of sufficient effort by the student.

American adults believe that virtually all education should take place at school within the defined school day. Homework, if assigned, should not require too much time or effort for the student. American parents expect their children to devote time at home to sports, television, part-time jobs, or other recreational or hobby pursuits. Thirty-two percent of high school students, for example, hold part-time jobs, many requiring twenty or more hours a week from the student. [24] The typical American elementary school student watches television for thirty-five hours per week. This compares with twenty-five to thirty hours per week, for only thirty-eight weeks per year, of direct classroom instruction.

By age eighteen a student has received approximately 12,000 hours of classroom instruction but has spent 25,000 hours watching television. This time expended on television is not merely wasteful, but is actually counterproductive to the development of attitudes and habits of mind conducive to work and learning.

Adults expect high school students to occupy their out of school time on the activities listed previously as well as part-time jobs and an active social life with their teenage friends. In all too many cases this social life includes drugs, alcohol, and premature sexual involvement, all of which, moral considerations aside, distract students from academic pursuits.

Two additional and related factors mitigate against a cultural thrust toward high academic expectations for American students. The first of these is that most Americans do not understand the magnitude of the economic challenges the United States faces as it attempts to compete in world markets. Most adult Americans reached maturity in an era when America was still the predominant economic force in the world. Unskilled and semiskilled workers could earn a comfortable living through strong union contracts in industries such as autos and steel. Formal education was not a prerequisite for these jobs, and, for a time, workers in these occupations earned more on average than their better-educated fellow citizens. Too many Americans persist in believing the comforting myth of continuing American economic supremacy. This wishful thinking blinds us to the critical need for educational improvement.

The enormous wealth of the United States in the 1950s and 1960s allowed for a dramatic expansion in the number of colleges and junior colleges. As a society we began to operate on the assumption that virtually everyone could be a college graduate. College enrollment exploded without a corresponding increase in the number of students academically equipped to succeed with the traditional college curriculum. Colleges created new and less demanding majors, while the number of college students enrolled in high-school level remedial courses soared.

By the 1980s there were enough college seats available to accommodate virtually every high school graduate who chose to attend. In the spring of 1988 about 2.9 million students graduated from high school. Three months later about 2.4 million students, many well into adulthood, enrolled as first-time freshmen in institutions of higher education. Allowing for the proportion of older students among this number, clearly there is no shortage of college places available to students in the United States.[25] The baby bust of the 1970s following the baby boom of the 1950s resulted in an oversupply of colleges relative to the number of high school graduates who were prepared to benefit from college-level study. The laws of supply and demand assured that even the most marginal of students could gain acceptance at some college or university. A recent study group of forty-six Rochester area college administrators and professors, when asked to discuss admission standards, responded "that they have no requirements, only preferences." [26] High school students now realize that a good scholastic record is not required as a condition for acceptance into college.

The local school boards in most localities show little enthusiasm for launching ambitious school improvement efforts. Such governing bodies concentrate on labor relations, personnel, school facility, and school funding issues. Public involvement in policy issues is typically restricted to tax increases, teacher strikes, and occasional controversial issues such as sex education, prayer at graduation, or drug abuse at the high school. There is virtually no constituency for school reform at the local level anywhere in the United States.

National politicians, newspaper pundits, business leaders, and academic researchers typically voice concerns about the quality of America's schools. None of these groups is able to have an impact on actual schooling at the local level. The day-to-day participants in the educational process—students, parents, teachers, administrators, and school boards—are comfortable with the status quo and see no urgent reason to undertake radical reform. This basic truth accounts for the startling fact that none of the major school reforms during the past thirty years has had a discernible impact on student achievement.

Public education in the United States is also singularly lacking in objective, agreed-upon standards by which to measure student achievement. For twenty years the U.S. Department of Education has been painstakingly gathering baseline information on student achievement through its NAEP studies. Only recently have the majority of states agreed to compare achievement results of these tests on a state-by-state basis.

An aversion to national testing and national standards is virtually universal within the educational community. There are no standards external to the school, or even the classroom, that students and teachers must work toward to demonstrate competence on the part of the student. The standardized achievement tests used by most school districts merely compare student performance to a norm for similar students. They do not represent external criteria for achievement that should be reached by the students. Teachers and administrators tend to resist even this modest attempt to gauge student performance.

America is a society that does not take education very seriously. There are no external standards of achievement which students must reach to graduate. There are no negative consequences for students who perform at only the minimal level necessary to graduate from high school. Acceptance at some college or university is virtually assured for anyone with a high school diploma. The prevailing youth subculture stigmatizes studious young people as nerds. The distractions of part-time jobs, cars, teenage romance, and similar factors all conspire to downgrade the importance of a sound education. Today there is no consensus to correct any of these impediments to improving our schools.

REFERENCES

1. Bernier, N. R. and J. E. Williams. 1973. *Beyond Belief: Ideological Foundations of American Education.* Englewood Cliffs, NJ: Prentice-Hall, Inc., p. 361.
2. Cremin, L. A. 1964. *The Transformation of the School.* New York, NY: Vintage Books, pp. 12 – 13.
3. Campbell, R. F. et al. 1985. *The Organization and Culture of American Schools.* Columbus, OH: Charles E. Merrill Publishing Company, p. 168.
4. Cremin, L. A., pp. 14 – 17.
5. Cremin, L. A., pp. 118 – 119.
6. Finn, C. E., Jr. 1991. *We Must Take Charge: Our Schools and Our Future.* New York, NY: The Free Press, p. 94.
7. Finn, C. E., Jr., p. 95.
8. Finn, C. E., Jr., pp. 95 – 97.
9. National Center for Education Statistics. 1991. *Digest of Education Statistics 1990.* Washington, DC: U.S. Government Printing Office, p. 90.
10. National Center for Education Statistics. 1991. *Digest of Education Statistics 1990,* pp. 77, 84.
11. National Center for Education Statistics. 1991. *Digest of Education Statistics 1990,* p. 77.
12. National Center for Education Statistics. 1991. *Digest of Education Statistics 1990,* p. 125.
13. National Center for Education Statistics. 1991. *Digest of Education Statistics 1990,* p. 244.
14. Kidder, T. 1990. *Among Schoolchildren.* New York, NY: Avon Books.
15. Sizer, T. R. 1984. *Horace's Compromise: The Dilemma of the American High School.* Boston, MA: Houghton Mifflin Company.
16. National Center for Education Statistics. 1991. *Digest of Education Statistics 1990,* p. 60.
17. National Center for Education Statistics. 1991. *Digest of Education Statistics 1990,* pp. 134 – 135.
18. National Center for Education Statistics. 1991. *Digest of Education Statistics 1990,* p. 103.

19. Cusick, P. A. 1973. *Inside High School.* New York, NY: Holt, Rinehart, and Winston, Inc.

20. Langlois, D. E. and R. P. McAdams. 1992. *Performance Appraisal of School Management: Evaluating the Administrative Team.* Lancaster, PA: Technomic Publishing Company, Inc.

21. Currie, G. and J. Rhodes. 1991. "Uncertainty and Fragmentation: The 'Realities' of the Principalship in the United States," paper presented at *The Annual Meeting of the American Educational Research Association, Chicago, April 3 – 7, 1991,* 35 pages.

22. U.S. Bureau of the Census. 1991. *Statistical Abstract of the United States, 111th Edition.* Washington, DC, pp. 53, 67, 86.

23. Myers, D. 1992. "A Social Recession Grips the Nation," *The Philadelphia Inquirer,* May 22.

24. National Center for Education Statistics. 1991. *The Condition of Education 1991, Vol. 1.* Washington, DC: U.S. Department of Education, p. 72.

25. National Center for Education Statistics. 1991. *Digest of Education Statistics 1990,* pp. 55, 177.

26. Tucker, M. 1991. Many U.S. Colleges Are Really Inefficient, High Priced Secondary Schools," *The Chronicle of Higher Education* (June 5):A36.

CHAPTER 3

Denmark — Education in a Welfare State

THE SMALL NATION of Denmark provides a worthy model of an educational system that effectively meets the needs of this highly developed modern European state. Located in Northern Europe, with Germany to the south, the North Sea and the British Isles to the east, and the rest of Scandinavia to its north, Denmark has for many centuries participated in the development of Western Civilization on the European continent. The discoveries of the astronomer Tycho Brahe, the philosophical insights of Soren Kierkegaard, the founding of the University of Copenhagen in 1479, and the fairy tales of Hans Christian Andersen each reflect a long tradition of intellectual achievement by the Danish people.

Present-day Denmark has a population of just over 5,000,000 on a land area that would fit very comfortably within the borders of all but our smallest states in the U.S.A. Denmark has an extensive welfare state system, some elements of which have been in place for 100 years. The educational system, a major component of this welfare state, has succeeded to such an extent that illiteracy is virtually unknown in Denmark. The Danish economy is dependent primarily on agricultural production and export, with a lesser emphasis on fisheries and manufacturing.

The Danes are governed through a constitutional monarchy, including a parliament and a cabinet of ministers under the direction of the monarch. The Lutheran Church is recognized as the official state religion. As in other Scandinavian countries, Denmark is noted for its high tax rates to support its welfare state. The steeply progressive income tax system effectively eliminates great disparities in wealth, ensuring that virtually all Danes enjoy a similar standard of living. The Danes constitute a homogeneous ethnic group with no significant minority population. Denmark provides a good example of an educational system that is not challenged by the disparities in wealth, varied ethnic subcultures, and fragmented governance that are characteristic of America's schools.

HISTORY AND DEVELOPMENT OF DANISH SCHOOLS

Primary school education in Denmark before 1900 featured free schools for the masses, and special private elementary and secondary schools for the more economically privileged. The prevailing political opinion of that time rejected the concept that free secondary and university education should be made available to the general citizenry.[1] A watershed period in the development of Danish education followed a radical change in the political climate in Denmark beginning in 1901. The Act on General Secondary Education of 1903 was a major step in the development of the principle ''that the state provides free education at all levels for all citizens—including all branches of higher education.''[2]

Throughout the twentieth century Denmark has periodically raised the number of years of compulsory education. Compulsory schooling laws originally required five years of attendance at a Danish elementary school, known as a people school or *Folkeskole*. This requirement later increased to seven years, and in 1958 the law changed again to require nine years of compulsory education from ages seven to sixteen.[3] After attending the Folkeskole for nine or ten years, a student may enter an upper secondary school, a vocational school, or may chose to leave the school system altogether.

The proportion of students choosing to attend the various secondary schools has increased dramatically in recent decades. Currently more than 90 percent of students are remaining in school after completing the ninth or tenth form (grade). Since Danish students do not begin first grade until age seven, almost all Danish students remain in school until at least age sixteen or seventeen. There is a low truancy rate and a low dropout rate in Denmark.[4] These school holding rates compare favorably with those of the United States for a similar age group.

Today about 50 percent of graduates of the Danish Folkeskoler attend vocational or other training programs, 40 percent attend the *Gymnasium* or other precollege preparatory schools, while the remaining 10 percent of students leave the school system (Figure 3.1). Until recent years the successful completion of the Gymnasium curriculum guaranteed admission to a university. This is no longer the case. Since 1976 supply and demand factors have influenced admission to particular fields at particular universities. High grades from the Gymnasium and on the national examinations are required for acceptance to university programs with limited openings or a high number of applicants. In recent years

Education is compulsory for nine years, starting the summer of the year a child is seven. However, more than 90 percent of the children start with a year in preschool before that.

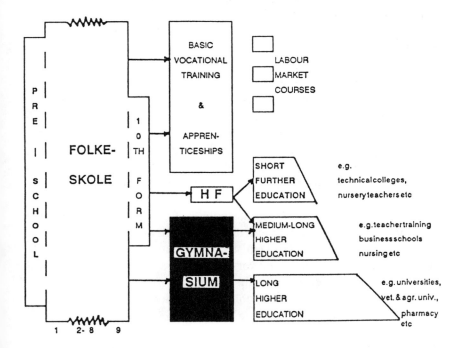

Following the ninth year of the Folkeskole, pupils have three choices:

- to stay on in the tenth form
- to go on to Basic Vocational Training (EFG) or apprenticeship
- to opt for the Gymnasium

Pupils who stay in the tenth form can go on to EFG/apprenticeship or Gymnasium after that year or they can go on to Higher Preparatory Courses (HF) at this stage. About 8 percent leave the education system altogether after the ninth or tenth form.

Although a number of general subjects are included, EFG is basically directed towards the labour market and the education and training lead to a vocational diploma.

The Gymnasium is a three-year course leading to *Studentereksamen* (upper secondary school leaving exam qualifying the students for university entrance). It is designed for academically able students aiming at higher education.

The HF is a two-year course, and the final exam qualifies for further and higher education.

Figure 3.1 *The main flows through the Danish education system (with permission from Ministry of Education and Research, Department of Upper Secondary Education, paper prepared for American Fulbright Exchange teachers, Copenhagen, Denmark, 1991).*

only about two-thirds of the graduates of the Gymnasia who have applied for university admission have been accepted.[5] Figure 3.1 provides a summary of the basic educational options available to Danish students as they proceed through the school system.

The Folkeskole

The Folkeskoler are the publicly provided elementary schools for Danish children between ages seven through sixteen or seventeen. Danish children begin formal schooling in August of the year in which they become seven years old. Students attend the Folkeskole for either nine or ten years, thus graduating from these schools at either age sixteen or seventeen. Although formal schooling begins at age seven, about 90 percent of Danish children also attend kindergarten or other preschool programs.[6]

There are more than 1,900 Folkeskoler in Denmark serving 550,000 students. The average enrollment in a Folkeskole is about 300 students. Approximately 90 percent of Danish children attend these schools while the remaining 10 percent attend various private schools. Although more than half of the Folkeskole contain all ten forms (grades), a significant minority of them provide classes only through form seven or form nine.[7] The local municipalities operate these elementary schools within guidelines established by the national government.

The maximum class size, by government regulation, is twenty-eight. Classes are usually much smaller, however, and nationwide classes average about eighteen students. All classes contain mixed-ability groups with no tracking or streaming in the first seven forms. Two groups of students (basic and advanced) are sometimes scheduled in forms eight and nine for courses such as English, German, and mathematics. The emerging trend, however, is to schedule mixed-ability groups throughout all forms of the school.[8]

A lesson or class in Danish schools, whether primary or secondary, is forty-five minutes in duration. First grade students receive 720 lessons per year while fourth grade students schedule 1,200 lessons.[9] The number of classes attended by students each day varies with their age. Students in form one, for example, have only four lessons each day, fifth form students have six lessons daily, and eighth form students attend six to seven lessons each day. Thus early primary grade students attend school for only several hours each day. Students in the Folkeskole remain with the same group of fellow students, as well as the same *class teacher* throughout their years in the school. The class teacher is usually a teacher of Danish or mathematics. This teacher forms very close relationships with both parents and students through many years of working with the same students.[10]

Danish students are not retained in grade and no formal written assessment of their performance is made until the fifth form or later. Danish elementary school students are not grouped for instruction, and do not take standardized achievement tests. Student progress is discussed at periodic parent-teacher conferences.

The 1975 Education Act established the curriculum for the Folkeskole. "Subjects that must be studied in every grade include Danish, arithmetic/mathematics, physical education and sport, and Christian studies. The following compulsory studies have to be provided in some years only: creative arts and music in years 1−5, history, geography, and biology in years 3−7, English in years 5−9, history in years 8−9, physics/chemistry in years 7−9, and contemporary studies (political and economic education) in years 8−9. Beyond these compulsory subjects pupils study differing numbers of subjects depending on their age, on their choices, and on the provisions the school is able to offer." [11]

The school year for students in the Folkeskole is 200 days. The Education Act allows classroom teaching to be temporarily discontinued for up to ten days for young students, and as many as thirty days for older students. These breaks in the school year allow students to participate in school camps, work experience, journeys, etc.[12]

DANISH UPPER SECONDARY SCHOOLS

All students attend the Folkeskole for either nine or ten years. About 10 percent of the students leave the educational system altogether after the 9th or 10th form.[13] Presently, about 40 percent of the students attend an upper secondary school that prepares them for some form of higher education, while the remaining 50 percent attend commercial schools, basic vocational training schools, or enter apprenticeships.[14]

The decision regarding which type of upper secondary school to attend is made jointly among the student, parents, and the teacher. In recent years there has been a significant increase in the numbers of students electing to attend the Gymnasium, which is the academic secondary school. In principle, students are to have free choice regarding the type of school that they will attend. This principle is modified in practice because of limited places in individual schools and limitations in the labor market restricting entry into certain vocational areas. About 50 percent of students take a job after ninth or tenth form, or after completing one year at a commercial or technical school following ninth or tenth form. The norm in Denmark currently is for virtually all students to attend a school of some type, at least on a part-time basis, for eleven or twelve years. Thus most students are at least eighteen years old before they complete a secondary school program.[15]

Gymnasium

Just under 40 percent of each age group enters a Gymnasium program at the conclusion of Folkeskole. Two-thirds of these students enter the Gymnasium after ninth form while the remaining one-third enter after tenth form. The Gymnasium offers the main route to admission to a university. The Gymnasium is a three-year program wherein students choose to follow either the language line or the mathematics line.

All students must take a common core of subjects including Danish, history, religion, and physical education. Language line students will study several languages such as German, French, or English at what is known as the *high level* of difficulty. Mathematics line students will study sciences such as chemistry and physics at the high level of difficulty. Gymnasia primarily offer traditional academic subjects, although there are some courses in music, visual arts, and physical education. The wide range of electives found in American comprehensive high schools is not available in the Danish Gymnasium.

Students attend the Gymnasium for 200 days each year, including the time for examination periods. Classes start at 8:00 A.M. and the school day ends at 1:30 or 2:00 P.M. Students typically attend six or seven forty-five-minute classes each day. Examination time is critical to Danish Gymnasium students since success on the written and/or oral examinations is required for admission to a Danish university.

Gymnasium students must take nationwide written examinations in certain major subjects after their second and third year at the Gymnasium. These exams are the same throughout the nation and are administered on the same day. Many courses also require an oral examination. Oral examinations are administered by the teacher of the subject along with a teacher from another school, known as a censor, who formally assigns a grade to the student for the oral exam. In practice, the student's teacher and the censor agree on the grade awarded to the student on the oral examination.

Students receive two grades for every course that involves national testing. Their classroom teacher assigns the term grade that represents the student's achievement in the classroom throughout the year. The second grade is based on the score in the national written exam, or when an oral exam is also given, on the average of these two exam scores. Two external examiners grade the written exams. A typical Gymnasium student will take a combination of ten oral and written exams during his or her final two years at the Gymnasium. These examinations are administered every year from mid-May to the end of June and are known as the *Studentereksamen.*

Students must earn satisfactory scores on these tests before being considered for admission to a university. The marking system for these, and other testing in Denmark, consists of a thirteen point scale. Possible scores include 00, 03, 5, 6, 7, 8, 9, 10, 11, and 13. The low score of 00 and the highest score of 13 are rarely assigned.[16] Gymnasium students may perform poorly in a few subjects but their overall average must be six or higher to move on to the next form. If their average is lower than six, they must either leave the school or repeat the year.[17]

About 10 percent of Gymnasium students leave the school during the three-year course of study for academic or other reasons. These students may return to the Folkeskole for tenth form, or transfer to a vocational or commercial school. By age twenty, from 25 to 30 percent of the age cohort has successfully completed the Gymnasium and is eligible for admission to the university system.

A further requirement for graduation from the Gymnasium is the *Danskopgaven.* This is a major written report that must be successfully completed by every third year student in a Gymnasium. Students use a full week free from required classes to research this report and consult with their teachers about it. The subject of this report may be Danish, history, or one of the optional subjects that the student is taking at high level. National educational regulations state that "the assignment shall be written during the course of one week in the period from 15th November to 31st January."[18]

Higher Preparatory Examination Courses (HF)

These precollege secondary schools, known as HFs offer courses of study similar to those of the Gymnasia. There are, however, several significant differences. They offer two-year courses of study rather than three years, and their students are older than those attending the Gymnasia. The coursework is rigorous, there are final examination requirements, and students in HF also must produce a major written paper as is required of Gymnasium students.

These schools offer a second chance for an academic education for those students who did not attend a Gymnasium after they left the Folkeskole, and for those who were unsuccessful at the Gymnasium as adolescents. Graduates of the HF schools generally will attend technical schools, teacher training colleges, or business schools.

Commercial Schools (HH)

Students typically begin study at a commercial school after completing ninth or tenth form at the Folkeskole. This school prepares students for entry into the business world as office workers in banks, manufacturing companies and retail businesses. The school offers a three-year course of study including many of the academic courses offered in the Gymnasium. There is also significant coursework in commercial subjects such as bookkeeping, typing/word processing, etc. The length of the student school day and school year is identical to that of Gymnasium students. Students may leave the commercial school after one year and enter an apprenticeship program planned cooperatively by the union and industry. Recently it has become difficult to find placements for all students.[19] This apprenticeship program requires two years during which time the student spends the equivalent of three weeks per year in school, and the balance of the time on an apprenticeship.[20]

Vocational Education and Training

Approximately 50 percent of Danish students enter a trade school or other type of vocational training upon completing the Folkeskole. These programs are typically three years in length and prepare students directly for jobs in the skilled labor force or other blue-collar occupations. Students preparing for skilled trades such as carpentry and plumbing will attend the technical school for one year, and then enter a three-and-one-half- to four-year apprenticeship program. During this apprenticeship they will attend the technical school for several weeks each year.[21] Apprenticeship programs in Denmark are much more formalized than in America, and are primarily under the direction of the various industries rather than the school system. "Vocational education and training is divided into the following branches: apprenticeship training, basic vocational education, basic technical or commercial exam courses, agricultural education and training, courses of social and health education, and other types of vocational education." [22]

PRIVATE EDUCATION IN DENMARK

Ten percent of Danish seven- to seventeen-year-old students attend private schools. The government pays 85 percent of the tuition costs and the parents pay the remaining 15 percent. These schools must offer a curriculum that parallels the national curriculum requirements. There is also a supervisor nominated or elected by the parents, subject to the approval of the local municipal government. This person testifies each year that the private school is satisfying state requirements regarding education. Since the tuition is largely paid by the state, students from all economic classes can attend private schools, and there is little social status attached to private school attendance. The schools are operated by a board of parents who can appoint teachers and a principal. Teachers usually possess the same qualifications as public school teachers, are paid on the same salary schedule, but do not have the same degree of job security as public school teachers. [23]

As noted elsewhere, the Lutheran religion, as well as comparative religions, is studied in the public schools. Since religious and moral instruction is provided in the public schools, parents typically do not select private schools for religious reasons. The Danish government supports private schooling as a method to ensure that people have a choice with respect to education. In Denmark, the overwhelming majority of parents choose to send their students to the public schools.

UNIVERSITY SYSTEM

Danish universities offer a more limited curriculum than do American colleges and universities, with degree programs in the hard sciences, social sciences, and the humanities. The lower enrollment level in the Danish universities, when compared with that of America, is partially related to their narrower range of course offerings. The education of nurses and elementary teachers, for example, takes place in separate schools, and not at the university level as in the United States. Considering all the types of higher education opportunities in Denmark, the proportion of the Danish population currently participating in higher education is about one-half the proportion of American students attending equivalent institutions in the United States.

THE TEACHER IN DANISH SCHOOLS

Educational requirements, daily worklife, and compensation of Danish teachers varies significantly depending upon the type of school in which they teach. Danish teachers begin their educational preparation by attending either a Gymnasium or a higher preparation (HF) program as adolescents. Teachers at the elementary, or Folkeskole, level generally receive their higher education at a teacher training college or seminary. This preparation program requires four years, including periods of student teaching experience.[24]

Since the school day for Danish students is shorter than in the U.S.A., the teacher workday is also shorter than that of an American elementary teacher. A full teaching load for a Danish Folkeskole teacher is twenty-four lessons per week of forty-five minutes each. Teachers in the upper forms of the Folkeskole teach only about eighteen to twenty-two lessons per week, since they are given released time for correcting homework in major subjects. Teachers are also given lighter schedules for serving as class teachers, leaders of the faculty, etc.[25]

Students experience a school day lasting from about 8:00 A.M. until 1:00 or 2:00 P.M. Danish students do not stay at school for lunch, but they do have a snack break sometime during the morning. Teachers are required to be at school only for their assigned lessons and may otherwise come and go as they please. Small group or general faculty meetings may require teachers to remain at school for an extra hour one afternoon per week.

The average class size in the Folkeskole is about eighteen students. There is little or no ability grouping before the eighth or ninth form and there is comparatively little ability grouping even at that level. Special schools are available for special education students, although some attempt is made to mainstream mildly handicapped students. The national government issues very general curriculum aims or goals. More detailed curriculum guidelines are recommended by the national government and these are generally adopted by the local municipalities operating the schools. Individual teachers are free to select textbooks and other materials in support of the general curriculum and teachers have a great degree of freedom in selecting the topics to be taught.

Relationships with parents of students are generally friendly and tend to extend over several years since a teacher instructs a student in the same subjects as the student moves through the forms. Folkeskole teachers teach two or more subjects to several grade levels, rather than teaching all subjects to a class of students for one year as is done in America. Relationships with students are less formal than in the U.S.A. and students often address teachers by their first name. Discipline standards tend to be more lax than those in American elementary schools. The judgmental role of the teacher is de-emphasized in Denmark since students do not receive written report cards until they are at least in the fifth form. In earlier years there are periodic parent-teacher conferences to discuss student performance.

Danish Folkeskole teachers work the traditional 200-day school year in Denmark. This time often includes overnight or week-long journeys or school trips where the teacher will accompany a class of students on an extended field trip. Elementary teachers in Denmark earn about 25 percent less than their better-educated and higher-status colleagues at the Gymnasium level. The typical Folkeskole teacher earns somewhat less than the current average salary for elementary teachers in the U.S.A.

Gymnasium teachers in Denmark enjoy the highest status and compensation in the Danish public school system. These teachers begin their academic career in a Gymnasium school, pass the required leaving examinations with the appropriate marks, and are then admitted to a university program. Many students take a year off from school between the Gymnasium and the university for travel, work, or to spend the year as an exchange student in another country. These future teachers usually spend six or seven years at the university and receive a master's level qualification in one subject, and a bachelor's level qualification in a second subject. All Gymnasium teachers must qualify to teach two subjects. Tuition at the university is free for all students. There are also provisions for living allowances for students in financial need.

Teacher candidates must pass the standard qualifying examinations to receive their degree from the university. The new Folkeskole teacher next spends four months as a student teacher. Gymnasium teachers must complete a five-month course in educational theory and practice before assuming their teaching duties.[26] The prospective teacher then applies directly to individual schools for a teaching position. The teacher is appointed to a position through an interview with the head teacher with, perhaps, some involvement with the school board of the particular school.

A full teaching load for Gymnasium teachers is twenty to twenty-one lessons per week. In a typical case a teacher may have four forty-five-minute classes per week with five different groups of students. These classes will not be held at the same time each day and may not meet every day during the school week. Teachers of subjects that require a significant amount of outside-of-class work teach on a reduced schedule. A teacher of English, for example, would have a total teaching load of sixteen to seventeen lessons per week rather than twenty-one. The teacher is required to be at school only for the assigned teaching periods. In addition, there may be one after-school meeting per week of the general faculty or specific department.

The teacher workday begins at approximately 8:00 A.M. and concludes by 1:30–2:00 P.M. Teachers generally will spend several hours at home in the afternoon or evening grading papers and preparing lessons. Danish teachers do not perform supervisory duties such as cafeteria supervision, bathroom patrol, or bus duty. Since the school day ends for most students shortly after noon, there typically are no cafeterias in Danish Gymnasia. Most schools schedule short ten- to fifteen-minute breaks after every few class periods. During these break times the students congregate in a commons area while the faculty members generally visit the staff room. Annette Priskorn, a Danish exchange teacher, noted that Danish teachers work the same number of hours as American teachers, but more of their time can be spent at home preparing lessons and grading papers, rather than in performing supervisory duties as do American teachers.[27]

Danish Gymnasium teachers work a 200-day work year. There is a six-week vacation during the summer, one week of vacation during the fall term, two weeks at Christmas, one week during the winter term, and two weeks at Easter. Some Danish teachers hold second, part-time jobs, but this practice is less common than with American teachers. Teacher salaries in Denmark are determined through negotiations between the national teachers' union and the national government. There is a standard salary schedule throughout the nation and there is no provision for merit pay for teachers. It takes fifteen years to reach the top of the salary schedule, which represents about $50,000 per year in American dollars. Thus average salaries of Gymnasium teachers are higher than salaries of American high school teachers.

There are national curriculum regulations and regional curriculum guidelines that teachers are expected to follow. Teachers at the Gymnasium must also consider the national written and oral exams that the students must pass successfully to gain admittance to the university.

Teachers operate within the broad constraints of the national curriculum and national written exams, while believing that they retain a reasonable amount of freedom to select teaching topics, textbooks, and instructional techniques.

Head teachers do not formally observe and evaluate Gymnasium teachers. Danish teachers would be both surprised and concerned if their head teacher entered their classroom to observe a lesson. Teachers feel that although they are not formally evaluated, the performance of their students on the national examinations provides a measure of their effectiveness. The head teacher will respond to parental or student complaints about a teacher by meeting with the teacher to discuss the concern. At the end of the school year, teachers must submit a report to the head teacher indicating the content that was taught during the year in each subject, as well as the textbooks and other instructional materials that were used.

Teachers in Denmark are able to support a middle-class lifestyle. Their status in the community is negatively affected by a perception among their fellow citizens that teachers have too short of a workday and too much vacation time.[28] In a 1988 study of international teacher salaries, Danish teachers, on average, were reported to earn 49 percent more than manufacturing workers in their nation.[29] This compares very favorably with data from the same document that indicates that American teachers earn only 3 percent more than the average American manufacturing worker.[30]

THE DANISH STUDENT

Ninety percent of young children in Denmark attend kindergarten before their entry into first form, or first grade. Danish students begin first grade at the end of the summer of the year that the child turns seven. Thus compulsory schooling begins one year later than is typical in the United States. During the first three years the student day is short, containing a maximum of from twenty to twenty-eight forty-five-minute lessons each week.

The actual time that these primary school age children spend in school is considerably less than that of their American counterparts. The students return home before lunch or, because many mothers work outside the home, they attend various day care establishments. Reading and writing in the Danish language constitute one-third to one-half of the curriculum during these early years. Mathematics receives the next largest time allocation. Physical education, Christian studies, music, and visual arts are each taught one or two periods every week.

Students are introduced to history, geography, and biology in third form. Home economics and woodworking occupy two periods per week in the middle elementary years. English is introduced in the fifth form, German in the seventh form, and physics/chemistry in form seven. By the middle Folkeskole years students are assigned to about twenty-eight lessons per week. This course load increases to thirty to thirty-two lessons per week in the ninth and tenth form. Even in the upper forms the school day ends by 1:30 − 2:30 P.M. and lunch facilities are normally not available at the school.[31]

All Danish students experience the curriculum outlined previously. There is no ability grouping within classes, except for a few subjects at the upper forms in a minority of schools. Students do not receive formal report cards before the fifth form. Periodic parent-teacher conferences provide the major communication link regarding student achievement. Thus Danish students are not overtly compared to one another through practices of the school system such as ability grouping, differentiation in courses of study among pupils, or written report card grades and evaluations.

Throughout their years in the Folkeskole, children attend classes with the same group of students. At least one teacher, known as the class teacher, will work with the same students for many years. This instructor is most often a teacher of Danish or mathematics. The class teacher is the major link between pupils, parents, and the school.[32] The ability of the classroom teachers to work successfully with these heterogeneous groups of students is facilitated by small class sizes, now averaging about eighteen.

Danish students, by law, must be involved in planning the content of their lessons and other classroom issues. Each week the class teacher provides a period to discuss such matters with students. In addition, each school has a pupil council that makes recommendations to the school board on matters of schoolwide concern. Student representatives sit on the school boards at both the Folkeskole and secondary school levels.[33]

By eighth or ninth form, at ages fifteen and sixteen, students must make a choice regarding their future educational path. The parents, the student, and the teacher collaborate in the decision-making process. The teacher makes a recommendation but the final decision is made by the family.

Students who aspire to enter the professions attend a Gymnasium in preparation for later admission to the university. In recent years, universities have been able to accept only about 25,000 of the 35,000 yearly applicants who have successfully completed the Gymnasium course.[34] This phenomenon has led to a greater competition among students in the Gymnasium to receive high grades and other academic distinctions. One Danish teacher expressed concern that this intensifying competition is hurting social relationships among students in Danish Gymnasia.[35]

Most students attend a Gymnasium for three years for forms eleven, twelve, and thirteen. There are short ten- to fifteen-minute breaks between some of the forty-five-minute classes. Danish students enjoy considerably more freedom in the school setting than their American counterparts. Students congregate in a commons area during these breaks and are not supervised by staff members.

Danish Gymnasium students do not remain at school for lunch and they are not assigned to study halls. Teachers are not required to supervise students in the halls or in the lavatories. Staff expectations of students regarding class attendance and completion of homework assignments are high. The principal has the authority to restrict a student's right to take a final examination whenever the student has missed 15 percent of his classes or has failed to submit 15 percent of his homework assignments.[36]

Students have four lessons each week in major subjects such as mathematics or English. Minor subjects such as music or physical education are taken two times each week. Danish Gymnasium students generally complete two to three hours of homework each day. Since students are dismissed from school very early, there are fewer opportunities for sports or other student activities than in American secondary schools. Young people in Denmark must be eighteen to obtain a driver's license, and both cars and gasoline are very expensive. Thus Danish teenagers are not involved in a lifestyle revolving around the automobile as are many young people in America. The above circumstances allow Danish students ample time to meet their homework obligations.

Recently many Danish teenagers have begun to hold part-time jobs. Danish teachers view this trend negatively since many of them believe that working students are being distracted from their studies.[37] While school-sponsored sports and other activities such as drama do exist, they are not accorded the same prominence and importance as similar activities in American schools.

About 50 percent of graduates from the Folkeskole attend a vocational education or training school. The great majority of these students remains in a vocational program for either three or four years. Participation in some form of upper secondary education is now considered the norm in Denmark, and nearly all students are engaged in a formal school program until age eighteen or nineteen.

Students who attend a commercial school are initially grouped according to previous performance in foreign language.[38] Students placed in level 1, the lowest group in academic ability, will attend the school full-time for only one year. At that point they will enter a two-year apprenticeship program that is operated primarily by industry. During this final apprenticeship students will attend school for about three weeks each year while the remainder of their time will be spent at a work site. Commercial school students assigned to higher academic groups will attend the commercial school on a full-time basis for an additional two years and will earn a higher level certificate when they graduate. Some of these students may ultimately be admitted to a university program. Most of them will enter two-year apprenticeships in banks, insurance companies, etc.[39] In any event, their higher qualification will enable them to attain higher level positions in the industrial work world.[40]

Students in the first year of the commercial school will experience a school day similar to that of Gymnasium students. They will study courses such as Danish, civics, economics, bookkeeping, and sales. The school year is 200 days long and students are scheduled for thirty to thirty-five forty-five-minute lessons each week. The school day starts at 8:00 A.M. and most students are finished by 1:45 P.M. Some students take additional courses and may stay at school until 3:30 or even 5:00 P.M. There are breaks between some of the class periods and students are given a thirty-minute lunch period. It is not necessary to supervise these sixteen- to twenty-year-old students in the halls or at lunchtime. Given the age of the students and the performance expectations placed upon them, there are few disciplinary problems at these schools.[41]

Recent legislation in Denmark has further refined the curriculum in vocational schools. Students may spend up to four years in these schools with no more than 50 percent of the time spent in academic studies. The remaining time is to be devoted to practical training. A third of the academic teaching in the vocational schools is to be in *core subjects* such as personal development, study skills, and information processing. A second third of the available time is for study within the student's broad area of interest. The final third of the time is allocated to subjects related to the student's specific field of study.[42]

During their first year of academic studies in commercial school the more able students typically will spend two or more hours per day on homework assignments. As in the Gymnasium schools, there is little provision for after-school athletic or other student activities. Students are free to come and go from the schools according to their class schedules. Student assessment for the academic courses in the commercial schools is similar to that of the Gymnasia.

Each student is assigned two grades at the end of the course. Students receive one oral or written grade for their class work, sometimes both grades are given.[43] Several tests, written work, and classroom participation determine this mark. Performance on national written and/or oral exams determines the second grade. As in the Gymnasium, oral exams are administered by the classroom teacher and a second teacher from another school. Thus external standards of performance apply to vocational students just as they do to academic students.

The expectations of students and the approach to their education differ markedly between the Danish Folkeskole and the various upper secondary school options. Students in the Folkeskole do not receive formal written grades until the fifth form or later, there is little ability grouping, and students are not retained in grade. Students remain with the same group of students throughout their years in the Folkeskole and typically work with the same teachers. Thus there is little academic pressure exerted on younger students in Danish schools.

By the ninth or tenth form of the Folkeskole, however, students and parents must make important choices about future schooling. Such choices significantly affect the future status and financial security of the student. All students, whether they select the Gymnasium or a vocational school, are expected to be serious students and to meet objective external standards of performance. The type of school that they select, as well as the grades that they earn on national exams, are critical factors in determining their future. Mechanisms are available for students who have chosen a less academically demanding route to change direction and pursue a more challenging course of study. The higher preparation program (HF) is a major method for older students to secure the background necessary to apply for university or other higher education options. It is also possible for students in vocational schools to receive *higher qualifications* from these schools that will enable them to pursue various forms of higher education.

The Danish education system retains approximately 90 percent of its students through twelve or thirteen years of schooling or school-related apprenticeships. Although standards for admission to certain programs are high, there are several avenues by which a student may ultimately qualify for higher education. The fact of external standards and examinations adds a seriousness to the educational enterprise that has a positive impact on teacher-student relationships and on general school climate. Students in Denmark attend school for twenty more days than their American counterparts, but the school day is somewhat shorter. It appears that throughout the school system students complete much more homework than is common in America. Until age fourteen, Danish students experience a virtually identical curriculum, regardless of their particular school or their individual abilities. This is certainly not the case in the United States.

Peddling along the bike path in Copenhagen, eighteen-year-old Britt reflects on her life at a crossroads. Her early morning ride to work on this Saturday takes her along Hans Christian Andersen Boulevard past the Tivoli, the world famous cultural and musical center of Copenhagen, and down Studiesstrade Avenue past Copenhagen University. Danish to the core, this young woman with blonde hair and blue eyes is attracted to the gaiety and fun symbolized by Tivoli and yet is confronted by the sobering reality of the hard work necessary to reach her goal of acceptance at the university.

Britt has both a part-time job and a steady boyfriend, two difficult distractions as she attempts to give top priority to preparing for the rigorous Studentereksamen, the school leaving exam from upper secondary school that also serves as an entrance exam for the university. It will not be sufficient to merely pass this test, since there are not enough university places for all qualified applicants, and therefore places are assigned to those with the highest test scores. Britt knows that she will have to put aside the movies, dances, and music that she and Anders love so well for the next six months, the time she needs to prepare for examinations in ten different subjects, in some cases both orally and by written test.

Britt found her three years in the Gymnasium to be much more difficult than her Folkeskole years. As a child Britt and her classmates stayed together as a class for ten years, with the same class teacher, Mrs. Angstrom, who she now views as she would a kindly aunt. Britt found her Folkeskole years to be pleasant rather than demanding. She was always able to do well in the mixed-ability classes that are a fixture of

(continued)

Danish schools. She was chosen as a student leader, served on the pupil council in her school, and even was elected as a student representative to the school board in her tenth year.

Once admitted to the academic Gymnasium Britt was expected to show some maturity and initiative. Her courses were very rigorous and out-of-class homework assignments were plentiful. She enjoyed the freedom to come and go from school depending on her schedule, and the freedom from adult supervision while at school. She had been told that in America only college-age students are given this degree of freedom.

Britt approaches adulthood with some anxieties. Although she knows that Denmark boasts the highest standard of living in Europe, she is troubled by the rising unemployment rates and the difficulty of gaining admission to the university. She enjoys an emotionally and financially stable family life shared with her parents and younger sister. While Britt would prefer to concentrate on the more enjoyable and recreational parts of her life, she intends to meet the rigorous standards that her nation requires for admission to higher education.

THE HEAD TEACHER

Principals, or head teachers, provide daily management of the Danish Folkeskole and the various upper secondary schools. Although these officials perform many of the duties that are staples of the American principalship, they exercise a more limited role than that of their American counterparts. A significant difference between Danish and American school administrators is that Danish administrators are not required to receive special formal training or certification in school administration. Such courses are available on a voluntary basis.

The average enrollment in one of the 1,900 Folkeskoler is about 300 students. "All Folkeskoler have a head teacher and most a deputy head. Head teachers act as administrators in addition to having considerable teaching commitments. Some see themselves as curriculum leaders, others do not. None of the Folkeskoler has formal management structures concerned, for example, with subject departments or year group organization." [44]

Each school has its own school board consisting of five to seven parents elected by the parents of children attending the school. There are also two teacher representatives, two students, a member of the municipal council, and the head teacher, who are usually nonvoting members of the board. Thus the direct influence of parents and teachers on the school program and policies is much stronger than in American schools. The head teacher in Denmark exercises a primarily managerial role in the operation of the school.

Head teachers in Danish schools do not directly observe or formally evaluate their teachers. The extent of their role as an instructional leader is dependent upon their own inclinations in this area. Their role in staff selection and budget development is advisory to the school board. The straightforward organizational arrangements, as well as the small size of the typical Folkeskole, make the management of the school rather uncomplicated. Teachers resolve most student discipline problems at the classroom level and thus discipline is not a major job task of the head teacher.

Head teachers work the same schedule as regular teachers and are not generally required to be at school during vacation periods. Their work-day is of similar length to that of a regular teacher and, as such, it is significantly shorter than the workday of an American elementary or middle school principal. There is some salary differential between the principal and a regular classroom teacher. In addition to the presence of a deputy head, the principal also relies upon the class teacher for most of the normal communications and interactions with parents. The class teacher is a higher status teaching position, although there is no additional compensation for the job. [45]

The role of the head teacher or principal in the Danish secondary school parallels that of the principal of a Folkeskole. The national regulations on curriculum and school organization frequently mention the role of the principal in interpreting the regulations at the local school level and in making decisions as to how the regulations will affect individual students. The role of the principal in these areas is quite authoritative. If a parent or student has a complaint about a decision affecting an individual student, the student may file a formal written complaint with the national Ministry of Education and Research.

The exact provisions for this complaint process are as follows:

1. Complaints against decisions of the principal in relation to this executive order may be submitted by the student to the Ministry of Education and Research within one month of the decision having been communicated to the student.

2. If the student is under parental custody, the complaint may also be made by the parent or guardian.

3. The complaint must be submitted in writing through the principal, who

shall forward it to the Ministry together with his own statement on the case. Before forwarding the complaint the principal shall give the complainant the opportunity to comment on the principal's statement within a time limit of one week. Any comments by the complainant shall also be sent to the Ministry.

4. The Ministry shall decide whether to confirm the decision of the principal or whether to alter it to the complainant's advantage.[46]

The formality of this process ensures that comparatively few decisions of a school principal are likely to be overturned. In America, by contrast, a parent unhappy with the decision of the principal will appeal directly to the local superintendent or members of the local school board. The American principal will often be unaware that a complaint has been filed until after the fact. Thus the Danish school principal has considerably more independent power and authority over decisions affecting students, than does his or her American counterpart.

The authority of the Danish principal relative to teachers, however, is considerably less than that of an American principal. As mentioned previously, Danish principals do not have formal evaluation responsibilities for their teachers. The principal in a Folkeskole is expected to supervise a teacher during the first two years in a school, but such evaluations are often perfunctory.[47] Teachers interviewed for this book report that the principal relies heavily on teacher input to develop a building budget, has little or no role in curriculum development, and plays a role supportive to the teacher with respect to student discipline.[48]

Danish principals do play a significant role in the development of the school schedule and organization. They also serve as the representative of the school to the community. The principal plays the major role in selection of new staff members, although the school board is consulted about teacher appointments. The principal's major function is to execute faithfully the national education regulations within his or her school. Thus the position is managerial, perhaps even bureaucratic. The American concept of the principal as an instructional leader is not an expectation in Danish secondary schools.

The education committee of the local municipal council selects the head teacher for each school. These are locally elected municipal officials having responsibilities for a number of governmental services, including education. Normally members of the school board are consulted about the appointment of a new head, but they do not make the decision.[49] Members of the school faculty have no role to play in the selection of a head teacher.

Teachers are generally not eligible to be appointed to the headship in their own school. Head teacher candidates typically have successful experience as a classroom teacher and have sometimes served as assistant heads in other secondary schools. Their experience as an assistant head serves as their on-the-job training for a headship. There are no formal university or other preparation programs for school administration in Denmark. It is possible, at least in the commercial schools, for a person to be appointed as head teacher who has had no teaching experience.

There is a salary differential between the principal and classroom teachers in Denmark. The magnitude of this difference is similar to the difference in salaries of principals and teachers in the United States.[50] In American dollars, a secondary school principal in Denmark earns approximately $70,000. Principals also teach from two to six lessons per week. They work the same school year as the teachers with, perhaps, an additional week at the end of the term and before the beginning of the next term. Their workday is similar in length to that of their teachers and, thus, considerably shorter than the typical workday of an American secondary school principal. The number of night meetings and other events for Danish principals is significantly less than for their American counterparts, primarily because of the lack of extensive athletic and other student activity programs.

Secondary schools in Denmark typically will have at least one part-time assistant principal. In addition, a small group of teachers will have a one-third reduction in their teaching schedule to serve as counselors to students. It is not necessary to have full-time assistant principals to deal with discipline and attendance problems, as is virtually universal in the United States. Assistant head teachers generally assume about one-half of a normal teaching schedule.

The Danish school administrator is essentially the representative of the national government at the local school level. He or she must ensure that all national and municipal rules and regulations regarding education are properly enforced. He or she is delegated a wide latitude of discretion regarding decisions relating to students. His or her powers vis-à-vis teachers seem to be more circumscribed. Since he or she has little to do with teacher evaluation or curriculum development, the Danish principal's job is less comprehensive than that of his or her American counterpart. The Danish principal's rather minimal involvement with student discipline also represents a significant role difference compared to an American school administrator.

EDUCATIONAL GOVERNANCE

The governance of education in Denmark is a shared responsibility among four levels of policymaking and administration. A strong commitment to democratic processes has produced a system of education designed to maximize the involvement of parents, students, and teachers in the decision-making process. The legal right of parents, students, and teachers to participate in the deliberations of the local school boards ensures that educational programs will reflect the concerns of those most affected.

The Ministry of Education and Research is the national governmental agency responsible for educational policy and administration. There is a Directorate for Primary and Lower Secondary Education, a Directorate for Upper Secondary Education, and a Directorate for Higher Education. The Ministry of Education implements educational laws passed by the Danish Parliament. This ministry is responsible for establishing broad aims for the educational system and for issuing recommended guidelines for the aims and content of specific courses offered in Danish schools. The ministry issues appropriate regulations and oversees the allocation of public funds for the schools.[51]

The national government negotiates with the national teachers' union to establish a single salary scale for all teachers. The Directorate of Upper Secondary Schools directly supervises the operation of the vocational colleges and commercial schools. In recent years the Ministry of Education has been active in promoting the decentralization of educational decision making as well as the concept of per-pupil allocation systems for distributing school funds.

The next lower level of government involved in education is the county council. There are fourteen such elected councils in Denmark whose task is to administer several functions of regional government. The county councils have an education committee to administer the Gymnasia and to provide a more generalized supervision of the Folkeskoler. Budgetary matters relating to the Gymnasia such as instructional materials, furniture and equipment, and school facilities are under the control of the county councils. These councils also appoint teachers and principals, in consultation with the school boards of the affected schools.

Each Gymnasium has its own locally elected school board consisting of five to seven parents elected from the parents of the students. The board includes two teacher representatives from the teachers' council as well as two student representatives. The principal is also a member of the school board. In the past, only the parents were voting members of these boards, although recent legislative changes have made it permissible, by local option, for teachers and students to have a vote.[52]

The school board for an individual school operates within budgetary and other parameters set by the education committee of the county council. These education committees consist of six members of the county council as well as five parents from throughout the county. School boards typically set general policies for the daily operation of the school that are then the responsibility of the principal to implement. School boards have only minor discretionary powers regarding the curriculum. They do, however, approve the number of lessons to be offered for each subject, the schedules or timetables for teachers, and the selection of textbooks.

Below the fourteen county governments are 276 municipal councils. These political bodies have direct responsibility for operating the 1,900 Folkeskoler in Denmark. These municipalities must approve the operating guidelines for implementing the general aims for education in the Folkeskole. In practice, most municipalities adopt the guidelines issued by the Ministry of Education regarding specific course objectives and content. These 276 municipalities are responsible for providing the financial support at the Folkeskole for school facilities, instructional materials and supplies, and furniture and equipment. The national government provides the money for staff salaries.

The daily operation of the Folkeskole is the responsibility of the school board at each school. The responsibilities of the school board at the Folkeskole level are very similar to those for the Gymnasium. Although attempts are being made to increase parental involvement in Danish schools, there is a low level of parent participation in school board elections. The national parents' organization in Denmark "estimates that, on average, only about 11 percent of parents vote in school board elections."[53] As is true in America, parents in the more affluent areas are more involved in school governance than are parents in less financially advantaged municipalities.[54]

School governance in Denmark and the United States can be contrasted in several respects. School boards in Denmark consist of parents of students, teachers, students, and the principal—each having a direct interest in the quality of the educational program. In America, school boards are composed of adults from the general community, who may or may not be interested primarily in education. American school boards are open to single issue candidates concerned about taxes, teacher salaries, or specific curriculum issues. Also, American school boards seldom involve teachers, principals, or students in their deliberations.

Decisions regarding tax rates, teacher salaries, and the determination of curriculum are not within the purview of Danish school boards. These decisions are all made at the national or the municipal level. Thus Danish school boards are seldom the focus of community hostility and controversy as is all too often the case in the United States. For these reasons Danish school boards are free to devote their energies to strictly educational issues.

An entire layer of school administration in America is totally absent in Denmark. The local school district central administrative apparatus is simply unneeded in Denmark. The role of the national government in educational policymaking and implementation, as well as the role played by existing municipal governments, makes it unnecessary to maintain a local school bureaucracy for each Danish school. By contrast, each of the 15,000 school districts in the United States must concern itself with financial, taxation, personnel, and curriculum matters.

The financial support for education in Denmark is much more broadly based than in the United States. The fact that teacher salaries are established nationally and financed nationally removes one of the major obstacles to providing educational equity. Unfortunately, the level of financial support for schools in the United States is very much dependent on the wealth of each local school district. This creates an enormous disparity in educational opportunities among American school districts. The Fulbright Exchange teachers visiting the United States each year consider this disparity to be one of America's most critical educational problems.

SOCIAL AND CULTURAL INFLUENCES ON EDUCATION

Denmark is a compact and ethnically homogeneous nation of only 5 million citizens. The school system is very egalitarian in the sense that virtually all Danish children have a similar schooling experience at least through age sixteen. The curriculum is similar throughout the nation and all students take the same courses, in mixed-ability classes, until at least form seven. Even the upper years of the Folkeskole offer very few classes that are ability grouped.

A common culture is formally transmitted by the schools through Danish studies, history, and religious studies. The school leaving examinations at the academic upper secondary schools further ensure that Danish students are exposed to a common core of values and educational experiences. The government also offers significant financial support to private schools, on the condition that they provide the essentials of Danish education offered in the public school setting.

The fact that staff salaries are set and paid by the central Ministry of Education ensures that all regions of the nation will be able to afford a quality school program. Local municipalities contribute to the less expensive areas of the education budget such as materials, supplies, and facilities. Danish school boards consist almost exclusively of parents, teachers, and students, and thus primarily concentrate on education-related matters. School board meetings are not battlegrounds for community controversies, taxation fights, or complaints about teacher salaries.

There is very little competition among students at the Danish Folkeskole. The absences of ability grouping, written report cards, or standardized testing all contribute to a team spirit among students and teachers. By the final year or two of Folkeskole, however, students must make important decisions about their future academic lives and career paths. In the upper secondary school years (forms ten to twelve) students are held to exacting and demanding standards of performance. It is a societal expectation that students at this age will work diligently to meet successfully the requirements of their particular school and program. A student who fails to meet the standards must either repeat the school year or transfer to a less demanding school or program.

The Danish policy of providing educational opportunities to all students, at no cost, confronts economic reality when students complete their upper secondary education. There are not always sufficient jobs available in those areas that students wish to receive training. This fact requires that some students select alternate vocational paths. Also, there are not sufficient places at the universities to accommodate all the students who annually pass the qualifying examinations from the Gymnasium, the higher preparation programs, and the commercial HH programs. Some students must select less popular areas for study. Even so, about 10,000 out of about 35,000 applicants are rejected by the universities each year.[55] Those who are admitted receive their education tuition free.

The disparity in socioeconomic levels among Danish students is much narrower than among American students because of the impact of the Danish welfare state. The funding process for education provides for a relatively similar level of financial resources in schools throughout the country. All students have access to adequate health care as an entitlement from the state. In addition, parents receive child allowances of approximately $800 per year per child until a student is eighteen years of age.[56] Students are also shielded from the negative effects of unemployment through the two-and-one-half-year payment of unemployment benefits to unemployed workers. Such payments equal approximately 80 percent of the worker's regular wage.[57]

In Denmark there is a problem with divorce and single parent households. Although the divorce rate is less than in America, births to unmarried mothers are the highest in Europe and twice the rate in the United States. Furthermore, the economic impact of the single parent phenomenon is ameliorated by direct government financial support for children and unemployed workers. There is also a greater availability of quality child care than is generally found in America.[58]

Denmark allocates more of its gross domestic product to education than does the United States (4.8 percent for Denmark versus 4.1 percent for the United States).[59] Additionally, Denmark has not been burdened with the cost of providing military security for the West for the past fifty years, as has the United States. Denmark does not have a national debt problem comparable to that of America's. The poverty-related educational challenges that the United States confronts with inner-city children are also absent in Denmark.

Danish society in general, and its educational system in particular, have produced a well-educated citizenry where illiteracy is virtually unknown. Over 90 percent of Danish students experience a very similar educational background until the age of sixteen to seventeen. Access to universities and other forms of higher education is based on merit and not economic ability. The very high proportion of citizens electing to patronize the public schools, in a nation that financially supports private schools, bespeaks an impressive level of citizen satisfaction with the school system. In summary, it is evident that the Danish school system meets the expectations of its citizens and is competitive in quality on a worldwide basis.

REFERENCES

1. Bjerg, J. 1991. "Reflections on Danish Comprehensive Education, 1903 – 1990," *European Journal of Education*, 26(2):133.
2. Bjerg, J., 26(2):133.

3. Ministry of Education. 1988. *The Folkeskole*. Copenhagen, Denmark: Ministry of Education, p. 7.

4. Ministry of Education. 1988, p. 17.

5. Bjerg, J., 26(2):137.

6. Ministry of Education. 1991. *The Main Flows through the Education System*. Copenhagen, Denmark: Ministry of Education, p. 2.

7. Department of Education and Science. 1989. *Education in Denmark: Aspects of the Work of the Folkeskole*. London: Dept. of Education and Science, pp. 1–3.

8. Department of Education and Science, p. 3.

9. Kurian, G. 1988. "Denmark," in *World Education Encyclopedia, Vol. 1*. New York, NY: Facts on File Publications, p. 312.

10. Kurian, G., p. 5.

11. Kurian, G., p. 4.

12. Kurian, G., p. 5.

13. Ministry of Education and Research, Department of Upper Secondary Education. 1991. *Danish Secondary Education*. Copenhagen, Denmark: Ministry of Education and Research, p. 2.

14. Andersen, A. Presentation at Fulbright orientation, Washington, DC, August 7, 1991.

15. Kolbaek, K. Correspondence with author, January 1992.

16. Ministry of Education and Research, pp. 5, 21.

17. Brondsted, A. Interview with author, October 1991.

18. Ministry of Education and Research, p. 10.

19. Kolbaek, K. Correspondence.

20. Kolbaek, K. Interview with author, October 1991.

21. Kolbaek, K. Correspondence.

22. United States Information Agency. 1991. *Your Year in Denmark*. Washington, DC, p. 10.

23. Department of Education and Science, p. 15.

24. Kolbaek, K. Correspondence.

25. Kolbaek, K. Correspondence.

26. Archer, E. G. and B. T. Peck. 1992. *The Teaching Profession in Europe*. Glasgow: Jordanhill College of Education, p. 83.

27. Priskorn, A. Interview with author, October 1991.

28. Priskorn, A. Interview.

29. Nelson, F. H. 1991. *International Comparisons of Public Spending on Education*. Washington, DC: American Federation of Teachers, p. 37.

30. Nelson, F. H., p. 37.

31. Department of Education and Science, p. 27.

32. Department of Education and Science, p. 3.

33. Ministry of Education. 1991, pp. 12, 15.

34. Bjerg, J., 26(2):137.

35. Priskorn, A. Interview.

36. Ministry of Education and Research, p. 7.

37. Brondsted, A. Interview.

38. Kolbaek, K. Correspondence.
39. Kolbaek, K. Correspondence.
40. Kolbaek, K. Interview.
41. Kolbaek, K. Interview.
42. Bjerg, J., 26(2):140.
43. Kolbaek, K. Correspondence.
44. Department of Education and Science, p. 3.
45. Department of Education and Science, pp. 3, 13 – 14.
46. Ministry of Education and Research, p. 15.
47. Kolbaek, K. Correspondence.
48. Kolbaek, K., A. Brondsted, and A. Priskorn. Interviews with author, October 1991.
49. Department of Education and Science, p. 13.
50. Kolbaek, K. Interview.
51. Department of Education and Science, p. 2.
52. Bjerg, J., 26(2):136.
53. Department of Education and Science, p. 14.
54. Department of Education and Science, p. 14.
55. Bjerg, J., 26(2):137.
56. Kolbaek, K., A. Brondsted, and A. Priskorn. Interviews.
57. Kolbaek, K. Interview.
58. Priskorn, A. Interview.
59. Rasell, M. E. and L. Mishel. 1990. *Shortchanging Education: How U.S. Spending on Grades K–12 Lags behind Other Industrial Nations.* Washington, DC: Economic Policy Institute, p. 5.

CHAPTER 4

Germany—A Tradition of Quality

STRATEGICALLY LOCATED IN Central Europe, Germany has for centuries been a major player on the world stage. Germany has had a dominant role in world affairs in the twentieth century, through two world wars and the domestic upheavals relating to them. As recently as 1990, Germany underwent the wrenching adjustment of reuniting the two sections of the country partitioned since the end of World War II.

The modern educational system in Germany originated in the Middle Ages with the church-controlled monastery schools, and later the church-chartered universities. The outlines of the current educational system took form by the early years of the twentieth century. The basic structure of the German system persisted through the cataclysmic events accompanying World War I, the Weimar Republic, the rise of Hitler, World War II, and the physical and economic destruction of Germany at the end of the war in 1945.

Germany has a population of approximately 79 million citizens living in an area somewhat smaller than the state of California. Germany enjoys an excellent reputation for the quality of its educational system and work force. The principal religious groups in the country are the Roman Catholics and the Lutherans. Economically, Germany has risen from the ashes of World War II to become a major world economic power.

German reunification has created a federal republic consisting of sixteen constituent states known as *Länder* (hereafter referred to as states). The new unified country is quickly adopting the governmental forms, policies, and ideology of the former West Germany. The former Communist regime in East Germany, the German Democratic Republic (GDR), has been totally discredited. It is apparent that this preference for West German policies and models will extend to the field of educational policy and practice.

The government of the united Germany follows the West German model in that it is a democratic, constitutional republic with two houses of the legislature and a strong executive branch. Each of the sixteen states has its own constitution and governing body. These individual states exercise broad latitude to govern in areas such as education, local government, cultural affairs, and the police.[1]

The federal government's role in education is to formulate broad policies and objectives for Germany's schools. Representatives from each state collaborate in developing educational goals for the nation through a mechanism known as the Standing Conference of Education Ministers. Each German state has its own Minister of Cultural Affairs to interpret the national educational framework into its own constitution. Each state develops its own curriculum guides, recommends textbooks, and organizes schools and teaching—all without any system of federal inspection or control. Each state also trains, appoints, and promotes teachers within the state.[2]

School administration usually operates at three levels, the top level being the state *(Länd)* education ministry. There is also a regional or intermediate level of school authority. The local district level includes towns, municipalities, and surrounding areas.[3] Educational governance at the state level in Germany is superficially similar to the model existing at the state level in many regions of the United States. In reality, however, the German model differs significantly from the most common systems of state educational control in America.

HISTORY AND DEVELOPMENT OF GERMAN SCHOOLS

The church's monopoly on education in the Middle Ages gave way to more secular influences during the Renaissance and the Age of Science that followed. Many of the German states, formed during the sixteenth and seventeenth centuries, viewed the creation of schools as a method to promote social cohesion. The first public schools appeared in the states of Gotha in 1642 and Prussia in 1716. ''The key figure who gave direction to the German and the world's secondary education system was Wilhelm von Humboldt (1767 – 1835), the Prussian minister of culture and education.''[4]

The Industrial Revolution of the nineteenth century created the need for a better-educated work force that would complement the needs of an industrial society. By the year 1900 the superintendent of schools in Munich, Germany, Georg Kerschensteiner, had developed his idea of the *Arbeitsschule* or industrial school. This marked the beginning of the vocational schooling programs for which Germany is still world renowned.[5] Current vocational programs in Germany closely reflect the principles of these early programs.

The present-day pattern of schooling in Germany developed during the Weimar Republic era of the 1920s. Then it became mandatory for students to attend a four-year *Grundschule* (primary school). Most students next entered the *Hauptschule* (main school), which was attended by students who were not chosen for one of the two other principal options. These additional paths were the *Realschule* (intermediate school) and the *Gymnasium* (grammar school).[6] The Realschule enrolled average- to above-average-ability students who would later fill the skilled technical and managerial ranks in the economy. The Gymnasium admitted only the best students, the top 15 percent as recently as 1960, who would prepare to attend the university and serve in one of the professions. By the middle decades of the century the majority of students attended the Hauptschule, while perhaps 10 to 15 percent of students attended the Realschule.[7] The proportion of students attending each of these three types of lower secondary schools has changed dramatically over the past twenty years.

The basic outline of this tripartite educational system persisted through the Nazi era as well as through the period of attempted reform by the victorious allies after the Second World War. More dramatic changes were mandated in Communist-controlled East Germany, but these changes are being abandoned rapidly with the reunification. It is likely that the existing basic structure of German education will continue into the next century (see Figure 4.1).

THE GERMAN PRIMARY SCHOOL (GRUNDSCHULE)

The Grundschule is the basic form of elementary education in Germany. Students begin first grade in these local schools at the age of six and remain in the school for four grade levels, until about age ten. The modern Grundschule (primary school) replaced the first four years of the former *Volksschulen* (elementary schools) during the period of the Weimar Republic in the 1920s.[8] Approximately 2.5 million children attended Grundschulen in 1989.

Virtually all German children attend some form of voluntary pre-primary school program such as kindergarten. These kindergartens also accept children of primary school age who are too immature to attend

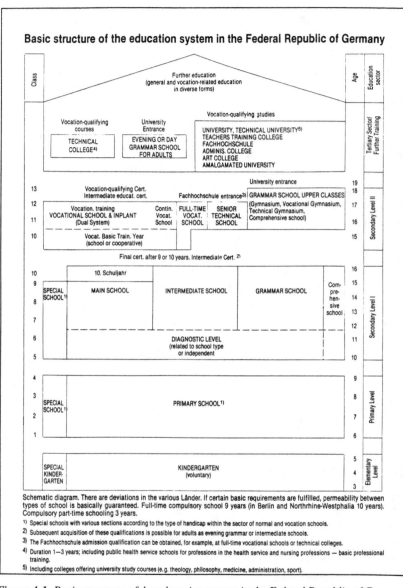

Figure 4.1 *Basic structure of the education system in the Federal Republic of Germany. Source: Monikes, W. 1991. "The School System in the Federal Republic of Germany,"* Education and Science, *3/4(e):12, with permission from INTER NATIONES, Bonn.*

98

first grade.[9] Preschool programs are under the direction of the Ministry of Health, Family, Youth, and Social Affairs. About 80 percent of the funding, however, is from private sources, including the church. Small fees are required only of those who can afford them.[10]

Primary school children in Germany have a shorter school day than older students. As in Denmark, children attend a series of forty-five-minute lessons each week that vary in number and subject according to grade level. In the first two grades, students schedule between twenty and twenty-six lessons each week. This translates into a school day that is about four hours long. In grades three and four, students schedule from twenty-four to thirty lessons per week. The primary school concentrates on the basics with supplemental compulsory lessons in religious studies, music, art, physical education, and local studies.[11] Specific basic subjects studied include reading and writing in German, social affairs, history, geography, biology, physics, chemistry, and mathematics.[12]

Students in the Grundschule are grouped by age but not by ability. The two concepts of *Anschauen* (see and enjoy) and *Heimat* (home world) form the basic philosophy of the elementary school curriculum. Education is to be an enjoyable experience that develops the students' natural positive responses to their immediate world. In these early years there is little evidence of the competition and performance orientation that are characteristic of German secondary education.[13]

German elementary school students are, however, subject to definite standards and expectations. The German reputation for neatness, order, and thoroughness is evident in the exercise books, handicraft projects, and homework assignments of elementary school students. There is great emphasis placed on working with tools and materials in the proper way. In day-to-day projects the teacher demands that the student produce a *whole job*. This might mean an illustration accompanying a homework written assignment, or the answering of questions in complete sentences. There is constant attention to the quality of the product, which becomes ingrained in the developing work habits of the child. There is a consistent emphasis in German elementary schools on developing high standards in the cognitive, affective, and practical domains.[14]

German elementary schools are usually modern structures, rebuilt as a result of bombing during the Second World War, or remodeled during the 1950s. Most schools are relatively small. Students typically walk to school or take a short ride by public transportation. Classrooms contain blackboards and movable desks similar to those found in the U.S.A. Students attend school six mornings per week, although in many regions

Saturday classes are held every other week. Teachers often schedule one full day each month to take the class on a day-long hike to a cultural, historical, or nature park site.

Classes begin at 7:45 – 8:00 A.M. and end very early in the afternoon, in time for most students to return home for a late lunch. Students are assigned homework, and parents are expected to assist students with these assignments. Homework will require perhaps thirty minutes for a first grade student and up to two hours for a fourth grade student. Students maintain separate exercise books for homework and classroom assignments. The emphasis in these exercise books is on neatness and completeness.

Students' tests are retained in the classroom by the teacher and kept for use in the year-end evaluation of the student. Report cards are issued twice every school year. Homework is usually corrected and is a part of the student's grade in each subject. The classroom teacher administers periodic tests and quizzes. Discipline problems are the responsibility of the classroom teacher. Five-minute breaks between lessons and a thirty-minute snack break after the second lesson each morning, when students are expected to go outside "for fresh air," are designed to minimize student restlessness, and thus keep discipline problems to a minimum.[15]

The school year contains several vacation periods totaling twelve weeks. There is a six-week summer vacation starting at various times in June, depending upon a rotating schedule among the sixteen German states. This rotating vacation schedule among the states is designed to avoid overcrowding at popular vacation and resort areas. There is a two-week vacation period in autumn, two weeks at Christmas, and two weeks at Easter. Students in some regions attend school five days per week for 200 days while in other regions the school year may have 226 days, including some half-day Saturday sessions.[16] Although German students attend school for more days than American students, the typical German school day is shorter than an American school day.

The total hours of instruction in German and American schools each year are similar. German elementary school students take many more day-long excursions away from school than do American elementary students. It is possible that German students actually spend fewer hours each year in direct classroom instruction than do their American counterparts.

Until recent decades, Grundschule teachers made significant unilateral decisions regarding the assignment of their students to various lower secondary schools. Students at age ten were formally assigned to one of three educational tracks. These tracks were relatively inflexible, with little opportunity for a student to make a later change to a higher academic level. In recent years, two-year orientation programs have been introduced at the fifth and sixth grade levels in most states to delay and improve decision making regarding student assignment to educational tracks.

TWO-YEAR ORIENTATION PROGRAMS (ORIENTIERUNGSSTUFE)

In modern Germany, students at the fifth and sixth grade levels usually attend a form of modified elementary school program designed to orient and prepare students for an appropriate form of secondary education. The purpose of the program is to provide teachers, students, and parents with a better basis for choosing a secondary school. These two-year programs are sometimes independent schools, but they are also frequently a division of a previously existing school.[17]

These two-year orientation programs provide additional opportunities for teachers and parents to recognize the abilities of the students, and for the students themselves to develop intellectually and emotionally. Parental involvement in choosing a secondary school track for the student has been enhanced in recent years. Where once the teacher and test results alone would determine the placement of a student in secondary school, the voice of the parent has now taken on greater weight as a determining factor in the placement of the child.

The changing academic expectations of parents for their children, the increased role of the parent in selecting a secondary school track, and the introduction of the two-year orientation program, have each contributed to a dramatic shift in the proportion of students selecting each of the secondary school options. In the 1990s, a far larger proportion of German students enroll in academic secondary schools than was the case a generation earlier.

LOWER SECONDARY SCHOOLS (SEKUNDARBEREICH I)

The aspect of the German education system that has been most criticized by Americans is the separation of students into three different types of schools, and career options, at a very early age. During most of this century the basic pattern in Germany was a tripartite system of education beginning after the primary school years. The best academic students enrolled in the Gymnasium in preparation for attending the university and entering one of the professions. The Realschule provided a middle academic path for students who possessed abilities in technical fields, or who offered promise as future managers. This path prepared students for work requiring independence, responsibility, and leadership.

The Hauptschule, or main school, was attended by all students who did not attend one of the other available schools. Students attending the Hauptschule would ultimately fill the ranks of skilled workers, as well as occupations that did not require independent action or highly developed skills. Assignment to one of these three types of schools was a result of prior academic performance and teacher recommendations. Until recent years, parents had little influence over the school to which their child was assigned.

In the late 1960s a fourth type of school appeared, known as the *Gesamtschule* or comprehensive school. This school attempted to avoid the early tracking of the existing system and to introduce an egalitarian element to the German school system. Such schools were particularly favored by Liberal and Socialist political parties and became relatively common in those few German states where these parties exercised political control. On a nationwide basis, however, only about 5 percent of an age group attends these comprehensive schools.[18]

Until a generation ago, the majority of German students attended the Hauptschule after completing their primary school years. Approximately one-fourth of the students enrolled at the Realschule, while an additional 15−20 percent of students attended the beginning grades of the Gymnasium. The proportion of students attending each of these schools has changed significantly in recent times.

Within the past thirty years Hauptschule enrollment has been halved, while enrollments in the Realschule and Gymnasium have almost doubled. Thus today about one-third of the students attend a Hauptschule, another third attend either a Realschule or a Gesamtschule, and the remaining third attend a Gymnasium.[19] These numbers indicate a sharp decline in enrollment at the Hauptschule, causing some concern that these schools will no longer be the main schools, but rather the remainder schools.

The shifting enrollment patterns described above indicate a fundamental change in German policy regarding public education. These shifts toward the more academic schools speak to greater parental influence on school selection, and an increasing awareness that higher forms of secondary education are critical to the financial and social well-being of the next generation. These changes are not universally applauded, particularly among many members of the teaching profession.

Interviews with Fulbright Exchange teachers from Germany revealed a concern with a dilution of academic standards as less able students are enrolled in the Realschule and the Gymnasium. There is a related concern that the Hauptschulen are increasingly populated by un- motivated students who can become discipline problems.[20] Available statistics indicate that the children of immigrant workers in Germany are disproportionately represented in the population of the Hauptschule.[21] These statistics suggest that attendance at the Hauptschule is increasingly becoming a function of social class.

The Main School (Hauptschule)

Students enter the Hauptschule at either grade five or seven, depend- ing upon whether their area offers a separate orientation school program for grades five and six. Students complete the Hauptschule after grade nine or ten, at which time more than 90 percent of them have earned a school leaving certificate. The schedule at this school follows the normal pattern of morning classes extending from about 8:00 A.M. until ap- proximately 1:00 P.M. In most regions, students attend school Monday through Friday and every other Saturday.

Subjects at the Hauptschule include German, foreign language, math- ematics, physics/chemistry, biology, geography, history, working world practices, religious instruction, music, art, politics, and physical educa- tion. The traditional academic subjects consist of four weekly classes while other subjects are taught two classes per week. Students attend a total of from thirty to thirty-three weekly lessons.[22] The working world practices course speaks to the German commitment to provide a career education emphasis to these students, who will be entering the work force, at least on a part-time basis, in their middle teen years.

Students may complete their full-time school attendance after finish- ing their ninth grade at the Hauptschule. All students are required, however, to attend school on at least a part-time basis until age eighteen. For most graduates of the Hauptschule, this part-time attendance will consist either of one or two days per week, or several full weeks per year of academic instruction. This academic instruction will be offered in conjunction with a three-year apprenticeship offered and operated by German businesses and industries.

Academically successful Hauptschule students have the option of transferring to the Realschule after seventh grade. Hauptschule students who perform well might also attend full-time vocational schools after completing ninth or tenth grade at the Hauptschule. Thus, there are avenues available for students in the Hauptschule to raise their academic and career ambitions beyond the limitations that assignment to a Hauptschule generally implies.

Realschule

Students enter the Realschule at either grade five or seven. Some students transfer from Hauptschule to a Realschule at grade seven. The curriculum at the Realschule is similar to the one described previously for the Hauptschule, but the instruction is more rigorous and comprehensive. The Realschule also offers an extended foreign language program (two foreign languages, one of which is compulsory). The number of weekly forty-five-minute lessons is between thirty and thirty-four. [23] These schools also offer more science studies as well as some business courses. They have traditionally proven to be a safe route for those who will seek positions in middle management. [24] Students attending the Realschule may transfer to a lower level Hauptschule or a higher level Gymnasium, depending on their interest and academic performance. The great flexibility that attending a Realschule provides to the student makes this school increasingly popular with both parents and students.

Gymnasium

The German Gymnasium is world renowned as a model for an academic high school with rigorous standards and well-educated graduates. This reputation developed during a period of stringent entrance requirements based almost solely on test results and teacher recommendations. Gymnasium students must pass course examinations, collectively known as the *Abitur,* as a condition of entry into the university. Acceptance to the tuition-free university system represented the surest route to financially rewarding careers with high social status. As recently as a generation ago, only about 15 percent of an age cohort would enter a Gymnasium program in fifth grade.

Modern orientation programs for fifth and sixth graders, as well as more parental involvement in school selection, have led to the enrollment of approximately one-third of each age cohort in the lower secondary school Gymnasium programs. During the lower secondary school years, some Gymnasium students will transfer to the less demanding Realschule, while some students from the Realschule will prepare to transfer to the Gymnasium after tenth grade.

The Gymnasien provide a general academic education leading to Abitur in nine years. Some Gymnasien provide an Abitur, or high school certificate, that allows students to enter any university program. Other Gymnasien offer an Abitur that restricts students to university admission for a specific subject or subject group.[25] Typical subjects studied by a tenth grade student at a Gymnasium include physics, biology, Latin, math, history, English, German, and chemistry as major courses that meet for three forty-five-minute periods each week. Minor subjects meeting twice per week include religion, sports, and civics.[26] Students attend class for between twenty-eight and thirty-two lessons per week. School hours are from approximately 8:00 A.M. to 1:00 P.M., Monday through Friday, as well as several lessons conducted every other Saturday morning.[27]

Academic standards at the Gymnasium are very demanding, with students expected to complete two to three hours of homework each evening. Students commonly repeat a year of work, since there are very strict academic standards applied for being advanced to the next grade in the school. American Fulbright Exchange teachers returning from a year in Germany report far greater concern for grades among German Gymnasium students than is found in the United States.[28] The level of concern of German students about grades has intensified in recent years as admission places to the university have become more competitive.

Comprehensive Schools (Gesamtschulen)

The Gesamtschule is the closest German approximation to the American comprehensive high school. Such schools represent a strategy to ameliorate the rigid tracking system existing in the traditional German tripartite system. Gesamtschulen are of two types, coordinated or integrated. A coordinated Gesamtschule incorporates the three basic types of schools previously discussed on one site. The integrated Gesamtschule considers all students as part of the same school but tracks them by ability for their basic subjects.[29] This integrated Gesamtschule closely resembles the tracking system in a typical American high school.

After more than twenty years of existence, the Gesamtschulen have failed to become a popular option in Germany. This is partly the result of the pull of traditional practices, but also reflects German concern that academic standards are being diluted, and that the traditional tripartite system offers the best chance to maintain academic standards. A German exchange teacher reports that "there has been a trend to establish more comprehensive schools like your high schools; but meanwhile people have realized that our traditional divided school system works a lot more efficiently."[30]

The popularity of comprehensive schools is further inhibited by the rapid rate of change in the policies and practices of the traditional school system. There is now much more opportunity for students to move among the various types of schools than was previously the case. Parents now have a greater influence in deciding the type of school that they would like their children to attend. The former power of school officials and teachers to make unilateral decisions on student placements has been weakened, if not eliminated.[31] During the current decade the proportion of students attending comprehensive schools is expected to remain at 5 percent.

UPPER SECONDARY SCHOOLS (SEKUNDARBEREICH II)

The lower secondary school program for Hauptschule pupils ends after grade nine or ten with a school leaving certificate. Most of these students then attend one of the apprenticeship programs described below. All students must continue in school, at least part-time, until age eighteen. Realschule graduates earn an intermediate certificate after grade ten that entitles them to attend a full-time vocational program. Some of these students transfer to a Gymnasium while others may enter a combination schooling and apprenticeship program. The Gymnasium is the only type of school that continues through to grade thirteen.

Gymnasium

Students who have succeeded in the lower levels of the Gymnasium are eligible to enter the *Oberstufe,* or senior level, consisting of grades eleven, twelve, and thirteen. The best academic students from the

Realschule transfer into a Gymnasium program at this point. The rigor of the academic work during these three years matches or surpasses that found in the most academic of American high school programs, and is comparable to the broad general studies programs pursued by American students during their first two years at a well-regarded American college.

Currently about 30 percent of the age cohort attends the oberstufe level of the Gymnasium. This represents a significant increase compared to the 10 − 15 percent figure of a generation ago. Some German educators and others are expressing concern that entrance standards have been lowered, and that the quality of student performance has diminished. The number of students earning the Abitur at the end of Gymnasium has increased to the point that the university system can no longer guarantee admission to all graduates of the Gymnasium. This has required an allocation system for entrance to universities, and has increased the grade consciousness of students in the Gymnasium.

The Abitur was formerly a very demanding test in all subjects. Four subjects − German, mathematics, one foreign language, plus another foreign language or either physics or chemistry − required written examinations. Other subjects were tested orally. Successful passage of this battery of tests was necessary to earn the Abitur and thus be eligible for university admission.[32] In recent years, the written test requirement has been reduced to two main subjects and one optional subject. There is also an oral test in one other optional subject. Subjects tested must include German, a modern foreign language, and mathematics or a natural science.[33]

Current regulations allow a Gymnasium, with the approval of the educational authorities, to offer new courses beyond the traditional academic subjects found in Gymnasien. Such courses might include pedagogics, psychology, sociology, legal affairs, geology, astronomy, technology, statistics, and data processing.[34] The Gymnasium of the 1990s is struggling to accept a wider range of students in terms of abilities and interests, while at the same time maintain its reputation for educational excellence.

Vocational and Technical Education

By eleventh grade about 30 percent of an age cohort attends a Gymnasium, about 10 percent of the age group has essentially completed formal schooling, and the remaining 60 percent are enrolled in various vocational and technical programs. Vocational training in Germany begins for most students when they complete their compulsory education after ninth or tenth grade. Most fifteen- to eighteen-year-old students are then trained within a dual system consisting of a *Berufsschule* (vocational school) and a *Betrieb* (firm).[35] The following is a brief description of some of the major types of vocational schooling available:

(*1*) *Berufsschulen* — These schools attract a plurality of school leavers who are either undergoing initial trade training or who already have a job. Students attend school for one or two days per week or else full time for several weeks each year. Some of the school time is devoted to general education studies such as German, social studies, and economics, while the majority of the time is spent on vocational subjects relating to specific trades.

This academic training is closely linked with training in inter-plant training centers operated by German industry. These programs can be as short as one year but typically continue for three years. By the early 1990s, approximately 1,500,000 students attended a Berufsschule program. Students completing this program successfully may gain admittance to a higher form of vocational training known as the Fachschule.

(2) *Berufsfachschulen* — These full-time, one- or two-year vocational schools receive students from Hauptschulen and Realschulen. Some of the programs offered include commercial, child care, and technical assistant training. Students in such schools take thirty to thirty-five lessons per week and the course culminates in a final examination. Success in the examination can lead to either a higher vocational training or a shortened apprenticeship. About 250,000 students currently attend these schools.

(*3*) *Fachoberschulen* — These schools provide a full-time two-year program for students in classes eleven and twelve. Acceptance depends upon a graduation certificate from a Realschule or an equivalent certificate. The courses consist of general education as well as specialized theoretical and practical knowledge. Graduates of these two-year programs are eligible to attend a *Fachhochschule* (polytechnic institute). Typical courses at these schools include German, social studies, mathematics, natural sciences, a foreign language, and physical education. Career paths for graduates of these schools include engineering, technical management, design, social services, and seamanship. About 75,000 German students attended these schools as of 1989.

(*4*) *Fachschulen*—These training programs offer working persons the opportunity for advancement through specialized training. They prepare students to manage firms in fields such as agriculture, domestic sciences, and the trades. Admission to these schools is restricted to persons who have completed their training for a specific occupation, and who have had relevant practical occupational experience. Such schools offer an alternative route for the skilled worker to enter the management sector of the business world. Today about 300,000 students are attending these schools.

(*5*) *Other types of vocational schools*—In recent years, several additional types of schools have emerged to provide qualifications necessary for vocational students to gain admission to a higher education institution. These schools have titles such as vocational secondary schools, technical secondary schools, senior technical academies, vocational academies, and sixth form colleges. Such schools offer a second chance for higher academic education for those young adults who have completed their trade training, or they may be attended in conjunction with vocational training. These programs address the American criticism that the German school system makes little provision for late-bloomers.[36,37]

PRIVATE EDUCATION IN GERMANY

The German constitution guarantees the right to private education. Private schools receive state subsidies in most states. Many such schools are operated by the Catholic and Protestant churches, as well as by private individuals and groups. These schools can select their own students and staff, and the curriculum and operating procedures are not as carefully controlled as in the public school sector.[38] While some states do not subsidize private education, other regions of the country reimburse parents for as much as 95 percent of tuition costs.[39]

In the late 1980s approximately 500,000 German students attended private schools. This number represents something less than 5 percent of the school age population in Germany. It is noteworthy, however, that religious studies is a required course in all German public schools. Students fourteen and older may elect not to participate in religious studies, but may study philosophy or ethics instead.[40]

HIGHER EDUCATION IN GERMANY

Higher education in Germany consists of the university system, technical universities, technical colleges, teacher training colleges, and polytechnical institutes. The German university system includes thirty-seven traditional universities plus seven technical universities and eleven comprehensive universities. Higher education establishments without university status include nine theological colleges, seventeen colleges of education and twenty-six fine arts and music institutions. Higher technical colleges offer three- to four-year programs in practical fields such as engineering or commerce.[41]

Programs of study at the universities typically require four or five years, while other types of higher education programs require three to four years of study.[42] Currently, approximately one-third of each age cohort attends some type of higher education program. Although these numbers do not yet approach the proportion of American students involved in higher education, they do represent a quantum level increase in the proportion of German students pursuing higher education compared to thirty years ago.

THE TEACHER IN GERMAN SCHOOLS

Teacher preparation, worklife, and compensation vary in Germany according to the type of school in which the teacher works. There are also small differences in teacher training requirements and compensation levels among the states that comprise the German Republic. A teacher in Germany typically is a graduate of the Gymnasium and has earned an Abitur before beginning teacher training.

These future teachers attend a four-year university or college of education program, including eight weeks of student teaching. At the conclusion of this program prospective teachers take the First State Examination, which is academic in nature. A second training period of two years follows the basic academic training period and emphasizes practical classroom skills and teaching competence. The prospective teacher must successfully pass the Second State Examination before being eligible to apply for a regular teaching position. The grades earned on this second examination influence the chances for securing a job and also partially determine the length of the probationary period that will be required. The probationary period is usually one to two years in duration. Because of this rigorous and extensive teacher preparation process in Germany, many teachers are twenty-eight to thirty years old before they obtain their first teaching position.[43]

During the probationary period the teacher is observed in class on several occasions and works closely with supervisory personnel. At the end of this time the supervisor must approve the teacher for permanent status.[44] The teacher then attains the status of a permanent employee and typically will be formally observed or supervised only once every five years.[45]

Teacher pay in Germany is determined at the national level, with supplements provided in some states to reflect differences in living costs in various parts of the country. The money to pay the salaries is raised at the state level and is uniform within each German state. Teachers are civil servants in Germany, which qualifies them for a supplemental salary for a spouse and children.

There is a formal salary schedule through which teachers advance one step every two years. The federal government makes cost of living adjustments to the salary schedule periodically. The previous procedures for determining salaries have mitigated the need for militant teacher unions. Germany enjoys good teacher labor relations, with an absence of strikes or other confrontational activities between teachers and school officials.[46,47]

As in Denmark, teachers at the different levels of German schools qualify for placement on different salary scales. Gymnasium teachers in Germany earn about 10 to 15 percent more than do their counterparts at the Grundschule and Hauptschule. This differential, while significant, is not as great as the disparity in pay scales found among Danish teachers. Teacher pay in Germany appears to be somewhat higher than the salary levels for the typical American teacher. Currently, salaries for German teachers average between $35,000–$40,000 in American dollars. In 1991 the average salary for an American teacher was about $33,000. A 1982 comparison to salaries for German and American teachers indicated that German teachers earned about 10 percent more than their American counterparts.[48]

A comparison of earnings of German teachers relative to the earnings of the average German manufacturing worker indicates that, on average, teachers in Germany earned 12 percent more than a factory worker in 1982. A Fulbright Exchange teacher expressed the situation concretely by her estimate that "teachers make somewhat more than a worker at a VW plant, and somewhat less than a supervisor at the same plant."[49]

This compares to an average 6 percent lower earnings for American teachers relative to American factory workers in the same year. By 1988, however, American teachers were earning 15 percent more than the typical American factory worker.[50]

The notion that teachers would hold a second part-time job was somewhat surprising to the German Fulbright Exchange teachers. One teacher indicated that in her region it was necessary to receive permission from the educational authorities to hold a second job. She also noted that such permission would generally not be given unless the job were related to teaching, such as instructing an evening course.[51] A second teacher made the observation that a second job seemed like a strange idea to her, and that Americans seem to live to work.[52] Several German teachers interviewed observed that many German citizens are critical of German teachers because of their apparently short workday and extensive vacation periods.

The worklife of the German teacher is similar to the pattern outlined for the Danish teachers. Teachers only need to be at the school for their actual teaching periods. Teachers typically provide instruction for from twenty-five to twenty-seven forty-five-minute lessons per week. There are few, if any, supervisory responsibilities such as cafeteria supervision, bus duty, or study hall monitoring. There is little need for such supervisory duties because of the way in which the school day is organized. Thus the workday for a German teacher, particularly at the Gymnasium level, corresponds more closely to that of an American college teacher than to an American public school teacher.

The teacher workday begins between 7:30−8:00 A.M. and typically concludes by 1:00 P.M. A teacher does not need to arrive in the morning until a few minutes before his or her first class. Teachers leave for home by 1:00 P.M., and typically spend several hours each afternoon on lesson preparation and evaluating student homework, compositions, and tests. After-school activities for students are limited. Activities, such as drama or the student newspaper, are supervised during the school day as part of a teacher's regular assignment. Faculty sponsors of such activities do not receive a supplemental contract for this work.

One interesting difference between American and German schools is that German schools do not employ substitute teachers. If a teacher is absent, the classes are covered by other teachers in the school. Students from the last class of the day are dismissed to go home early, and first period classes are also canceled if it is known beforehand that a teacher will be absent. Class sizes in Germany are similar to those of the United States with about twenty to twenty-five students per class for the lower grades or slower academic classes, and as many as thirty per class at the Gymnasium level and upper-ability classes. An overall average class size of twenty to twenty-five seems to be standard in Germany. [53]

Student discipline is the responsibility of the classroom teacher in Germany. Only in extreme cases is a student sent to the principal or assistant principal. Teachers report that student discipline is not a major problem in most situations. Some of the Hauptschule classes at the upper grade levels present somewhat of a problem. Students are sometimes suspended, but they are seldom transferred or expelled. [54] Students are sometimes transferred to a lower level school because of academic reasons, which may be related to poor behavior.

American teachers returning from a year as Fulbright Exchange teachers in Germany provide interesting insights regarding German students and German classroom life. Returning Fulbright teachers report that it is accepted classroom practice for German students to talk among themselves during class. The pressure for grades also produces a lax attitude toward cheating among some German students. German students tend to be more analytical and more critical than their American counterparts. They are also more likely to challenge grades they receive and to require detailed explanations of how a grade was determined than is common in the United States. Absenteeism tends to be quite high in the upper classes, since older students may write their own excuses. [55]

THE GERMAN STUDENT

Young children in Germany attend a Grundschule for their first four years of compulsory schooling. Most students attend kindergartens and preschool before their entrance to first grade at age six. During primary school there is little attempt to group students by ability or differentiate instruction among members of the class. This is a low-intensity educational experience that differs greatly from the competitive nature of the upper secondary years.

As mentioned previously, the curriculum consists of the usual basic academic courses, with the addition of religious instruction. Students in these grades begin to be trained in the habits of thoroughness, good order, and neatness that are the hallmarks of the German worker. The schools emphasize the concept of *Heimat,* incorporating curriculum experiences that draw on the everyday life of students, and that will develop in students a love for learning and their physical and social world. [56]

The student school day at the Grundschule is shorter than that of American students at a similar age. During the first two years of school German students attend twenty to twenty-five lessons per week. This generally includes attendance at classes every other Saturday morning. By the third and fourth grades the number of classes per week approaches thirty. This translates into a typical school day that is about four hours long. The tradition of one day per month for an excursion, or field trip, further diminishes the time available for strictly academic instruction. Young children are assigned some homework on a regular basis. Parents assist students with their homework and most often the homework is checked carefully by the teacher.

Students' schoolwork tends to be graded critically by the teachers, which helps to develop a critical attitude in students toward the quality of their work. Students' notebooks are extremely neat, and these documents are graded and kept throughout the school year.[57] This contrasts with the American practice of extensive use of fill-in-the-blanks worksheets, which are frequently misplaced by the students, and do not constitute a formal record of progress. The transitory nature of worksheets, when compared with the permanence of notebooks, may influence the differing attitudes of American and German students toward the importance of their school work.

The responsiveness of the typical German student may be enhanced by the pace of the daily school schedule. The school day is comparatively short, with five-minute breaks between each forty-five-minute period. There is a thirty-minute snack break after the first two class periods. Children leave their classrooms during these break periods so they will have a chance to move around and so the classroom can be infused with fresh air. The morning hours are reserved for the more difficult academic subjects while afternoon classes, when they are held at all, are reserved for courses such as arts and crafts, music, and home economics. Students have the afternoon hours free to participate in Boy Scouts, community athletic clubs, or musical organizations. Local municipalities and private clubs sponsor these activities, rather than the schools. There was an attempt to establish full-day school in some cities in the 1970s, but the result was an immediate increase in truancy and failure rates in these schools.[58]

In past generations the decision as to which academic path a student would pursue was made at the end of fourth grade. Teacher recommendations and a week-long battery of tests formed the basis for this decision. This system was criticized because of the life-determining decisions that were being made about students at a very young age. The concept of a two-year orientation period, in fifth and sixth grade, was introduced to allow teachers and parents a longer period in which to observe the academic performance of the student. The role of the parent in the decision-making process was also enhanced, which further diminished the possibility that a student would be prematurely assigned to a lower academic track than might be warranted.

Students attending these special programs for fifth and sixth graders experience a school day modeled after the elementary school routines. They attend classes for about twenty-eight to thirty-two lessons per week. Students return home in time for lunch each day, and participate in group recreational activities sponsored privately or by the local municipality. By this stage in their schooling, students typically complete about two hours of homework each night. Homework is not assigned over the weekend or over vacation periods.

By seventh grade all German students are attending one of the three types of secondary schools described earlier in the chapter. These are the Hauptschule (lower level), the Realschule (middle level), and the Gymnasium (higher level). Regardless of the academic level, students must meet strict standards of performance and generally complete several hours of homework each night. There is a six-point grading scale in German schools with a 1 denoting highest performance and a 6 denoting lowest performance.[59]

Individual course grades are based upon performance in major tests, called main tests, periodic quizzes, class participation, and quality of homework assignments. There are usually from four to six main tests each year, with average grades of between 2.8 and 3.8. Two report cards are issued each year, in February and July. If a student fails two subjects, he or she must repeat the school year or transfer to a less demanding secondary school. By ninth and tenth grade, about 10 percent of the students fail for the school year and must repeat the grade or transfer to another school. It is not uncommon in Germany for a student to require an extra year to meet the graduation requirements from his or her particular school.[60]

German students in the upper secondary years experience a school life that is strikingly different from that of their American counterparts. Students must be at school only for their assigned classes. They may leave school during the day if they have open periods. During break periods, students congregate in a commons area with little or no adult supervision. Students generally finish school by 1:00 P.M. and leave the premises for lunch at home or some other location. Many students have an afternoon class or two once or twice each week.

Students must be eighteen years old in Germany to apply for a driver's license. Thus few students have access to a car. Many of the teachers interviewed reported that German students seldom hold part-time jobs. These teachers often expressed surprise at the question, since they felt that students did not have the time to meet their academic obligations and hold a job. While it is true that some full-time students do have jobs, the presence of students in the German work force does not approach student work force participation in the United States. There is a consensus in Germany that school takes priority in the life of the student.[61]

German teachers almost uniformly report that discipline in German schools is good. Student misbehavior is most likely to occur at the sixth to eighth grade levels and at the Hauptschule. There is some concern that the Hauptschule is becoming the dumping ground for students who are not interested in school. Discipline problems are addressed by the classroom teachers through traditional means such as student conferences, detentions, or parental contacts. A school administrator intervenes in discipline matters in only the most extreme cases. There is little or no violence, vandalism, or malicious mischief in the typical German school. Students are seldom suspended from school and are almost never expelled.[62]

German students are less likely than their American counterparts to form strong romantic attachments at a young age. They most often participate in group activities rather than pair off as couples. The inability to own or drive a car, the absence of part-time work commitments, and the tendency to postpone intense boy-girl relationships, all contribute to a subculture that reinforces the concept that schooling is the major priority for a teenager. This social reality, coupled with strict academic standards with clear consequences, lead to a student body that is both motivated and conscientious. The practice of having students attend classes with a fixed group, their *form,* might also contribute to their positive social and academic attitude.[63]

Living just outside Munich, a twenty-minute ride from the city, Greta's suburban lifestyle is typical of eighteen-year-olds of her class and region. An athletic, attractive, young woman with an engaging personality, she is less than enthusiastic about the time and energy that she must now devote to preparing for her Abitur in eight months.

(continued)

Spending a late summer afternoon by a nearby lake with friends, she reflects wistfully upon her last year in school. Each day her lessons began at 8:00 A.M. and continued until 1:00 P.M. On Mondays she had a later class that ended at 2:00 P. M. and on Fridays her classes ended at 11:15 A.M. There was a fifteen-minute schoolwide morning break at 9:30 A.M. when Greta and her classmates would gather in the outdoor student commons area for conversation and relaxation. Lessons in her state of Bavaria are forty-five minutes long, although her school schedules almost all courses in double periods lasting ninety minutes. Greta has chosen the areas of business and English as her major areas of concentration. She has been attending classes with the same students for several years now, and feels comfortable with both her classmates and teachers.

When school ended at 1:00 P.M., Greta almost always returned home for lunch with her mother and younger brother, a common practice in her home village. She would then spend from about 1:30−3:30 P.M. working on her homework assignments in her room. At least several afternoons each week she would use the hours from 3:30-6:00 P.M. visiting with friends in her neighborhood. Since the driving age in Bavaria is eighteen, it is only in recent months that it has been possible for Greta and her friends to enjoy the mobility of visiting the lake which is a short drive from her home. Until gaining access to a car at age eighteen, Greta's social life was centered on the area within walking distance of her home.

Greta, unlike most of her classmates, held a part-time job during the last school year. She worked only two four-hour shifts each week, however, a typical light work load for the minority of academic students in Germany who do work. Thinking about her job, she reflected that she didn't know much about the work habits of the working-class students in her region, since neighborhood residential patterns reflected economic status. In school Greta attended the academic Gymnasium while the working-class students attended the Hauptschule, and then entered the work force in various apprenticeship training programs. Thus Greta and her school friends had little opportunity to interact with students of other social classes.

Marc and Hans interrupted her reverie to invite her to join the rest of the group for a walk in the woods. She declined, and as they walked away her thoughts turned to her group of close friends, four boys and four girls, who frequently traveled together to the lake, to soccer matches, or to concerts. She had been surprised during her three-month visit to the United States to see the romantic intensity and degree of sexual activity among many couples in the American teenage culture. In Germany boys

(continued)

and girls had little to do with one another until about age fifteen, and then they tended to travel in mixed-sex groups of six or eight during the next several years, rather than to form intense romantic attachments with one person.

Greta's thoughts returned to her next and last year at the Gymnasium, scheduled to begin in two weeks. From September through April she would follow her regular school routine, although her commitment to study would increase markedly. By February she needed to submit her thirty-page special written project, a requirement for all students in Bavaria who would be taking the Abitur. From April through June she would be scheduled to take three sets of both written and oral tests in her three major subjects. A full day would be allotted for the written test in a subject followed by a full day for the oral test in the same subject. The testing dates would be spread out over the two-month period to allow time for intense private study prior to the tests. A final two-week holiday in June would precede Greta's final oral test in her minor subject. Preparing for even this minor subject, however, would leave her little time for recreation during this holiday period.

Greta's motivation to study hard for the Abitur is the harsh reality that there are not sufficient places at the German universities for all students who successfully pass the Abitur. Greta will need a high score on the exam to be admitted to the university directly after graduation from the Gymnasium. Many of her classmates will need to wait one or two years to gain university admission, and some may never be admitted.

Greta was thankful that at least she would have the time to devote to studies during the next year. The actual number of hours spent at school would be relatively few. Also, she would not be heavily involved in school activities, a situation she found to be common for top students in the United States. Her job commitments were also minimal and she could simply quit if her work hours interfered with her study time. As her summer drew to a close, Greta clearly understood that school and studying for the Abitur would be the top priorities in her life for the next year.[64]

THE HEAD TEACHER

Teaching in Germany is recognized as a true profession. For this reason the relationship between the head teacher and the teachers in the school is more collaborative and collegial than is typically the case in the United States. The American concept of the teacher as worker and the principal as manager is less pronounced in Germany's schools. Candidates for the headship in Germany are recommended by the local and regional school authorities, and must be officially appointed by the state-level Ministry of Culture.[65]

There is no special training required for a teacher who wishes to apply for a headship. Head teacher vacancies are advertised and interested teachers apply. The local school and faculty have no role to play in the selection process. Local and regional school officials seek candidates who have been successful teachers, and in some cases, candidates who are active with the political party currently in power. New head teachers receive some training in school administration once they are selected. The heads have lifetime tenure in their positions and often seek promotions to higher administrative jobs with the regional and state educational offices.

Head teachers generally play no role in teacher selection and a very limited role in teacher evaluation and supervision. A German head teacher does not typically conduct classroom observations, nor does he or she prepare written evaluations of the teachers. The head or other teacher supervisor will review the lesson plans of teachers during the school year to ensure that they are following the prescribed curriculum. The head teacher has no role in curriculum development, but is responsible for monitoring the implementation of the curriculum by the teachers.[66]

The political skills of a head teacher in Germany are often important. His or her relationship with local municipal authorities can influence the degree of financial support for equipment, instructional materials, and school facilities. Local municipalities have some role to play in the financing of each of these functions. The head is also responsible for the general public relations of the school with the larger community. The head has ultimate responsibility for school discipline, although the classroom teacher is expected to resolve all but the most difficult cases. The school schedule is a collaborative effort of the head and the teachers. The head teacher will generally develop a schedule for classes that conforms to the desires and recommendations of the teaching staff. In larger schools, the assistant head develops the schedule.[67]

The head teacher's responsibilities in budget development are limited to consulting with teachers regarding the allocation of limited funds for textbooks, other instructional materials, and equipment. He or she also interacts with the local municipal authorities regarding the school's financial needs in these areas. In essence, the head and the faculty operate in a collegial manner to reach joint decisions.

The head teacher's workday and work year are similar to those of teachers. The head teacher works a slightly longer day, but is frequently able to leave school by mid-afternoon. The work year is several weeks longer than that of a teacher, although there remains a generous amount of time for vacation. Head teachers in Germany also teach from two to six periods per week, and they attend special evening functions held by the school. The number of such events, however, is limited by the small number of extracurricular activities that are sponsored by the schools. Assistant heads teach about fourteen to fifteen classes each week. Head teachers hold a higher level of civil service status than teachers and therefore receive a higher salary. This salary differential is relatively modest, however, on the order of 10−20 percent.[68]

The scope of the position of head teacher in Germany is more limited than that of the principalship in the United States. For this reason the amount of administrative support for the head is less than is typically found in America. A large school of 1,400 students might have two assistant heads, but each of these administrators carries a half-time teaching assignment. Teachers generally perform a counseling function in German schools. They conduct their counseling duties during a five-period-per-week reduction in their teaching assignment. Germany does not employ full-time counselors as we do in the United States. The scope of the counseling function in Germany is essentially restricted to academic and career concerns. The homeroom teacher, who remains with the same group of students for several years, routinely helps the student deal with more personal and developmental concerns.[69]

The headship in Germany is primarily a managerial position. The head teacher is not expected to be an instructional leader or to facilitate innovation or change. A basic role is to monitor the staff and students to ensure that curricular and other state educational policy matters are conducted according to regulations. Because the teachers are considered professionals, the head must perform his or her duties by collaborating and cooperating closely with the teaching staff. The difficult issues of selecting staff and evaluating new teachers before granting them permanent position status are left to the regional educational authorities. These same regional authorities are responsible for observing and evaluating all teachers once every five years. Teachers from Germany report that even these minimal requirements are not always met.[70]

EDUCATIONAL GOVERNANCE

The governance of education in the Federal Republic of Germany is primarily the responsibility of each state. The federal government, through a committee of ministers from each state, has developed broad goals and principles for education throughout Germany. Its role is essentially advisory, however, including little real legislative or financial power.[71]

The attempt to coordinate major educational policies and practices throughout Germany through cooperative planning by the individual German states has allowed for the free movement and career choice by German citizens throughout Germany. "The object of this cooperation is to coordinate the school and higher education systems in respect to structures, facilities, teaching content, and final qualifications."[72] This cooperation on final qualifications is especially critical in Germany where heavy reliance is placed upon qualification by testing for higher education, and to enter most professions and occupations.

The two major vehicles for establishing similar goals and practices among the German states are a joint Federal Government/Federal States Commission of Educational Planning and Research Promotion (BLK) and a Standing Conference of the Ministers of Education of the Bundeslander (KMK). Agreements reached by these groups over the years have provided standardization among the states regarding the beginning, end, and length of the school year, the designation of different types of educational facilities, the organizational form of these facilities, the sequence in which languages are taught, and the evaluation of student achievement.[73]

The operational responsibility for education in Germany rests with each of the sixteen German states. Each state has a Minister of Education and Cultural Affairs, whose office interprets and implements the goals and policies established by the previously mentioned committees at the federal level. Funding of elementary and secondary education is primarily the responsibility of each state. Few federal funds are available for schooling, while local municipalities do play a minor role in school funding. A basic teacher salary schedule is set at the federal level. This scale may be modified at the state level to reflect differences in cost of living among the sixteen states. Salary schedules are uniform within each state.

Tax monies to support teacher salaries and other major expenses are raised and distributed at the state level. The states are responsible for training, appointing, and promoting teachers. The curriculum for each course is established by the states and is the official course of studies for each course within the state. Decisions regarding the list of acceptable textbooks are also made at the state level. The organization of schools and teaching is another responsibility of the state educational authorities.

There is no system for federal monitoring of school operations in each state. [74]

Educational administration in most German states is further divided into several regions, each under the jurisdiction of the head of the government district. It is at this intermediate level that teacher appointments and transfers are approved. This office supports a number of inspectors who periodically visit individual schools and provide supervision for probationary teachers. Staff development programs for teachers are generally the responsibility of this intermediate level of school administration. This office is also generally responsible for the vocational schools within the region. The direct supervision of the Gymnasien is most often the responsibility of state officials. [75]

The local level of school governance in Germany is the district, which can either be a town or a large rural area. This local educational office is called the *Schulamter* and this office is generally responsible for supervising the Grundschulen, Hauptschulen, Realschulen, and *Sonderschulen* (special/remedial schools) within the district. Officials from these district offices interact most directly with local school principals and local municipal officials.

Schools operated at these local levels must rely for some of their funding for textbooks, furnishings, facilities, and salaries for nonteaching personnel, such as secretaries and custodians, on allocations from the local municipal governments. School boards as we know them in the United States do not exist in Germany. Individual schools have parent councils that serve as advisory bodies to school authorities. Members of the general public do not serve on these councils. [76] Local communities do have some input regarding the location of school buildings. They also have some financial responsibilities regarding school construction and maintenance. [77] We have seen that decisions regarding curriculum, funding, staffing, and salary levels are made at the state level in Germany, with no role in these areas for the local school board.

Thus the local school board in Germany is much less likely to be involved in community controversies regarding taxes, curriculum, and teacher salaries than are school boards in the United States. German educational policy and practice are left to educators and parents to a greater extent than is true in America. The lack of a ready local outlet for public dissatisfaction, and the diminished opportunity for pressure groups to influence local school operations, both foster a school system that is insulated from the day to day hurly-burly of political influence.

Direct parent involvement in the schools in Germany is officially promoted but is rather unusual in practice. German parents and laymen prefer to leave education to the educators, and do not directly involve themselves in school affairs except in extreme circumstances. The more direct role that parents now play in selecting schools and educational paths for their children is having a rather dramatic effect on the schools in Germany. There is some concern among teachers, and many laymen, that educational standards are deteriorating due to the more open access to school options that were formally more restrictive.[78]

The political organization of the German educational system parallels that of the American system. In Germany, however, the federal government plays a stronger role in coordinating educational policies among the states. Also, educational authorities at the state level in Germany exercise more direct authority over the schools than is the case in most of our states. The regional school authorities in Germany also have counterparts in many of the states in America. Local educational governance in the United States exercises more power and control over the schools than the comparable local governing bodies in the German states.

SOCIAL AND CULTURAL INFLUENCES ON EDUCATION

Germany is a mixed economy with a strong welfare state component. The social *safety net* concept is apparent in the special provisions for family support. Every family in Germany receives a government monthly stipend for each child. Women are granted up to two years of maternity leave for each child. Children receive annual physical exams at school and parents are expected to resolve health problems that are reported to them. Since health care coverage is required for workers in Germany, virtually all children have ready access to health care, at no direct cost to their parents.[79]

Divorce and single parent families are a growing phenomenon in Germany, although the rate of family dissolution is less than half that of the United States. There appears to be a greater stigma attached to the single parent in Germany than in the United States.[80] Single parent households tend to be better off financially than those in America. Supplemental child support grants, free medical care, and liberal maternity leave policies all contribute to this stronger financial condition. One of the Fulbright Exchange teachers from Germany stated that she thought that we in the United States could learn a great deal from Germany about properly caring for our young people.[81]

In the earlier discussion of elementary schools, we saw that strong work habits and a work ethic are instilled in German students from their earliest school days. In addition, the student must meet rigorous performance standards to qualify for the more difficult levels of schooling and occupational training. Whether a student wishes to enter the university or become an automobile mechanic, there is an appropriate skill and knowledge level that must be attained to reach the goal. German government and industry cooperate closely with the schools to promote career awareness, and to provide apprentice and other programs to students as early as age fifteen and sixteen.

Most students in Germany take their schooling very seriously because of the dramatic and immediate effects that poor performance can have on their future livelihood and social status. The German culture does not share the American notion that adolescents should have a diversified lifestyle consisting of school, work, and recreational activities in almost equal measure. The German family views education as by far the most important responsibility of the adolescent. The Fulbright teachers interviewed reported that few teenagers hold part-time jobs and those that do, work a minimal number of hours.

The fact that German teenagers cannot obtain a driver's license until age eighteen eliminates many of the aspects of American teenage subculture that distract our students from their studies. German schools also relegate school athletics to a more peripheral role than they play in America. Students might participate in a sports activity one or two days per week, but in most cases the sport is sponsored by a private club or by the municipality, and does not consume a major portion of student time or energy.

German students, on average, seem to be more engaged in their studies and more goal oriented than their American counterparts. The fact that German students must meet specific educational standards at a relatively young age may serve as a source of motivation and may also lead to a quicker maturation process. The Fulbright Exchange teachers all reported that discipline in German schools was rather good, except, perhaps, at some Hauptschulen. It appears that many of the students in the German Hauptschulen share a lack of motivation and direction that is common to a much larger proportion of students in American schools.

The German culture also seems to have a higher regard for the teaching profession than is found in the United States. The requirements to become a teacher in Germany, particularly at the Gymnasium, are more stringent than teacher qualification requirements in the United

States. The working conditions of teachers in Germany are clearly superior to those of American teachers. Compensation levels for German teachers are also somewhat better than those of teachers in America. All of these factors indicate a culture that places a high value on education.

Schools in Germany reinforce societal values such as competence or a *whole job,* definable and strict achievement standards, and significant individual effort to achieve a goal. Education is very much controlled by the state bureaucracy with little opportunity for individual parents or parent and community groups to directly influence the schools. Some tensions have developed as parents have sought to make the more desirable options of the school system available to their children, while the controlling state bureaucracy, including the teachers, seeks to ensure that current academic standards are maintained.

The close collaboration between German industry and the schools in providing vocational training is the most unique aspect of schooling in Germany. German vocational students spend the greater part of their time in an industrial setting during middle teen years, with this major component of training costs being borne by industry. This tremendous monetary contribution that German industry makes to the German educational system needs to be considered when comparing international data on governmental contributions to education.

The German nation has experienced repeated upheavals throughout the twentieth century. The current challenge is to absorb the states that were formerly a part of East Germany. Since the end of World War II, attempts have been made to expand educational opportunities in Germany and democratize the schools. Much progress has been made in this direction. Nevertheless, the German people seem determined to maintain the best elements of their existing system so that traditional German quality can be preserved in the schools. Preserving and enhancing school quality, while continuing to expand educational opportunity, is a primary concern to German citizens as they approach the next century.

REFERENCES

1. 1968. *Encyclopedia Britannica, Vol. 10.* p. 344.
2. Department of Education and Science. 1982. Paper prepared by Her Majesty's Inspectorate, "Federal Republic of Germany," London, p. 24.
3. Monikes, W. 1991. "The School System in the Federal Republic of Germany," *Education and Science,* 3/4(e):6.

4. Schieser, H. 1981. "West German Education," *Comparative Education Systems,* E. Ingnas and R. Corsini, eds., Itasca, IL: F.E. Peacock Publishers, Inc., pp. 387–388.

5. Schieser, H., p. 388.

6. Monikes, W., 3/4(e):3.

7. Rust, V. D. 1988. "West Germany," *World Education Encyclopedia, Vol. 1.* New York, NY: Facts on File Publications, p. 448.

8. Rust, V. D., p. 3.

9. Department of Education and Science, p. 20.

10. Department of Education and Science, p. 20.

11. Department of Education and Science, p. 20.

12. Monikes, W., 3/4(e):15.

13. Schieser, H., pp. 393–395.

14. Schieser, H., pp. 406–407.

15. Schieser, H., pp. 419–420.

16. Archer, E. G. and B. T. Peck. 1992. *The Teaching Profession in Europe.* Glasgow: Jordanhill College of Education, p. 313.

17. Monikes, W., 3/4(e):15.

18. Monikes, W., 3/4(e):18.

19. Monikes, W., 3/4(e):14.

20. Kolling, U. and U. Nold. Interviews with author, October 1991.

21. Monikes, W., 3/4(e):10–11.

22. Monikes, W., 3/4(e):15.

23. Monikes, W., 3/4(e):16.

24. Department of Education and Science, p. 21.

25. Monikes, W., 3/4(e):16.

26. Riel-Kermann, S. Interview with author, October 1991.

27. Korte, R. and S. Riel-Kermann. Interviews with author, October 1991.

28. Report from American Exchange teacher to Germany for 1989–1990 school year, name not available, released under the Freedom of Information Act.

29. Department of Education and Science, p. 21.

30. Korte, R. Interview.

31. Mitter, W. 1991. "Comprehensive Schools in Germany: Concepts, Developments, and Issues," *European Journal of Education,* 26(2):163.

32. Department of Education and Science, p. 22.

33. Department of Education and Science, p. 22.

34. Monikes, W., 3/4(e):17.

35. Monikes, W., 3/4(e):19.

36. Monikes, W., 3/4(e):19–23.

37. Department of Education and Science, p. 22.

38. Monikes, W., 3/4(e):10.

39. Korte, R. Interview.

40. Nold, U. Interview with author, October 1991.

41. Department of Education and Science, p. 23.
42. Department of Education and Science, p. 23.
43. Archer, E. G. and B. T. Peck, pp. 141 – 143.
44. Monikes, W., 3/4(e):15, 16.
45. Nold, U. Interview.
46. Korte, R., U. Nold, and U. Kolling. Interviews with author, October 1991.
47. Schieser, H., pp. 414 – 415.
48. Nelson, F. H. 1991. *International Comparisons of Public Spending on Education.* Washington, DC, p. 37.
49. Nold, U. Interview.
50. Nelson, F. H., p. 37.
51. Nelson, F. H., p. 37.
52. Kolling, U. Interview with author, October 1991.
53. Baeuml, S., D. Pohl, R. Korte, U. Kolling, U. Nold, and S. Riel-Kermann. Interviews with author, October, 1991.
54. Kolling, U. and U. Nold. Interviews.
55. United States Information Agency. 1991. *Your Year in Germany.* Washington, DC, pp. 21 – 22.
56. Schieser, H., p. 395.
57. Schieser, H., pp. 406 – 407.
58. Schieser, H., p. 405.
59. Riel-Kermann, S. and U. Kolling. Interviews with author, October 1991.
60. Korte, R., U. Nold, and S. Baeuml. Interviews with author, October 1991.
61. Korte, R., S. Riel-Kermann, and U. Nold. Interviews with author, October 1991.
62. Nold, U., U. Kolling, R. Korte, and S. Riel-Kermann. Interviews with author, October 1991.
63. Nold, U. Interview.
64. Baltus-Michaelsen, M. Interview with author, August 1992.
65. Schieser, H., p. 415.
66. Nold, U., R. Korte, U. Kolling, S. Baeuml, and S. Riel-Kermann. Interviews with author October 1991.
67. Nold, U., R. Korte, U. Kolling, S. Baeuml, and S. Riel-Kermann. Interviews.
68. Kolling, U., U. Nold, and S. Baeuml. Interviews with author, October 1991.
69. Korte, R., S. Baeuml, and S. Riel-Kermann. Interviews with author, October 1991.
70. Pohl, D., U. Kolling, U. Nold, and R. Korte. Interviews with author, October 1991.
71. Monikes, W., 3/4(e):5.
72. Monikes, W., 3/4(e):6.
73. Monikes, W., 3/4(e):6.
74. Department of Education and Science, p. 24.
75. Monikes, W., 3/4(e):6.
76. Rust, V. D., pp. 451, 461.

77. Postlethwaite, T. N. 1988. *Encyclopedia of Comparative Education and National Systems of Education.* Oxford: Pergamon Press, p. 296.

78. Baeuml, S., R. Korte, D. Pohl, and U. Nold. Interviews with the author, October 1991.

79. Schieser, H., pp. 420–421.

80. Baeuml, S. Interview with author, October 1991.

81. Korte, R. Interview.

CHAPTER 5

England—A Nation Reforms Its Schools

OUR CULTURAL HERITAGE from England is as rich and diverse as the Magna Carta and the language of Shakespeare. The military and economic preeminence of Great Britain in the nineteenth century, and of the United States in the twentieth century, has caused English to emerge as the world's primary international language. England's contributions to the Industrial Revolution, world exploration and trade, and governmental guarantees of individual rights, have significantly influenced world history and human progress.

Today the United Kingdom (England, Scotland, Wales, and Northern Ireland) is engaged in a vigorous effort to reverse the economic decline that accelerated at the end of World War II. The former status of the United Kingdom as a leading industrial nation has eroded steadily over the past several decades. During the past ten years educational reform has been recognized as a critical element in the revival of Great Britain's economic and political fortunes.

England's achievements in the field of education have never matched accomplishments in the political, economic, and cultural arenas. Impeded by its strong class consciousness, England was one of the last countries in the industrialized world to commit itself to universal, free public education through the secondary school level. This commitment was not achieved until passage of the Education Act of 1944. The nation that can boast of Oxford and Cambridge in the realm of higher education is still striving to create a high quality system of primary and secondary schools.

The England of the 1990s has a population of 46 million citizens living in a country approximately the size of New York State. The nation is governed by a constitutional monarchy in which the Queen's role is largely ceremonial, with true power residing in the elected Parliament. England developed an extensive welfare state system during the middle years of this century. Recent decades have been marked by economic stagnation and decline at home, and a corresponding decrease in power and influence on the world stage. The election of Margaret Thatcher in 1979 signaled a disenchantment with the welfare state philosophy and a mandate to create a free market economy with a diminished role for the government sector.

During the 1980s, the educational system became a major battleground in the Thatcher Revolution. The Education Act of 1988 marked a radical departure from the educational policies and practices that had evolved since the Second World War. Many of the mandated educational changes mirror educational reform proposals currently being discussed in the United States. A study of present day English education provides an early indication of how similar initiatives might fare in the United States.

HISTORY AND DEVELOPMENT OF ENGLISH SCHOOLS

Since the time of the Industrial Revolution, elementary and secondary schools in England have developed independently of each other. Voluntary groups, primarily the churches, originally operated elementary schools for the benefit of the working poor. Endowed private schools conducted secondary education to prepare middle and upper class students for the professions.[1] The principal agent for providing elementary education by the end of the eighteenth century was the Sunday school movement, motivated by a desire to ensure that church members could read the Bible as an aid to the salvation of souls.[2]

The central government, through monetary support and a system of inspection, became involved with these voluntary elementary schools by the middle of the nineteenth century. Such indirect government control proved insufficient to fulfill the educational needs, and in 1870 local school boards were created to supervise the first state-sponsored elementary schools. The tradition of private schools continued, however, and in 1902 church schools began to receive public funding. This same year Local Education Authorities (LEAs), which were created to replace the school boards, were authorized to provide secondary education.[3]

The 1944 Education Act formed the legal and philosophical basis for education in England following the Second World War. The most radical feature of this legislation was the notion that secondary education should be provided to all students. As a result of this legislation, the age of compulsory schooling was raised to fifteen in 1947 and to sixteen in 1973 (see Figure 5.1). At the end of the Second World War it was anticipated that secondary education would be tripartite in nature. Highly academic students would attend grammar schools, which would mirror the elite private secondary schools. Technical schools would provide appropriate education for skilled craftsmen and technical workers. A third type of school, the secondary modern school, was expected to provide an education for students who did not qualify for the other two options.[4]

The tripartite secondary education system never fully developed. The model of a comprehensive high school, to include all students, gained favor and influence during the period from 1950 – 1975. A resistance to the early tracking at age eleven implied by the tripartite system, the demand of the middle class that its students have access to a rigorous education program, and the practical impossibility of supplying alternate types of schools in rural communities, all contributed to the growth of the comprehensive high school. In the early post-war years, ever more students attended the grammar schools. Only the students with lesser academic ability attended secondary modern schools, causing the reputation of these schools to deteriorate steadily. Although still a somewhat controversial subject in England, comprehensive schools had established themselves as the preferred organizational system for English secondary education by the 1980s.[5]

In spite of the move toward comprehensive schools, England still sends a comparatively small proportion of each age group to the university. Even today, only about 20 – 25 percent of secondary school students remain in an academic setting for sixth form (school years twelve and thirteen), which is the traditional preparation for attending a university or college.[6] England's traditionally strong class system has been slow to assimilate the trend toward democratization of schooling characteristic of most other industrialized nations.

England's chronic economic weakness and loss of international influence fueled reform efforts in many areas of English life. English educational critics assign much of the blame for the failings of the general society to the deficiencies of the school system. The Education Act of 1988 mandated radical changes in English education that are currently being implemented at a rapid pace. American Fulbright Exchange teachers who were assigned to England over the past few years report that English educators and schools are finding it difficult to cope with and accommodate the radical changes that are being implemented.[7]

The major educational reforms required by the 1988 law include parental choice in selecting schools, site-based management at the local

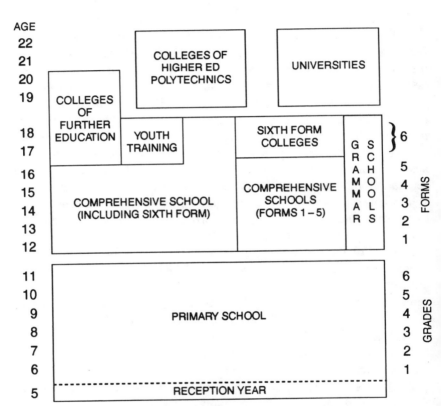

Figure 5.1 Structure of the English education system.

school with parental involvement, a diminished role for the local educational authority, a national curriculum, and a national student assessment program. Few nations have attempted the rapid and revolutionary educational changes currently occurring in England.

ENGLISH PRIMARY SCHOOLS

English students enter primary school at age five and continue at such schools until age eleven. The first year of school, known as the *reception year,* corresponds to kindergarten in other nations.[8] The first three years in the primary school, known as the *infant stage,* feature a child-centered, individualized, self-paced academic program. The child explores, through various types of project work, individual interests, and talents. There is little pressure on students to meet objective academic standards during these years. Students work at their own pace, without set deadlines to complete their tasks.[9]

The term *junior stage* describes the final three years of primary school. The classroom is somewhat more formal, with standards and time demands becoming a more common part of student experience. The project approach is still favored, with little evidence of teaching specific subject areas in isolation.[10] Subject areas frequently explored through the project approach are English, math, history, religious studies, science, art, drama, dance, and music. English primary schools do not generally have special subject teachers for art, music, or physical education, although many areas have visiting specialists who serve groups of schools. The regular classroom teacher often must integrate art and music into class project work and also supervise the physical education program.[11]

A recent report by a member of an American study group that visited English primary schools describes a typical primary school setting.[12]

Individualization was extensive in the English schools, and there was much less whole-class lecturing . . . than is typical in American schools. The approach was child-centered and often experiential. Projects were a main vehicle for instruction in primary schools.

Usually students sat in groups at tables—desks were seldom seen—working alone and sometimes consulting one another. Classes . . . were organized heterogeneously rather than homogeneously. Teachers were coordinators of differentiated learning, and they moved around the room—from table to table, from student to student—attempting to guide the process. (with permission of *Phi Delta Kappan*)

Student discipline in English primary schools is less structured than in American schools. American visitors find these schools to be quite noisy, with students engaging in a steady chatter as they perform their individual or group projects. Many American exchange teachers returning from England note the informal, if not laissez-faire, approach to student discipline in the English primary schools. These teachers, as well as others returning from England, report that harsh reprimands and raised voices are frequently used tools for enforcing required discipline.[13] One English Fulbright Exchange teacher noted, with approval, the American practice of relying more on positive reinforcement and developing self-esteem in students as methods to promote positive discipline.[14]

Schools in England operate for 190 days each year. There is a six-week summer vacation period with shorter vacations distributed throughout the year, principally at Christmas and Easter. Thus the school schedule in England is similar to that found in Denmark and Germany. Classroom teaching supplies in England are very limited in comparison to the typical situation in an American classroom. Textbooks and workbooks are not commonly used in English classrooms. Only recently have teachers begun to be provided with curriculum guides to direct their teaching efforts.[15]

The school day in a typical English primary school begins at 9:00 A.M. All students attend an assembly for thirty to forty-five minutes to fulfill the national requirement for an act of daily worship. This activity must be nominally Christian in content and features inspirational readings, music, and presentations by students. This daily ritual promotes a sense of community within the school.[16]

Classes begin at 9:45 A.M. and continue until lunch at noon. There is a fifteen-minute break during the morning, during which time most teachers gather in the staff room for coffee and conversation. The lunch break extends for one hour with afternoon classes scheduled from 1:00 – 3:00 P.M. There is a ten-minute break in the afternoon for the five- to seven-year-old students.[17] Actual classroom instructional time totals about four-and-one-half hours per day. This time allotment is similar to that found in elementary schools in Denmark and Germany, but is somewhat less than is common in the United States.

Student assessment practices in English primary schools consist of written anecdotal records which teachers must record several times each week for each child. There is a formal end-of-year written report to parents that is in essay form. English primary school children do not receive letter or numerical grades and do not generally take group tests. There are about three parent-teacher conferences during the school year. Students seldom receive homework assignments during their early primary school years.[18] The new national student assessment program will test all students at ages seven and eleven. The details and procedures for this national assessment of student achievement are currently being completed. The national assessment will mark a radical departure from past practice for students and teachers in English primary schools.

The English primary school serves as a model for educators who champion a child-centered, self-paced, low-stress schooling approach to elementary education. There is evidence that the British themselves, however, believe that this approach might have been overemphasized to the detriment of reasonable performance standards for elementary school students. The national assessment requirements for seven- and eleven-year-old students represent an attempt to ensure a greater degree of academic rigor in the English primary schools. English secondary teachers, not unlike their counterparts in other countries, are often critical of the lack of preparation in the students they receive from the primary schools.[19] English primary school teachers, however, are quick to defend their child-centered and humanistic approach to early childhood education.

ENGLISH SECONDARY EDUCATION

As noted, there has been a move toward comprehensive high schools in England during the past few decades. By the late 1980s the comprehensive high school had become the predominant form of secondary education in England. Less than 5 percent of English pupils in a *maintained,* or public school setting, now attend the traditional academic grammar schools.[20] While high school students in America enroll fourteen- to eighteen-year-old students, the English comprehensive high school serves students ages eleven to sixteen. The minority of English students attending sixth form in preparation for university entrance continues in the comprehensive school until age eighteen, or enters a separate sixth form college.

Upon leaving the primary school at age eleven, English students enter the first form of the secondary school. Virtually all students move through the first five forms over a period of five years. At age sixteen students either leave school, attend sixth form, attend a college of further education, or enroll in a vocational or technical education program. These programs may require either part-time or full-time school attendance for an additional one or two years. Currently about 40 percent of sixteen-year-old students enter the sixth form or colleges of further education, about 25 percent enter two-year government training programs (usually on a part-time work and part-time training basis), and another 25 percent enter directly into the full-time work force.[21]

Secondary schools in England operate for 190 days each school year, with vacation schedules similar to those discussed for the primary schools. Many of the comprehensive high schools are in fairly modern buildings and serve from 1,000 − 1,500 students. The school day begins at approximately 9:00 A.M. with a brief homeroom, or registration period. Most schools also have a brief daily assembly to comply with the Act of Daily Worship law in England. There are no study halls in comprehensive schools and students are free to eat lunch in the cafeteria or leave the school during the one-hour lunch period.

The school day may consist of six or seven class periods of forty-five minutes each. There is a five-minute period between classes and most schools have a twenty-minute schoolwide break after second period. During this time staff members gather in the staff room while the students congregate in various commons areas of the school. Teachers provide some supervision of students during these break periods. Lunch is offered on a staggered schedule to accommodate the large number of students in the school. A short registration (homeroom) period occurs before the start of the two or three afternoon classes. There will generally be a brief ten-minute break during the afternoon session.[22,23] The formal school day ends at 3:30 P.M. A student attending such a school will have about five hours per day of actual instructional time. Thus the English secondary school student's day is comparable in content and length to that of an American high school student.

During their first few years in the comprehensive schools all students study a similar curriculum. Students take ten to twelve different courses that meet from two to four times each week. Courses required include English, math, geography, science, art, religious studies, and physical education. There are also optional courses such as music, foreign languages, crafts, and home economics.[24]

Many American teachers returning from a year in England reported concerns with the state of student discipline in many schools. These teachers reported that little support was given to teachers by the administration in resolving disciplinary problems.[25] Some English schools, particularly in economically depressed areas, must combat the same peer pressures against academic achievement that exist in similarly located American schools.[26] Both England and America seem to share the problems of poor student discipline and low motivation in a number of their schools, particularly in disadvantaged areas.

The curriculum in English comprehensive schools was, until very recently, largely the prerogative of individual teachers. This was particularly true during the first several forms in the school. By fourth and fifth forms the teaching was shaped and constrained by the external exams, which students must pass successfully to receive a school leaving certificate. The creation of a national curriculum and national student assessments will impose an unprecedented uniformity in the English secondary school curriculum.

The English exam system plays a large role in defining the last two years of compulsory schooling for English students. Virtually all fourteen- to sixteen-year-old students follow a course sequence leading to the GCSE (General Certificate of Secondary Education). This course sequence includes a required core of English, math, a modern foreign language, and a science course. Grades are assigned for each subject at the end of the two-year course. A public exam is also a major factor in determining the final grade to qualify for the certificate.[27]

Sixteen-year-old students interested in pursuing further schooling of an academic nature will enter sixth form for a program with the following characteristics:

College-bound students and others of an academic bent will at the age of 16 select a specialized course of studies. Typically a "sixth former" will embark on a two-year course of 3 GCE A-levels (General Certificate of Education Advanced level) with some general studies to balance the narrow focus that results from the limited subject range. For example, a student aspiring to study medicine at the university level is highly likely to study physics, chemistry, and biology. The grades that the sixth former achieves in the public (i.e. national, not school-based) exams at the end of the two-year course will determine whether or not he or she is admitted to a course of higher education at a preferred location or indeed at all.[28]

College-bound students in the United States receive a broader general education than do their counterparts in England. English academic students, however, receive a far more intensive education within their chosen area than is possible for American students exposed to a more general curriculum. Currently about 50 percent of English students remain in some type of full-time school program after age sixteen. This compares to a similar proportion of American students attending some type of post-secondary training after remaining in high school until age seventeen or eighteen. Thus, despite recent increases in the number of English students remaining in school for more years of instruction, the English system does not yet approach the holding power of American secondary schools.

The grading system in English secondary schools relies primarily on continuous assessment. Written work on essays and homework assignments forms the basis for student assessment. Students also submit projects for assessment and perform practical demonstrations in areas such as science. Parents receive two reports each year on student progress. There is less reliance on periodic testing to determine grades than in the United States. Homework is assigned to academic students on a regular basis but is only nominal in the case of less academic students. Classes consist of mixed-ability groups, except in some subjects where prerequisites limit course enrollments. [29,30]

After-school activities in the English secondary school closely follow the American pattern. There are athletic teams for boys and girls in sports such as soccer, rugby, field hockey, tennis, and cricket. A school play is typically produced once each year, a school orchestra gives occasional concerts, and a school magazine may be published. English secondary schools are alive with activity from early morning until mid-evening. [31] The traditional practice of teachers voluntarily performing these unpaid extra assignments has diminished somewhat as a result of the teachers' *industrial action* in the mid-1980s. There is a concern among English educators about the long-term viability of these activities in this less cooperative environment. [32]

PRIVATE EDUCATION IN ENGLAND

English terminology describing private education can be confusing to an American observer. Many church-operated schools in England are part of the maintained school system in that they receive public funds on the same basis as other publicly funded schools. About one-third of these maintained schools, known as *voluntary* schools, were founded and are operated by religious institutions, chiefly the Catholic Church or the Church of England. [33] These schools must meet the same national and local LEA requirements as all other publicly funded schools.

There are also private schools in the sense that we think of them in the United States. These schools are known as *independent* schools. Currently about 7 percent of English students attend such schools. These schools charge tuition, although the government provides about 5,700 scholarships, known as *assisted places,* to permit some lower income students to attend these schools. Independent schools are subject to national curriculum requirements, are registered with the Department of Education and Science, and are inspected periodically by a team of Her Majesty's Inspectors.[34]

These independent private schools are also known in England as *public* schools. They include the traditionally elite private boarding schools such as Eton and Harrow that were and are attended by the British aristocracy and other members of the upper classes. Students attending these schools have the greatest chances of being admitted to prestigious universities such as Oxford and Cambridge. There are currently about 400 of these traditional, private, independent, public schools. All schools in England, whether maintained, voluntary, independent, or public, must follow national educational regulations and are subject to periodic monitoring by Her Majesty's Inspectorate.

HIGHER EDUCATION IN ENGLAND

Sixteen-year-old students in England enter sixth form, leave school, or attend some other type of *further education.* Further education may consist of a *sixth form college* outside the regular secondary school system, attendance at vocational or technical training schools, or participation in some form of adult education. *Advanced further education* is the term used to describe educational options most similar to American colleges and universities. Approximately 500,000 English students pursue advanced further education, about 300,000 pursue nonadvanced further education, and more than three million students attend school part-time.[35]

Traditional universities in England were supplemented by so-called *new universities* during the 1950s and 1960s. These colleges are typically controlled by LEAs.[36] Such additional avenues to higher education created major increases in the number of English students enrolling in higher education. Even so, the proportion of English students attending higher education is significantly lower than similar ratios in the other countries reviewed in this book.[37]

Higher education in England is financed through tuition grants to students administered through their local LEA. Students are responsible for meeting living expenses, although grants are available for students demonstrating financial need.[38] A student loan program was expanded in 1990 to ensure that students would ultimately pay for a larger portion of the cost of their education. Higher education is still not a likely option for lower-class students in England, and thus does not represent a path to upward mobility to the extent that college attendance does in the United States.

THE TEACHER IN ENGLISH SCHOOLS

''Remarkably free though English teachers are, the freedom that they most cherish is that of deciding how to teach and how to manage their own classrooms.''[39] This analysis by noted English educators in a 1981 publication explains the low morale, anxiety, and malaise felt by teachers in England as the 1990s unfold. Many of the reforms enacted by the 1988 Education Act directly challenge the prerogatives and professional latitude traditionally enjoyed by teachers in England.

American Fulbright teachers returning to the United States over the past three years consistently mention the sense of foreboding and even fear felt by teachers in England as the new requirements are implemented.[40] Teachers are experiencing a sense of powerlessness as decisions regarding a national curriculum and student assessment are made with little or no involvement from classroom teachers. Their traditional sovereignty in the classroom is being challenged by plans for periodic evaluation of teacher performance, with teacher pay and promotion tied to student performance.[41]

The Education Act of 1988 marked the culmination of a twenty-year period of intense criticism of English schools and teachers. The low esteem in which teachers are held in England, as well as their lowly socioeconomic status, bears a striking resemblance to conditions in the United States. Teacher compensation, for example, has long been a topic of controversy both in England and in the United States. The increasing militancy of English teacher unions in the 1970s and 1980s culminated in the revocation of the right of teachers to bargain over salary and working conditions. This situation has led to a further deterioration in teacher living standards during the past five years.

Further similarities between American and English teachers appear in work schedules and working conditions. English teachers work a 195-day school year, including five days for teacher workshops and meetings. The formal school day for a teacher begins at about 8:30 A.M. and ends at approximately 3:30 P.M. Teachers will frequently remain at school for an additional hour or two for inservice meetings, staff meetings, or to sponsor student clubs or other activities. A primary school teacher might supervise children on the playground for several periods each week. [42]

Supervisory duties for secondary teachers are limited, since there are no study halls for students and many students leave the school premises for lunch. English teachers typically have "a proper lunch of one hour's duration," [43] as compared to the American standard of a thirty- to forty-minute lunch period. English teachers at both primary and secondary levels also enjoy a morning tea or coffee break, when most staff members can gather to socialize and relax. These morning breaks and long lunches allow English teachers an opportunity to form a cohesive work unit. [44]

English secondary teachers generally instruct students for all but one period each school day. Thus, student contact time at the secondary level is similar to that of teachers in American schools. The time available for breaks, lunch, and planning taken together, indicate that English teachers have somewhat more unscheduled time each day than their American counterparts. The fact that English teachers have fewer out-of-class supervisory duties accounts for this difference.

English primary school teachers work with students in an individual classroom for about four-and-one-half hours each day. The remaining time in the day is devoted to schoolwide assemblies, lunch, and a morning break. Since teachers often instruct students in all areas, including music, art, and physical education, English classroom teachers are not as regularly relieved of classroom responsibilities by subject specialist teachers, as is common in the United States.

The work load of English teachers outside the classroom is heavier than that of their American counterparts. The limited supply of textbooks, workbooks, and other instructional materials places the full burden for lesson construction and the creation of materials on the classroom teacher. Until recently, teachers constructed lessons without the assistance of a standard curriculum guide.

Student assessment practices in England also require a high level of teacher effort. At the primary level, the teacher generally makes at least three anecdotal records each week on the performance of each child.

Reports to parents provide written summaries of performance, as compared with the American practice of letter or numerical grades. Student tests are usually of the essay variety rather than the short answer, true and false, and multiple choice type tests common in American schools. [45] This level of out-of-class preparation and assessment responsibility may explain the English Fulbright Exchange teachers' amazement over the fact that many American teachers hold second jobs. They reported that this is very unusual in England. [46]

Teachers in England are paid according to a single national pay scale known as the *main professional scale*. Primary and secondary teachers earn the same amount for equal experience. A supplement is provided for teachers working in London and its environs. As noted previously, English teachers are not legally permitted to bargain for salaries. Teachers in the church-operated voluntary schools, which receive public funds, are also paid on the main professional scale. Incentive allowances, or supplemental contracts, compensate teachers who assume additional duties such as counselors or department heads. [47] Salaries of teachers in England are lower than those of American teachers. In a 1988 comparison based on 1984 data, teachers in the United Kingdom earned an average salary equal to 79 percent of the average American teacher's salary. This study also indicated that a teacher in the United Kingdom earned 120 percent of the salary of an average factory worker in the United Kingdom. [48] An English teacher earns ''somewhat less than a police officer and somewhat more than a nurse.'' [49]

A teacher in England can become qualified to teach in one of several ways. Prospective teachers finish their secondary education by completing sixth form and earning an A-level exam grade in at least two subjects. They may then enroll in a four-year concurrent academic training and student teaching program leading to a bachelor of education degree. These programs are offered at polytechnics and colleges of higher education or at a university department of education.

A person may enter teaching by earning a degree, over a three- or four-year period, in a field other than education, and then pursue an intense one-year pedagogical and practical training course leading to a post-graduate certificate of education qualification. [50] All beginning teachers must serve a one-year probationary period. Individuals who are not formally qualified to teach may become teachers in areas where there is a shortage of qualified teachers by becoming *licensed* teachers. After two years of successful experience, such teachers will gain qualified teacher status. [51]

Class size in England ranges from twenty to thirty. Lower class sizes tend to be found at the secondary level. The precipitous decline in student enrollment in recent decades has produced a steady decline in class size at all levels. Teachers are responsible for maintaining proper discipline in their classrooms. Visiting Fulbright Exchange teachers, as well as English teachers themselves, consider administrative support for teachers in discipline cases to be inadequate.[52] Secondary teachers in England will usually teach classes across four or five age levels and will seldom present the same lesson to more than one group of students.

American Exchange teachers marvel at the range of age levels and the number of teaching preparations required of English secondary school teachers. Relationships between secondary teachers and their students and parents are somewhat more formal in England than in America.[53]

Teachers have not typically been formally evaluated by their head teachers once they complete their probationary year. The government is currently implementing a formal and continuous teacher evaluation procedure as part of its reform efforts. There is an intention to link such appraisals to salary and promotion decisions.[54]

In general, the professional recognition granted to teachers in England is low, although the professional status of American teachers is even lower. A recent study of the relative professional status accorded to teachers in the United Kingdom and the United States considered factors usually associated with professional status. These factors included size of the relevant work force, the relationship of the client to the professional, the method of payment of fees for service, degree of unionization, and professional autonomy. Teachers in both the United States and the United Kingdom do not qualify as true professionals when measured against these criteria.[55]

THE STUDENT IN ENGLISH SCHOOLS

Compulsory schooling in England includes students from ages five through sixteen. The Education Act of 1988 requires all students to study the following nine foundation subjects: English, mathematics, science, technology, history, geography, art, music, and physical education. Study of a modern foreign language, the tenth foundation subject, begins at age eleven.[56] Students will take national tests in each of these subjects. Such assessments for seven-year-old students are already in place, with assessments for eleven-year-old students to begin shortly.[57]

The subject approach to learning, as well as the formal assessments, is likely to interact poorly with the traditional, and still widespread, teaching practices of the English primary school. These schools emphasize self-pacing of students through a project-oriented curriculum that does not emphasize the accumulation of subject-specific knowledge. The teacher in such an environment views himself/herself as a facilitator of learning rather than as a dispenser of knowledge. Students are of mixed ability, although a teacher might use a flexible grouping approach to assign students to groups for particular projects.[58]

Individualization is extensive in English primary schools. There is much less whole-class lecturing than in America. The approach is child-centered, with students proceeding at their own pace and with little concern for deadlines by either student or teacher. There is little discussion about whether students are on grade level or keeping up with their classmates. Students are rarely retained in grade and the entire American concern with school readiness is moot, given that students proceed at their own pace.[59] Homework is not an integral part of the early primary school years in England.

Students from a middle-class background tend to be deferential toward authority while students from the working class, with few academic aspirations, are less so. The public schools (i.e., private independent schools) still expect very formal relationships between students and teachers. Students in many of the comprehensive high schools often rise when a teacher enters a room, and in many instances such schools require students to wear school uniforms.[60] Even so, English teachers and American visitors would agree that English classrooms tend to be somewhat noisy by American standards.

The demographic distribution of students in English schools is similar to the American pattern. Urban centers serve mainly lower-class, economically depressed children, many of whom are immigrants. These schools share the American problems of poor student performance and high dropout rates. Vandalism, graffiti, and theft, however, are not as large a problem in these schools as they are in similarly situated American inner-city schools.[61]

Children of middle-class parents tend to reside in the suburban or *ribbon developments* surrounding the large cities. Schools in these communities usually feature modern facilities, good staffing ratios, and well-motivated students.[62] In the more rural areas, schools have fewer resources. The students are less motivated and have lower aspirations than their suburban counterparts. In all, the distribution of students within the English school system bears a marked resemblance to the American educational landscape.

By age eleven the English student is completing primary school and is ready to enter the first form of secondary school. The student has been nurtured in a supportive educational environment that has de-emphasized both competition among students and the attainment of external academic standards. Many secondary teachers in England complain that the students they receive have not been academically challenged at any point in their schooling.[63] This is also a familiar complaint among American secondary school teachers.

Students in the first three forms of secondary school all take a standard curriculum mandated by the national government. Such students study ten to twelve subjects, some of which meet three or four times each week, with others meeting only once or twice each week. The school day is organized by periods, as is the practice in middle and high schools in the United States. In England, however, the morning session usually contains a fifteen- to twenty-minute break at mid-morning for socialization and relaxation. The lunch period is longer than in American schools, typically lasting for a full hour. Afternoon classes are in session for from two to two-and-one-half hours.

A full range of athletic and other extracurricular activities is generally available after school, although sports are not as central to English school life as they are in American schools.[64] Academic students are assigned one to two hours of homework each night, while homework assignments for the less-able students are nominal or nonexistent. Students submit written work for correction by their teachers. Unlike in an American classroom, there are few periodic formal tests. Parent conferences are scheduled regularly and parents receive two teacher-prepared evaluations of their children each year.

By the early teen years, the class consciousness still prevalent in English society begins to exert its influence on student aspirations and achievement. As students enter fourth and fifth forms, at ages fourteen and fifteen, greater diversity among students in course selection patterns begins to appear. The mixed-ability grouping of the first few forms is replaced by ability grouping in subjects such as math and English. Prerequisites and student selection patterns begin to effectively divide students according to their academic aspirations.

Students in forms four and five begin to prepare for the external GCSE (General Certificate of Secondary Education) exams that are based on a range of courses that students select according to their own aptitudes and interests. For more than 60 percent of English students, the GCSE earned at age sixteen will mark the end of their full-time school attendance.[65] About half of these school leavers enter the full-time work force at this time and totally discontinue their schooling, while the other half attend vocational training schools on a part-time basis while working in a related industrial job.

It is during the final two years of compulsory schooling that the social class and attendant peer pressure inhibit the aspirations and motivation of many students capable of additional schooling. An American education writer, after a recent visit to England, expressed this tendency as follows: ''There appears to be a tendency among students . . . to hide their interest in education and in achievement. . . . These students assume that social mobility is nearly impossible and appear not to aspire to higher education to the degree that poor Americans do.''[66]

College-bound students remain in school after taking their GCSE and become sixth form students. Such students pursue a two-year program concentrating on a maximum of three subject areas and culminating in the General Certificate of Education Advanced level (GCE A-level). The grades earned by students on these exams will determine whether or not they will be admitted to the university system.[67] Sixth form studies may be pursued either at a comprehensive high school or at special sixth form colleges. From 20 to 25 percent of an age cohort completes the GCE A-level and enrolls at a university or college. England is attempting to increase the proportion of its students who participate in higher education. This proportion enrolled in higher education has risen from 16 percent in 1980, to 20 percent in 1990, and is projected to reach 33 percent by the year 2000.[68]

The Education Act of 1988 is designed to correct the perceived lack of standards and rigor in English primary schools and the lower levels of secondary schools. Students who respond seriously to the GCSE and GCE exams do experience a rigorous academic program during their final few years of school. The half of the English student population that previously reached the school leaving age of sixteen without having been seriously challenged or motivated academically, should find the new requirements more demanding.

The English themselves perceive that this situation must be reversed if England is to maximize its human resources to produce economic and social improvement. The challenge for the English is to extend the rigorous education provided to their elite to a greater cross section of English society. The task of educational reform in England appears even more daunting than the similar challenge facing American schools.

Nigel, with his flaming red hair, his preference for black clothing, and passion for rock music, is still in his early teens, and yet life is becoming difficult. He fights with his parents constantly and, until recently, he was a poor student in school. His ambition was to join a rock band, but he realizes that this hope is unlikely to be realized. He comes from a middle-class family, but his Midlands accent marks him as less sophisticated than those who speak with the standard BBC accents.

Nigel appeared to be following the path of his older brother, who quit school entirely at age sixteen and went to work full time. In recent years, corresponding to Nigel's first years in secondary school, he experienced far more academic pressures and demands than his brother had met only a few years earlier. Nigel didn't understand the reason, but it was obvious to him that his teachers too were under more pressure to meet curriculum objectives. He found that he was assigned one or two hours of homework every night. Along with his teachers and classmates, he was preparing for the national assessment tests that he would take as a sixteen-year-old student.

Where his older brother's plans to leave school were greeted with indifference, or even encouragement, he was being urged to stay in school and raise his career aspirations. Nigel couldn't see himself as a sixth former, preparing to enter the university. He did, however, have an interest in engineering. Only recently he decided to apply to a polytechnic institute after fifth form, and pursue his interest in engineering. This new ambition seems more realistic than playing for a rock band. A concrete future career plan motivates Nigel to meet his new academic demands and to perform at a higher level than at any time in his school career.

THE HEAD TEACHER

As the name implies, the English school principal, known as the head teacher, is considered to be a teacher among teachers. A teacher in England must acquire fifteen years of teaching experience before becoming eligible to apply for a head position.[69] The head teacher is considered a member of the teaching profession and will often retain at least minimal teaching responsibilities. Successful teaching experience is a major factor in becoming appointed a head teacher.

English faculties and administrators enjoy a more collegial relationship than is often the case in American schools. There is not yet the sense in England that school administration is a separate profession with its own training requirements and prerogatives. There is some fear among

English educators that the administrative requirements made on heads as a result of the Education Act of 1988 might force English head teachers to assume a management role similar to that of American principals. [70]

The power relationships of the English head teacher vis-à-vis parents, community, and teachers have evolved in England in much the same manner as they have in the United States. The former hierarchical and paternalistic leadership styles in both America and England reflect themselves in the following description of the headship written in 1971 and reported in a 1981 essay on English education.

> The power exercised by the head in an English school is formidable, and the head can be compared to the sovereign of a state whose powers are limited only by the willingness of his subjects to obey his commands but whose right to give commands is not disputed by his subjects. [71]

The above description should be compared with more recent reflections on the English headship such as:

> Various writers have argued that it is possible to conceive of any school as working within a particular set of community parameters. This is what Charters called the "margin of tolerance" or . . . the "zone of tolerance" – the latitude . . . granted to the leadership of the schools by the local community. [72]

> In practice head teachers are generally loathe to infringe in any direct way on those areas of subject expertise (pedagogy and curriculum) that are traditionally regarded as the province of "the department." [73]

Reflecting on the changes to the headship that will be required by the Education Act of 1988, Hill makes the following observation:

> . . . The head will carry an increased responsibility for all staffing matters. His or her relationship with the unions will be critical and he or she will have to take great care over contracts of employment, equal opportunities, racial discrimination and other conditions. . . . Like an education officer, the head will be responsible for making certain that the system works. [74]

Schools have traditionally displayed elements both of hierarchical work organizations and member-controlled organizations. Teacher autonomy remains as a symbol of the professional status of teachers and it is taken for granted as an effective limitation on the power of the head teacher. [75] As the 1990s unfold under radically different educational laws:

Teachers, advisors, parents, and heads themselves seem to disagree as to the scope and responsibilities of the role. Heads are frequently faced with irreconcilable expectations of performance within their audiences; this produces practical and political dilemmas which may be irreconcilable.[76]

The tensions of these conflicting expectations are familiar elements in the worklives of American school principals and local superintendents. The new education law in England adds the additional elements of parental choice of schools, a national curriculum, and a national student assessment program. These radical departures from past practice are expected to be implemented successfully by local school leaders who consider themselves to be members of the teaching profession, and who are accustomed to a collegial style of decision making within the schools. The leadership challenges facing English head teachers are formidable indeed.

The daily worklife of an English head bears many similarities to that of an American principal. The head will collaborate with teachers through department heads to allocate instructional budgets for the school. The head, who has the power to suspend pupils from school, will resolve major discipline problems. As mentioned previously, there is some concern among teachers that English school administrators do not offer sufficient support to teachers in matters of student discipline.[77]

English heads have not traditionally observed or evaluated experienced teachers in the classroom. They have been responsible for preparing written reports on first-year probationary teachers. The Education Act of 1988 requires that teachers be formally evaluated by the head teacher. By 1991 plans were in place for all teachers to be assessed on their classroom performance once every two years.[78] Head teachers traditionally rely upon advisory personnel from the local education authority to provide teachers with guidance in the areas of curriculum and instruction.[79] Secondary schools also have a strong department system, where the department head assumes responsibilities to help teachers resolve problems relating to classroom methods and materials.

The workday of the head teacher is similar in length to that of an American principal. The extent of after-school activities in English schools requires some administrative supervision from early in the morning to late in the afternoon. English heads share in the frequent vacations accorded to teachers, although they will spend some time during vacations preparing for the new school year and attending LEA-sponsored meetings and workshops. The salary of a head teacher may be two to two-and-one-half times that of an average teacher.[80] Thus the differential in salaries between building administrators and teachers in England is greater than that typically found in the United States.[81]

In large comprehensive schools, the head teacher will have deputy head teachers, grade or form leaders to serve a counseling or pastoral care role, and department heads. These personnel generally have major teaching responsibilities in addition to their administrative duties, and they receive an incentive allowance in addition to their regular salary. English exchange teachers to the United States report that there is a greater role differentiation between teachers and administrators in America than there is in England.[82]

English head teachers interact with two different supervisory entities. The LEA has traditionally exercised a powerful supervisory influence on the head teacher. It was through the LEA that the daily administration of English schools was directed and monitored. Head teachers were selected by a committee of LEA officials with little or no input from the local community or teachers in the schools. Head teaching jobs are typically advertised nationally and in regional newspapers.[83] Each local school has its own board of governors with elected representatives of parents, teachers, and the community. These bodies historically have had little power, however, and often served as rubber stamps for the decisions of the head teacher.[84]

The above authority relationships have been essentially reversed by the Education Act of 1988. Local school governing bodies now possess much greater power vis-à-vis the LEA and the head teacher. The element of parental choice in selecting a school and the ability of schools to opt out of direct LEA control have critically diminished the role and power of the LEAs. The head teacher is thus relieved of some of the bureaucratic constraints imposed by the LEA governance system, but is more directly influenced by the wishes and directives of his/her more powerful local board of governors. The national curriculum and student assessment will place new demands on the head teacher.

Research evidence and common experience demonstrate the critical role that a school principal plays in developing an effective school in the United States. A researcher on English school governance writes that "the evidence suggests that it is usually the head teacher who takes the initiative in introducing innovations into the school, and even where this is not the case, his support is necessary for any innovation proposed by a member of the staff."[85] The head teacher in England is destined to play a pivotal role in piloting individual schools through their educational reform voyage of the 1990s.

SCHOOL GOVERNANCE IN ENGLAND

School governance is the defining issue in English schools for the 1990s. References to the Education Act of 1988 have occurred throughout this chapter. The fundamental changes in governance wrought by this legislation point to a profound level of dissatisfaction and frustration among the English concerning their educational system. The changes required by this act are of particular interest to Americans, since many of the new initiatives in England are currently the topics of heated debate in the United States.

Four provisions of the education act represent major change in English school governance. Similar proposals exist for restructuring the United States' education system. The major elements of each of these four initiatives are as follows.

National curriculum — A standard curriculum in ten subject areas is currently being developed by the national government. This curriculum must be taught in all schools, both public and private. Time allocations for topics within the curricula are part of the curriculum package. The teaching profession in England now has an affirmative obligation to deliver a prescribed course of studies, even though teacher involvement in creating the curriculum has thus far been minimal.[86] Many teachers resent the lack of teacher participation in the decision to create a national curriculum and in the development of it.[87,88]

Although disenchanted with the process of developing the national curriculum, teachers do see the need for it and are generally supportive of the concept.[89] The national curriculum is being promoted to satisfy the English concept of *entitlement*. This refers to the right of every student, regardless of the school attended, to have access to essentially the same curriculum.[90] During its four years of development and implementation, the national curriculum has gained widespread public and professional support.[91]

National student assessment — This new initiative serves to ensure that the national curriculum is actually implemented and mastered by students. All students will be tested, on nationally devised assessments, at ages seven, eleven, fourteen, and sixteen. These tests were originally intended to provide an equal emphasis on all the curriculum areas. Already, however, there have been changes made to provide greater emphasis on the more basic academic courses.[92] The format of the tests is a matter of concern and controversy. English educators want to avoid the brief answer, multiple-choice format of American standardized tests. They favor the traditional English reliance on essay tests. The English are attempting to develop a national testing system that is economically and administratively practical, and yet one that allows students to demonstrate knowledge through practical demonstrations, portfolios, and essay responses.

A second purpose for national testing is to provide information on the relative performance of different schools. Thus parents will have access to the information that they will need to make informed decisions regarding the schools that their children will attend under the parental choice element of the new education laws. The availability of comparative testing results will provide a method to promote a market approach to school selection.

Parental choice — The most radical aspect of the new education law is the provision that parents can freely choose the school that their child will attend. Market forces are expected to direct students toward the more desirable schools while at the same time decreasing the enrollments in the less desirable schools. Poorly performing schools are then expected either to improve dramatically, or eventually close. The more successful schools, on the other hand, will grow and prosper and thus provide a superior education to a growing proportion of the student population.

Parental choice is limited by practical considerations such as the geographic proximity of the school and the availability of places within the more popular schools. Parents have traditionally had choices in England among private and quasi-private schools, as well as the genuinely public schools that have been under the authority of the local educational authority. The new law allows parents to select schools among those operated by the LEAs. In addition, a new type of school known as a *grant maintained* school has also been created.

The board of governors of an individual school may petition the national government to operate independently of the LEA, and be financed directly with a grant from the national government. A majority of the parents of such a school must approve this proposed change before application is formally made. Education writer Gene Maeroff compares this option to giving a neighborhood school in Los Angeles or Dayton the right to secede from its school district and receive funding directly from Sacramento and Columbus.[93]

Very few schools have elected to pursue grant maintained status during the first few years under the new law. The most recent figures indicate that only about 2 percent of publicly maintained schools have thus far applied for grant maintained status. Further investigation shows that many of the schools that have applied would have been likely candidates for closure had they remained in the LEA system. In other cases the particular schools were experiencing various types of difficulties and disagreements with their LEAs.[94] Thus, the decision of a school to apply for grant maintained status may have more to do with political considerations than with educational issues.

Interviews with students, parents, and head teachers in these new grant maintained schools indicate that operationally they differ little from their previous years under LEA control. Students and parents do report that the schools seem cleaner and more attractive, with more attention to general maintenance. There seems also to be a greater interest in student deportment and dress issues. These differences most likely reflect a public relations emphasis to recruit students.[95]

By September 1991 the parental choice concept in England had evolved to a point where the government published a *Parents' Charter* guaranteeing that each year parents would receive the following information about their student and his or her school:

(*1*) Yearly report on child's progress

(*2*) Performance tables with full information on all schools

(*3*) Summary of recent inspection report on their child's school (government inspections take place every four years)

(*4*) Action plan for correcting weaknesses identified by the school inspection

(*5*) Annual report from school governors regarding school test and exam results, truancy rates, future academic or career plans of school leavers, the school budget, and election procedure for parent governors[96]

The above charter indicates clearly that after four years of school reform, the English remain dedicated to producing radical changes in their educational system.

Local management of schools — This feature of educational reform took effect in many schools in April 1990. This device "gives the board of governors of the individual schools much greater influence. This devolution of power from the local education authority to its constituent schools will be achieved by the delegation of control over the school budget.''[97] Whereas previously the head teacher was subject to LEA directives with the board of governors playing a peripheral role in school management, the new structure makes the head teacher primarily answerable to the local board of governors. Staffing decisions and decisions relating to the distribution of budget resources within the allocation provided by the LEA are now under the control of each school's governing board.

This new organizational structure diminishes the influence of the so-called bureaucrats from the LEA and gives direct power and responsibility to the parents, teachers, and head teacher of each school. The previously influential LEAs are being relegated to a strictly advisory and support role in many sections of England. The guiding philosophy of the ''local management of schools'' initiative is that with this change, schools will become more responsive to the particular needs and interests of their clientele. Individual school governance will also create greater diversity in schooling, thus providing true options to parents in a marketplace environment for school selection. The local management of schools initiative is similar in concept to the school-based management proposal in the United States.

The board of governors' approach to local school governance is analogous to, but not identical with, the system of local school boards in the United States. Boards of governors consist of representatives of parents elected by parents, representatives of teachers elected by teachers, and political leaders in the region appointed by the LEAs. There are usually an equal number of parents and LEA appointees.[98] Thus members of these boards typically have a genuine interest in the educational program of their schools. These boards are less likely to contain the ''watchdogs of the public purse'' or other defenders of special interests who often serve on American school boards.

Local schools in England are not community schools in the same sense that local schools are in the United States. Although most of the students will be local, parental choice is weakening the tie between geography and school attendance. The board of governors primarily represents the interests of those involved directly with the schools and is not broadly representative of the community. Even the financing of the schools is less a matter of local concern in England than is commonly the case in the United States.

Schools in England continue to receive about 80 percent of their funding from national resources and about 20 percent from local property and income taxes. This system greatly decreases the disparity between LEAs of different wealth with respect to school funding.[99,100] National funds flow from the Department of Education and Science (DES), through the LEAs, and to the individual schools. A modified procedure is used to accommodate the new grant maintained schools that receive funding directly from the DES rather than from the LEA.

A complete picture of educational governance in England must include the role of Her Majesty's Inspectors (HMI). This elite cadre of 500 inspectors provides the central government with an independent assessment of educational programs in LEAs and individual schools. Members of this corps are recruited from the ranks of very successful classroom teachers, usually at about age forty. These knowledgeable educators devote the remainder of their educational careers to their work as inspectors. Their salaries are comparable to those of the head teachers of large secondary schools.[101]

These inspectors participate in from twenty-two to twenty-six school inspections each year and serve as members of a team that varies in size. The team arrives at a school on Monday and observes classes steadily until midday Friday. Team members meet during the evenings to discuss their first impressions while they are still fresh, and a preliminary report is prepared within days of the conclusion of the visit. A written report is ultimately published and presented to the school and the LEA. The LEA must provide a formal response to each significant item in the report. These HMI evaluations represent the only type of close supervision that is recognized as valuable and valid by the teaching profession. Even independent private schools receive periodic inspections by Her Majesty's Inspectors.[102]

SOCIAL AND CULTURAL INFLUENCES ON EDUCATION

England supports one of the most extensive welfare state systems in the industrialized world. More than a decade of conservative political leadership under Margaret Thatcher and John Major has failed to reverse the public preference for liberal, if not socialistic, approaches to government policy issues. England has experienced a precipitous decline in political and economic power since the end of World War II, which many critics attribute to the lack of economic vitality and competitiveness characteristic of government-supported industries. The ready availability of government-provided social services, and the high tax rates necessary to support them, are blamed for undermining the English work ethic, diminishing motivation, and lowering worker productivity.

In certain respects, however, the welfare state does provide for the basic needs of its student population. The National Health Service provides necessary medical services to all children, regardless of their economic condition. American Fulbright Exchange teachers consistently report, however, that the quality and efficiency of medical care in England are inferior to that of the United States.[103] While the English system may be inferior to private health plans in the United States, children from the lower classes in England receive better health care than do their uninsured counterparts in the United States.

Fulbright Exchange teachers from England report that divorce rates in England are significantly lower than in America.[104] The problem of broken and dysfunctional families is most severe in the poverty-stricken urban areas of England, a pattern that mirrors the situation in the United States. Children from such families do receive a family supplement in England. All families with children also receive a small child allowance each week of about eight pounds, or about $15.00 (1992). Parents receive this allowance until the child reaches age sixteen, and sometimes longer.[105]

England is experiencing a growing problem with assimilating its immigrant minorities into the mainstream of English life. English social policy appears to be far behind the United States in this regard. Even the collection of information on race and ethnic origin is rare in England. Affirmative action programs are equally scarce.[106] Writing on English education and the immigration question, Taylor and Lowe concluded that ''Whether the schools will be harnessed to the cause of racial harmony or whether they will be used as instruments by which one social group will seek to sustain its advantages may well be critical in determining the future harmony of English society.''[107]

In a broader sense, the issue of England's commitment to eliminating traditional social class barriers remains an open question. The movement for comprehensive schools in the 1950s and 1960s, and the current countervailing impetus for school choice and diversity, are not purely educational issues in England. The Labour party, in its support of comprehensive schools and mixed-ability classes, would argue ''that a mobile and highly differentiated labour force to be effective must share a common culture. A modern economy is hampered by deep social and class divisions.''[108] Arguing a different perspective, a leading Conservative figure in government during the 1980s declared that England had never been able to afford a good education for all its people, and implied that it never would. A senior educational official remarked that "it was time, once again, to educate people to know their place in society." [109]

Political opponents of the Conservative government and its educational reform program charge that the initiatives on parental choice and grant maintained schools represent an indirect attack on the concept of comprehensive schools that serve all classes of students. [110] Thus there is some question as to the extent that the English really want an egalitarian and democratic school system.

At the level of the individual student, however, the tradition of the class system is still a significant influence on educational aspirations. In his report on English education Gene Maeroff notes that:

> In England, there is an overlay of a historically intractable system of social class that has a devastating effect on the aspirations of young people in the lower class, who in England are overwhelmingly white. These students assume that social mobility is virtually impossible and appear not to aspire to higher education to the degree that poor Americans do. In turn, higher education in England does not play the role that it does in the U.S., where the educational hopes of the disadvantaged are reinforced by nonselective admissions policies and lots of available spaces. [111]

Student motivation in England is further depressed by the high unemployment rate and a corresponding sense that academic effort will not translate into a good job. As is true in the United States, a scandalously high proportion of students leave school in England without the critical technical skills and work attitudes necessary to succeed in a technological society. [112] An educational underclass in England is a mirror reflection of a similar malady in America. Issues relating to social class represent an additional burden that must be borne by the English educational system.

English education is at a crossroads. The economic and political realities of the 1990s have brought about a radical educational reform program in England. Implementing these reforms will require a break with past traditions and practices. Early indications on the fate of reforms are that while they are causing some frustration and discomfort, they are enjoying a high level of support from teachers and parents. The initial attempts at student assessment, while not totally successful, have produced changes in the testing program to make them both more practical and more useful.

The educational reforms appear destined to produce a more rigorous and standards-oriented curriculum at both the primary and secondary school levels. The proportion of secondary students meeting the standards for university admission can also be expected to rise, while the standards themselves will remain high. The local management of schools and school choice programs can be expected to provide parents with a more direct influence over the education of their children. The government's adoption of the Parents' Charter in 1991 demonstrates its commitment to fully implementing the parental involvement initiative contained in the Education Act of 1988. All of these reform efforts are worthy of careful study in the United States.

REFERENCES

1. Taylor, P. H. and R. Lowe. 1981. "English Education," *Comparative Education Systems*, E. Ignas and R. J. Corsini, eds., Itasca, IL: F.E. Peacock Publishers, Inc., p. 140.
2. Taylor, P. H. and R. Lowe, p. 141.
3. Taylor, P. H. and R. Lowe, p. 142.
4. Tomlinson, J. R. G. 1991. "Comprehensive Education in England and Wales, 1944 – 1991," *European Journal of Education*, 26(2):103 – 104.
5. Tomlinson, J. R. G., 26(2):105 – 108.
6. Central Office of Information. 1992. *Britain 1992, an Official Handbook.* London, p. 157.
7. United States Information Agency. 1989, 1990 and 1991. Reports submitted by American Fulbright Exchange Teachers in England (individual identities protected by Freedom of Information Act), Washington, DC.
8. Potter, A. Interview with author, January 1992.
9. Taylor, P. H. and R. Lowe, pp. 151 – 152.
10. Taylor, P. H. and R. Lowe, p. 152.
11. Potter, A. Interview.
12. Maeroff, G. I. 1992. "Focusing on Urban Education in Britain," *Phi Delta Kappan*, 73(5):355.
13. United States Information Agency documents.
14. Potter, A. Interview.
15. United States Information Agency documents.
16. Maeroff, G. I., 73(5):358.
17. Potter, A. Interview.
18. Potter, A. Interview.
19. Maeroff, G. I., 73(5):356.
20. Tomlinson, J. R. G., 26(2):112.
21. United States Information Agency. 1991. *Your Year in the United Kingdom.* Washington, DC, p. 15.

22. Cox, A. Interview with author, January 1992.
23. Taylor, P. H. and R. Lowe, pp. 176–177.
24. Taylor, P. H. and R. Lowe, p. 157.
25. United States Information Agency documents.
26. Maeroff, G. I., 73(5):357.
27. United States Information Agency, pp. 17–18.
28. United States Information Agency, p. 17.
29. Cox, A. Interview.
30. Taylor, P. H. and R. Lowe, p. 153.
31. Taylor, P. H. and R. Lowe, p. 177.
32. Cantley, J. Correspondence with author, June 1992.
33. United States Information Agency, p. 16.
34. United States Information Agency, pp. 16–17.
35. United States Information Agency, p. 18.
36. Taylor, P. H. and R. Lowe, p. 139.
37. Nelson, F. H. 1991. *International Comparisons of Public Spending on Education.* Washington, DC: American Federation of Teachers, p. 35.
38. Coalter, V. and A. Potter. Interviews with author, January 1992.
39. Taylor, P. H. and R. Lowe, p. 169.
40. United States Information Agency documents.
41. Maeroff, G. I., 73(5):358.
42. Potter, A., V. Coalter, and A. Cox. Interviews with author, January 1992.
43. Potter, A. Interview.
44. United States Information Agency documents.
45. United States Information Agency documents.
46. Potter, A., V. Coalter, and A. Cox. Interviews.
47. Potter, A., V. Coalter, and A. Cox. Interviews.
48. Nelson, F. H., p. 37.
49. Coalter, V. Interview with author, January 1992.
50. Archer, E. G. and B. T. Peck. 1992. *The Teaching Profession in Europe.* Glasgow: Jordanhill College of Education, pp. 108, 352.
51. United States Information Agency, pp. 19–20.
52. United States Information Agency documents.
53. Cox, A. and V. Coalter. Interviews with author, January 1992.
54. Maeroff, G. I., 73(5):358.
55. Judge, H. G. "Cross-National Perceptions of Teachers," *Comparative Education Review,* 32(2):143–158.
56. Maeroff, G. I., 73(5):354.
57. Potter, A. Interview.
58. Potter, A. Interview.
59. Maeroff, G. I., 73(5):355–356.
60. Taylor, P. H. and R. Lowe, pp. 172, 178.
61. Maeroff, G. I., 73(5):355.

62. Taylor, P. H. and R. Lowe, p. 176.

63. Maeroff, G. I., 73(5):356.

64. Cox, A. and V. Coalter. Interviews.

65. Central Office of Information, p. 157.

66. Maeroff, G. I., 73(5):357.

67. United States Information Agency, p. 17.

68. Central Office of Information, p. 144.

69. Ball, S. J. 1987. *The Micro-Politics of the School.* London: Methuen and Company Ltd., pp. 174–175.

70. Ball, S. J., p. 358.

71. Taylor, P. H. and R. Lowe, p. 168.

72. Ball, S. J., p. 257.

73. Ball, S. J., p. 40.

74. Hill, D., B. O. Smith, and J. Spinks. 1990. *Local Management of Schools.* London: Paul Chapman Publishing Ltd., p. 67.

75. Ball, S. J., pp. 9, 121.

76. Ball, S. J., p. 156.

77. United States Information Agency documents.

78. Archer, E. G. and B. T. Peck, pp. 111–112.

79. Taylor, P. H. and R. Lowe, p. 167.

80. Archer, E. G. and B. T. Peck, p. 22.

81. Potter, A., V. Coalter, and A. Cox. Interviews.

82. Potter, A., V. Coalter, and A. Cox. Interviews.

83. Potter, A., V. Coalter, and A. Cox. Interviews.

84. Taylor, P. H. and R. Lowe, p. 168.

85. Ball, S. J., p. 78.

86. United States Information Agency, p. 14.

87. Cox, A. Interview.

88. Maeroff, G. I., 73(5):358.

89. Potter, A. Interview.

90. Maeroff, G. I., 73(5):354.

91. 1992. *New York Times* (January 8):A1, B7.

92. Tomlinson, J. R. G., 26(2):112.

93. Maeroff, G. I., 73(5):355.

94. Halpin, D., S. Power, and J. Fitz. 1991. "Grant-Maintained Schools: Making a Difference without Being Really Different," *British Journal of Educational Studies,* 39(4):410–411.

95. Halpin, D., S. Power, and J. Fitz, 39(4):416–420.

96. Central Office of Information, p. 144.

97. United States Information Agency, p. 14.

98. Central Office of Information, p. 149.

99. Cox, A. Interview.

100. Taylor, P. H. and R. Lowe, pp. 167–168.

101. Pearce, J. 1986. ''School Oversight in England and Wales,'' *European Journal of Education,* 21(4):333.
102. United States Information Agency, p. 17.
103. United States Information Agency documents.
104. Potter, A., V. Coalter, and A. Cox. Interviews.
105. Central Office of Information, p. 138.
106. Maeroff, G. I., 73(5):357.
107. Taylor, P. H. and R. Lowe, p. 181.
108. Tomlinson, J. R. G., 26(2):115.
109. Tomlinson, J. R. G., 26(2):113.
110. Tomlinson, J. R. G., 26(2):110−111.
111. Maeroff, G. I., 73(5):357.
112. Maeroff, G. I., 73(5):357.

CHAPTER 6

Canada — Our Cultural Cousins

CANADA, FOLLOWING THE dissolution of the former Soviet Union, has been thrust into first position as the nation with the world's largest land mass. This huge expanse of territory covers more than half the total land area of the North American continent. The vast Canadian nation is sparsely inhabited, having a total population of only 26 million citizens. The attempt to mold the diverse peoples of this immense region into a common nation continues to be a major political challenge in the 1990s.

Canada is a young country characterized by the pioneer spirit of fur traders of the sixteenth and seventeenth centuries, and the settlers of its Western provinces less than one hundred years ago.[1] The British and French influences have been dominant, along with the cultural contributions of British Loyalists who fled to Canada during the American Revolution. Currently about 40 percent of the population claims British heritage, about 27 percent are of French descent, with an additional 20 percent representing other European cultures. The remaining portion of the population is Native Canadian. Forty-six percent are Roman Catholics and 41 percent belong to various Protestant denominations.[2] The historical cultural clashes between British and French, Protestant and Catholic, profoundly affect the educational systems of several Canadian provinces.

The largest population centers in Canada are found along the Atlantic and Pacific coasts, and across a band of territory running east to west along the 3,700-mile border with the United States. More than half of the total Canadian population lives in the two central provinces of Ontario and Quebec. These provinces provide the industrial base for modern Canada and produce many of the goods for foreign trade with Canada's primary trading partner, the United States. The western plains provinces of Saskatchewan, Manitoba, and Alberta together form one of the major breadbaskets of the world, producing a significant percentage of world grain supplies. Pulp and paper mills in Canada account for

163

15 percent of world newsprint supplies. Auto manufacturing in the Central provinces represents a major industry in Canada.[3]

Canada is a constitutional monarchy under the British crown, with a Canadian governor-general representing the Queen. The Prime Minister is the head of government, sharing power with the Senate and the House of Commons. Membership in both the Senate and the House is roughly proportional to the population in the provinces. Each of the ten provinces has its own unicameral legislature, while the territories are administered by commissioners and small elected councils. Elected councils govern the 4,500 local municipalities in Canada.[4]

The British North America Act of 1867 laid the foundations for the Canadian system of educational governance. This act explicitly states that "in and for each province the legislature may exclusively make laws in relation to education."[5] Thus in reality there is no single Canadian education system but rather a series of ten provincial and two territorial systems. There is no federal department of education, although there are federal offices that collect educational statistics and related information. The federal government is active in the financing of higher education and in supporting vocational and technical education.

Among the six nations in this survey, the Canadian educational system is most similar to that of the United States. While educational policies and practices differ to some degree among the provinces, Canadian schools throughout the nation share many common characteristics. The marked similarity between educational systems in Canada and the United States should facilitate the adaptation of successful Canadian practices to American schools.

HISTORY AND DEVELOPMENT OF CANADIAN SCHOOLS

Seventeenth-century missionaries introduced the first formal schools in Canada. The Catholic and Protestant churches were a strong force for educational development in the Canadian colonies throughout the seventeenth and eighteenth centuries. The Hudson Bay Company provided the impetus for the establishment of schools in the western expanse that it controlled, which later would become the Western provinces.[6]

Schools made the transition from private to public control between 1750 and 1850. Moral and religious ideals permeated all school programs from reading and writing instruction to the training of apprentices.[7] An act in 1807 and the School Act of 1816 marked the first use of government funds to support people's schools. By the 1840s most provinces were building provincial educational systems within which local school boards operated tax-supported nondenominational schools under provincial departments of education.[8]

In 1841, Ontario and Quebec provinces authorized public support for denominational schools. This provision allowed religious minorities to operate tax-funded schools separate from the schools of the religious majority. The predominant Catholic population of Quebec developed distinctly Catholic public schools, while at the same time providing publicly supported schools for its Protestant minority.[9]

The period from Canadian confederation in 1867 to 1900 marked the development of the Canadian provincial school systems of today. The British North America Act of 1867 provided the basic governmental sanction for the strong provincial educational systems that were to develop. The period was marked in most provinces by the development of strong central educational authorities, free schooling at both the elementary and secondary levels, and local taxation and provincial grants to finance the schools. The newer Western provinces developed educational systems modeled after those of the older and more settled Eastern and Central Canadian provinces.[9]

The story of twentieth-century education in Canada parallels that of the United States. An increasing demand for higher educational attainment by a growing population caused a vast increase in the size of the educational enterprise. Canada was especially convinced of the link between education and economic and social development, and thus invested more heavily in education at all levels than most other industrialized countries. By the 1970s, Canadian educational expenses were among the highest in the world.[10]

During the 1950s and 1960s there was a wave of enthusiasm for a child-centered and progressive curriculum. This enthusiasm has waned in recent years, however, to be replaced with a concern over a perceived decline in quality and excessive cost. Educational budgets have been tightened, curriculum guidelines have been strengthened, and student assessment procedures have been implemented.[11] Educational controversies, challenges, and reforms in the Canada of the 1990s are evolving in tandem with those of its American neighbor to the south.

ELEMENTARY EDUCATION IN CANADA

Most Canadian provinces provide publicly funded kindergarten for five-year-old children. The compulsory school age begins at six or seven and continues through age sixteen in most provinces, although a minority of provinces end compulsory schooling at age fifteen. Canadian students attend school for approximately 190 days per year, a number that varies slightly among the provinces. Teachers often work an additional five or more days for inservice training and building, district, or provincial level meetings. [12] Summer, Christmas, and Easter vacations tend to follow the American pattern. These vacation schedule patterns in the United States and Canada differ from the practice in all other countries in this study. Denmark, Germany, England, and Japan each have more frequent, but shorter vacation periods.

The traditional grade organization of elementary schools (grades one through eight), and secondary schools (grades nine through twelve), has been modified in recent years in most Canadian provinces. The change is toward middle schools for grades six to eight or junior high schools for grades seven through nine. Thus, elementary school now most often encompasses kindergarten through grade five or six. There is also a strong trend toward bringing all teacher education, both elementary and secondary, into the university system. School boards are now more likely to include both elementary and secondary schools under their jurisdiction, rather than following the previous practice of separate elementary and secondary districts. [13]

These changes have produced a more unified and coordinated system of elementary and secondary education in the Canadian provinces. Many of the changes mirror similar American educational trends over the past thirty to forty years (see Figure 6.1). Educational practices in the United States have directly influenced individual Canadian provinces, particularly the Western provinces of Canada.

The curriculum in Canadian elementary schools is similar to that of American elementary schools, with perhaps a greater attempt to integrate subjects and provide for group project work. Special subjects such as music and art are often taught by the regular classroom teacher in less populated regions of Canada, rather than by special subject teachers as is common in the United States. Curriculum guides are created at the provincial level and are expected to form the basis for instruction in all schools within the province. Provincial departments of education employ subject specialists, who work with committees of teachers, to create curriculum materials and supervise their implementation throughout the province. Textbooks and other teaching materials are in good supply in most Canadian schools. Plentiful instructional materials represents another similarity between American and Canadian schools.

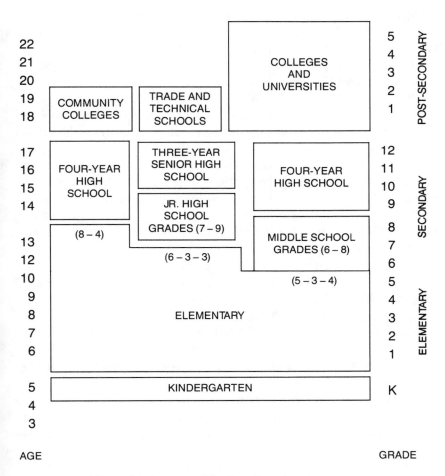

Figure 6.1 *Structure of the Canadian education system.*

In the upper years of elementary school, students study either French or English as a second language, whichever is not their language of daily instruction. The strong Canadian desire to retain cultural traditions has led to a system where the primary language of instruction in a given school is determined by the ethnic heritage of the community. It is recognized, however, that civil peace and cooperation require all Canadians to interact and work well together. Thus instruction in French is provided to students in English-speaking schools while instruction in English is provided to students in French language schools. This system ensures that most Canadian students will be bilingual.

The Canadians' determination to preserve their various cultural identities reflects itself in the phenomenon of denominational public schools. Forty percent of Canadian students attend schools that are religious in character and are fully or substantially funded by public taxes. In Saskatoon, Saskatchewan, for example, taxpayers designate whether their local taxes will be sent to publicly supported Catholic schools, or nondenominational public schools.[14] Such taxpayer-supported Catholic schools provide religious instruction to their students and are permitted to hire certified teachers who fulfill religious and character requirements set by the school.[15]

Grading and assessment in Canadian elementary schools, particularly in the early years, is informal and largely anecdotal. Teachers are concerned with both social and academic development and communicate progress to parents through parent conferences and written reports. Standard formal examinations are no longer common in Canadian elementary schools. During the upper elementary years, teachers begin to introduce more formalized tests and grades and hold students to stricter academic standards.[16]

Canadian schools at the elementary level are often nongraded and feature a continuous progress curriculum. The Year 2000 initiative in British Columbia mandated the combination of two or more age levels in one classroom beginning in 1991. Elementary classes in this province are to contain students of mixed-ability and mixed-age groups. Instruction is to be child-centered with an emphasis on whole language and cooperative learning.[17] An educational researcher from British Columbia has noted with some irony that British Columbia is moving toward a more child-centered, self-paced program, at the same time that England is moving away from this approach and instituting a standard curriculum and student assessment program.[18] The continuous progress, ungraded approach to instruction ensures that relatively few Canadian elementary students are retained in grade.[19]

Elementary class sizes in Canada typically range from twenty to thirty students. Rules of school behavior are similar to those found in the United States, although one teacher interviewed reported that her Canadian school allowed students far more freedom of movement within the school than did her exchange school in the United States.[20] Homework assignments to Canadian elementary students are minimal.[21]

The school day for students in Canadian elementary school begins at about 9:00 A.M. There is generally a recess during the morning and a full hour for lunch from 12:00−1:00 P.M. The school day ends at 3:00 or 3:30 P.M.[22] Thus the student day is similar in length to that of many American students, although actual instructional time may be somewhat less than in most American schools.

CANADIAN SECONDARY SCHOOLS

American visitors to a Canadian high school would feel quite at home. Familiar features of American high schools, such as six to eight forty-five-minute classes, study halls during unscheduled periods, and student cafeterias monitored by teachers, are all characteristics of Canadian secondary education. Canada also shares America's commitment to the comprehensive high school, designed to meet the educational needs of all students in the community.

As was noted at the elementary level, the history of Canadian secondary schools in the post-World War II period closely parallels developments in the United States.[23] Until recent decades Canadian secondary schools followed the European model of an elite academic education for the few, with a lesser concern for the majority of students. During the 1950s and 1960s Canadian educational policy shifted rapidly toward universal access to a comprehensive high school education, and a virtual open door policy toward higher education. The higher education expansion was fueled by the creation of two-year community colleges and the rapid growth of the existing college and university system.

The commitment to expansion of educational opportunity led to a perceived decline in student achievement. The Canadian tradition of provincial examinations at the end of the high school years was largely abandoned.[24] By the 1980s, high unemployment, rapidly escalating educational costs, and the perceived drop in achievement combined to produce a more critical attitude among Canadians regarding their schools. Again there was concern for getting more educational value for the dollar and establishing more objective standards of student achievement.[25] In some provinces there was a return to provincial exams at the end of secondary school. Other provinces instituted assessment tests at various grade levels for various subjects. These tests generally use sampling techniques to establish achievement results that are valid for the province as a whole.

The minimum age for leaving school is fifteen in about half the Canadian provinces and sixteen in the other half. The dropout rate in Canadian schools is similar to that of the United States. More than 60 percent of Canadian high school graduates proceed to some form of higher education, a figure that is somewhat lower than that of the United States, but substantially higher than that of other countries in this study.

Tracking or streaming of students is not common in Canadian secondary schools until tenth grade. By this grade level, students are effectively ability-grouped by means of the pattern of courses that they select.[26] Canadian students generally pursue a core of required subjects during their first two years of high school and select more specialized courses during their final two years. Students qualify to graduate by accumulating a series of credits in both required and elective courses, as in the United States. Vocational courses are now offered either at or in cooperation with Canadian comprehensive high schools. Students wishing to enter a college or university will pursue an academically rigorous program during their final two years in secondary school.[27]

School leaving examinations, once common but now largely abandoned, are staging a comeback in some provinces. Manitoba province has initiated a new assessment program for twelfth graders whereby one or two subjects are tested each year, with the grade that the student earns counted toward his/her final course grade.[28] In Saskatchewan, twelfth grade students must take a provincial exam in certain subjects if their teacher is not accredited. An accredited teacher is a fully certified teacher who has taken extra courses and workshops in the provincial curriculum and testing practices.[29]

There are a few exceptions to the general rule that students graduate from secondary school at the end of twelfth grade. Secondary school in the provinces of Newfoundland and Quebec ends after eleventh grade.[30] In 1967, Quebec created a new type of school between secondary school and the university. This institution is known as a *college of general and vocational education*. After completing eleventh grade, students attend this school for two or three years to prepare to enter a university or professional school. It corresponds roughly to a junior college in the United States and other parts of Canada.[31]

An American student transferring to a Canadian high school would likely experience a smooth transition. Teachers rely heavily on textbooks as a major instructional support. Audiovisual materials and equipment are as common as they are in American schools. Students proceed through a series of classes in different subjects taught by different teachers.

Some Canadian schools operate on a semester basis with students having only four or five subjects, most of which meet for two periods each day. These two periods are sometimes scheduled together and sometimes occur at different times during the day. Teachers in such a semester organization have only half as many different students as they would in a year-long organization structure, and the students have only half as many subjects at one time as they would under a year-long course structure.[32] Other schools achieve the same effect of fewer courses for the student by scheduling five one-hour classes each day. A teacher in this five-period-day system will teach four classes each day, thus limiting his or her total student count to 80 to 100 students. This five-period-day system is followed in all eight high schools in one Saskatchewan district.[33]

At the end of the regular school day the American transfer student will find an extracurricular program of athletics and other activities similar to that of American schools. Teachers usually volunteer to supervise such activities. Grading in Canadian secondary schools consists of teacher evaluation of quizzes, unit tests, and student projects and reports. Again, the Canadian practice with respect to grading closely parallels that of the United States. In homework too, Canadian teachers duplicate American practice by assigning perhaps one-and-one-half hours of homework to the more academic students, and half an hour or less to the nonacademic student.

One striking difference between American and Canadian secondary schools is the high proportion of Canadian publicly supported schools that are affiliated directly with religious groups. Denominational religious instruction is offered in these schools, although the religion classes are often not mandatory for students. In addition, the rules and ethos of the schools reflect the religious principles of the sponsoring religious body.

PRIVATE EDUCATION IN CANADA

The clear distinctions between public and private education that exist in the United States do not apply to Canada. The pattern of public support and control of private education described for the European nations in earlier chapters is found, with some variations, in all Canadian provinces. Slightly more than half of Canadian students attend nondenominational public schools analogous to public schools in the United States. More than 40 percent of students in Canada attend church-related schools that enjoy various levels of public support, along with varying degrees of public control.

Private schools in the American sense enroll less than 5 percent of Canadian students. These schools are largely free of governmental control, can employ teachers according to their own standards, and can establish their own criteria for selecting students. In the Eastern provinces and Ontario such schools are very loosely regulated but receive no public funds. In Quebec and the Western provinces there is greater governmental control, along with a correspondingly greater degree of governmental financial support. [34]

Such financial support is directly proportional to the degree of provincial control. Support ranges from virtually full support in Saskatchewan to about a 15 percent level of support in Manitoba. Quebec differentiates among private schools in that schools that it declares to be of *public interest* receive 80 percent support, whereas other private schools receive 60 percent support. [35] Private, also known as *independent* schools, have enjoyed a surge in popularity in recent decades – this during a period when public school enrollment has declined markedly.

Regardless of the degree of provincial control, private schools in Canada closely follow provincial curriculum guidelines and course requirements. Private school graduates are subject to school leaving examinations in provinces that require them, and must meet the same requirements for admission to colleges and universities as public school graduates. [36] Private schools are more common at the secondary level and function primarily as academic prep schools for the universities. Virtually all the private schools are religiously oriented.

The great majority of denominational schools in Canada receive state funds on an equal basis with nondenominational public schools. More than two million Canadian students attend such denominational schools throughout Canada. Almost 90 percent of these students attend Catholic schools. Two-thirds of this number are in Quebec province. About 200,000 children attend Protestant public schools, half of these being in Quebec province. Virtually all publicly supported denominational schools in Canada are Christian in character. [37]

The mechanism for funding these denominational schools varies among the provinces. In most provinces the major funding source for denominational schools is the province itself, which is also the case for public schools. Christian schools are fully integrated into the public school system, must follow all curriculum and teacher certification requirements, are subject to provincial supervisory oversight, and participate in provincial school leaving examinations and student assessment programs. Individual schools determine the religious content of instruction and the operating procedures for the school. Assuming a teaching candidate is otherwise certified and qualified, the denominational school may apply denominational criteria to teacher selection.[38]

HIGHER EDUCATION IN CANADA

By the 1980s, Canada supported about seventy public universities enrolling close to 400,000 full-time students. Most of these universities evolved over time from private religious schools to more secularized institutions, with an increasing dependence on public funding. The federal government offers substantial support to higher education. The provinces also provide a large portion of the budget.[39] Endowments, gifts, and student tuition provide the remaining financial support. Tuition rates vary greatly among the provinces but tend to be comparable to tuition rates at public universities in the United States.[40]

Students enter colleges and universities after completing high school at age eighteen. In Quebec, students attend a two- or three-year preparatory school after completing eleventh grade, before entering college at nineteen or twenty. A bachelor's degree can be earned in either three or four years by completing fifteen or twenty full-year courses. The school leaving examinations, common in the provinces until recent years, were once a major determinant of college admission. In the absence of these exams, colleges rely on high school grades and aptitude tests.[41]

Community colleges in Canada, following an explosive growth rate in the 1960s, provide students with a convenient and inexpensive alternative to the university. They typically offer two- or three-year diploma-granting programs in technical and vocational areas. Admission requires a high school diploma, although nongraduates with relevant work experience can be admitted to some programs. These less expensive schools, closer to the homes of the students, account for a substantial amount of the rapidly increasing enrollments in higher education.

Student enrollment in all types of Canadian higher education increased from 640,000 to 1,300,000 between 1970 and 1987, an increase of 100 percent. Fifty-eight percent of the twenty- to twenty-four-year-old population in Canada participated in higher education in 1987. This is comparable to the 65 percent figure for the United States in the same year.[42]

The Canadian system of higher education closely parallels the United States system. Canada is the only country in this study approaching the United States in the proportion of the populace attending post-secondary school institutions. Most of this dynamic growth in the higher education sphere has occurred during the past twenty years.

TEACHING IN CANADA

The similarities between the Canadian and United States educational systems extend to the worklife of the classroom teacher. Like their American and English counterparts, Canadian teachers have a heavier daily teaching schedule than do teachers in Germany, Denmark, or Japan. The required school day for Canadian teachers typically extends from about 8:30 A.M. −3:30 P.M. Teachers will usually have a full hour for lunch, a luxury not available to most United States teachers. An elementary teacher may have two or three free periods during the school week,[43] or perhaps a thirty-minute free period each day.[44] Secondary teachers usually have one period each day for planning. All remaining periods are scheduled for classes or supervisory responsibilities such as study halls or cafeteria duty.[45]

A school work year for Canadian teachers is from 195−200 days, including several days of workshops and meetings. The length of the teacher year in Canada is comparable to that of the European countries studied and is about two weeks longer than the school year for American teachers.

Canadian teachers do not receive supplemental contracts for coaching sports or other student activities. Teachers volunteer for such activities with the expectation that every teacher will perform his or her share of such work. Peers and supervisors exert pressure on teachers who do not voluntarily participate in these programs. This broad involvement of teachers in after-school activity programs may partially explain the fact that Canadian teachers seldom hold second part-time jobs.[46]

In 1984, Canadian teachers earned 35 percent more than American teachers, on a purchasing power parity basis. At that time Canadian teachers earned 40 percent more than the average manufacturing worker in their country. Thus Canadian teachers are the best paid of the six countries in this study, and rank second only to Japan when their wages are compared to those of manufacturing workers within their own country.[47] Canadian teachers interviewed for this study confirm that teacher salaries in Canada are indeed higher than teacher salaries in the United States.

Although procedures for establishing teacher salaries vary among the Canadian provinces, there are several common compensation practices throughout the nation. Both elementary and secondary teachers are paid on the same salary schedule. Teachers earn additional salary increments for years of teaching experience and advanced degrees. Teachers in Catholic and other denominational schools, as well as public school teachers, are on the same salary schedule.[48]

Teachers in British Columbia, who recently acquired the right to strike, negotiate at the individual district level to establish their salary schedules.[49] Teachers in Manitoba also negotiate salaries at the local level, but they do not have the right to strike. Salary disputes in Manitoba are resolved through arbitration.[50] In Saskatchewan there is a single salary schedule throughout the province, although teacher groups do negotiate at the district level regarding fringe benefits and working conditions. Teachers in Saskatchewan do have the right to strike.[51] Teachers in Ontario, who won the right to strike in 1974, conduct contract negotiations at the local level.[52]

Discussions with Canadian teachers from several provinces reveal the same concerns over professional autonomy, testing and accountability, class size, and professional status that are common concerns among American teachers. The recent public demand for more educational accountability and productivity has led to increasing work loads and an erosion in salary levels for teachers in many Canadian regions.[53]

Evaluation of classroom teaching performance is not a priority in Canadian schools. A teacher from British Columbia reports that teachers are formally evaluated once every five years, although principals do occasionally visit a class for an informal visit.[54] A second teacher reported that classes are formally observed during the first two years of teaching, and that an experienced teacher is observed informally, if at all.[55] Another teacher reports that a formal evaluation with a checklist and descriptors is completed once every three or four years. A single page summary report is prepared each year following a discussion between the teacher and the principal.[56] A teacher from Manitoba province indicated that formal evaluations in his district occur every two years.[57]

Teacher education and certification requirements differ among the ten provinces. Most provinces now require a minimum of a bachelor's degree, which is typically earned in an education major during four years of college. At least one province requires a fifth year of training with one semester devoted to student teaching.[58] Some teachers attend college for an additional two years to earn a second degree. There are still teachers in Canada, nearing retirement age, who have only one year of university preparation.[59] Educational requirements for teacher certification in Canada generally correspond to existing practice in the United States.

Daily classroom routines for Canadian teachers closely resemble those of American teachers. There is a reliance on instructional materials and texts, which are generally as plentiful as they are in the United States. The move toward ungraded primary schools encourages more project and cooperative learning activities, as are commonly found in English primary schools. Secondary teachers continue to rely primarily on teacher-centered presentations of information. Class sizes in Canada are typically in the range of twenty to thirty students. Because of various scheduling procedures, Canadian secondary teachers may interact with fewer than one hundred students each day, a somewhat smaller number than is common for an American secondary school teacher.[60]

Canadian teachers do not consider themselves to hold high status in their own country. They are being criticized for the perceived poor performance of the schools. People complain about their long vacations and there is frequent grumbling about high teacher salaries whenever local contracts are being negotiated.[61] All the above are familiar refrains to American educators.

The Canadian teacher's worklife is comparable in almost every way to that of an American educator. There does, however, appear to be a significant difference in salaries in favor of the Canadians. It should be noted, nonetheless, that the work year for a Canadian teacher is two weeks longer than that of American teachers, and that Canadian teachers typically perform extensive extracurricular duties on a voluntary noncompensated basis. American teachers routinely receive extra pay for such extra duty.

STUDENTS IN CANADIAN SCHOOLS

The parallel organizational pattern of Canadian and American schools has been previously noted. A Canadian student will begin kindergarten at age five or six and remain in an elementary school until fifth or sixth grade. Many students will then transfer to a middle school or junior high school for grades six to eight or seven to nine. Senior high school incorporates grades nine to twelve or ten to twelve. More traditional grade organization patterns, particularly in rural schools with low enrollment, will feature eight years of elementary school and four years of high school. As in America, individual school boards generally make decisions regarding grade organizational patterns. [62]

Students in Canada attend school for about 190 days each year, approximately two weeks longer than their American counterparts. The student day at the elementary level begins at approximately 9:00 A.M. and ends between 3:00 and 3:30 P.M. There is generally a full hour for lunch. Schools normally schedule a fifteen-minute recess break in the morning session so that actual instructional time each day is about five hours. [63] This is comparable to the length of the school day for American and English students and is somewhat longer than the elementary school day in Denmark and Germany. Students eat lunch at school, either in the school cafeteria or — more likely — in their classroom.

Secondary students begin the school day at 8:30 – 9:00 A.M. and remain in classes until 3:00 – 3:30 P.M. Depending on the particular daily schedule of their school, students may attend as few as five one-hour classes or as many as seven or eight forty-minute classes. Students will have an hour for lunch, and will have study halls during unscheduled class periods. Exchange teachers report that procedures and rules for student discipline are somewhat less stringent and formal in Canadian schools, and that Canadian students generally behave better than American students. All agreed, however, that the perceived differences in this area were not great. [64]

Canadian high school students follow a lifestyle that mirrors that of the American teenage subculture. The schools provide extensive after-school sports and other activities, many students hold part-time jobs, and students can begin driving at age fifteen or sixteen. The fact that the majority of the Canadian population lives along a 150-mile band of territory bordering the United States ensures that students have ready access to American television, as well as to services and products reflecting the American culture. The American teenager's tendency toward early sexual involvement, and to participate in a weekend party culture, are characteristics shared by many Canadian students.[65]

Even though Canadian teenagers may hold part-time jobs, the time commitments required are less than is typical for American teenagers. Stores and shopping malls in Canada operate fewer hours each week than in America, thus reducing the need for part-time workers. In Quebec province, for example, shopping malls remain closed on Sundays and close at 5:30 P.M. during the first few evenings of each week. Shopping malls in Saskatchewan still close on Sunday, although this tradition is being challenged by the retail stores.[66]

Many provinces have introduced some type of continuous assessment program system for grading, leading to a decrease in the number of students retained in grade.[67] In British Columbia, recent legislation has mandated heterogeneous and cross-grade grouping for students with a continuous assessment, continuous progress model of instruction.[68] Student reports in the lower elementary grades contain descriptors such as ''meets expectations'' rather than letter grades or percentage grades.[69] Canadian elementary schools are moving closer to the English primary school model, which de-emphasizes competition and pressure on students to meet strict achievement standards.

Student assessment practices at the secondary level, meanwhile, are beginning to become more stringent. Provincial school leaving examinations and standardized testing, while once common, were abandoned over the past twenty years. They are now being reinstated as provincial student assessment programs. In Manitoba province, the testing program appears in two forms. There are required school leaving exams in certain subjects for high school seniors, which count as part of their grade. There are also tests in certain subjects given to a random sample of students at various grade levels.[70]

Provincial school leaving exams are required for twelfth grade students in Saskatchewan only if their instructor does not possess a special accreditation to prepare and evaluate his or her own final examinations.[71] Ontario province has established a series of standardized test questions for academic courses, has reestablished compulsory subjects at the basic, general, and advanced levels, and has compressed the time available for advanced students to complete the same amount of work.[72] The Canadian Council of Ministers of Education has approved the goals and objectives for a School Achievement Indicators Study (SAIP). Every province, except Ontario, has agreed to participate in this assessment of reading, writing, and mathematical skills of thirteen- and sixteen-year-old students. The first assessment is scheduled for 1993.

This trend toward a return to mandated testing reflects current nation-wide Canadian concerns about the quality of schooling. Evidence is growing that Canadian secondary school students are experiencing the same tightening of academic standards and rising academic expectations as their American counterparts. There is concern in Canada, as in the United States, that higher expectations alone may lead to higher dropout rates.[73]

The similar cultures of Canada and the United States affect Canadian and American students in a similar fashion. Canadian high school students participate in many extracurricular and out-of-school activities. These activities, plus the availability of cars and part-time jobs, diminish the importance of schooling in the life of the Canadian teenager. Easy access to higher education lessens the need to compete with other students for admission to college. Homework requirements tend to be minimal, except for the most academic students. There is some evidence that as the Canadian culture and schooling patterns come to more closely mirror those of America, Canadian secondary school students will increasingly project the same lack of motivation and commitment that are pandemic among American students.

Alberta province, north of Montana and North Dakota, is the home of seventeen-year-old Paul. He is among the many students in his rural high school, five hours from Edmonton, the closest major city. He will work on the farms once he completes high school. He bought his own pickup truck, complete with gun rack, and dresses in the jeans and cowboy boots that are practically a uniform among workers on the vast ranches in the plains states of both Canada and the United States. Paul works a part-time job at one of the stores in his small town on Thursday and Friday evenings, the only nights that retail stores are open in his area. In his ample spare time Paul likes to cruise around town in his pickup truck, hang out with friends at a local diner, or take his girlfriend to the movies.

Paul has noticed that the minority of his classmates who will be attending college are spending much more time studying than he is. These students must take the Alberta provincial exams as seniors to qualify for admission to college. The grades that these students earn on these tests will have greater weight than their course grades in determining their

(continued)

chances for admission to various schools. As tenth grade students, Paul and his classmates were separated into different ability groups for the first time, a fact that further accentuated the differences between Paul and his college-bound peers.

The differences between Paul and his group of friends, and the more academic students, are most pronounced at lunch time. Paul's group uses the one-hour lunch to walk into town, buy a hamburger, and stroll along the main street. The college-bound students, however, use this hour to meet in study groups to prepare for the provincial exams. They have gained some practice in studying for such exams by taking mid-term and final exams in their regular courses throughout their high school years. The study-group setting is very relaxed since teachers do not supervise students over the lunch period, whether they remain at school or visit town as Paul and his friends commonly do.

Paul does participate in a community ice hockey team but does not play any of the several sports offered by his high school. He likes sports but doesn't want to face the three-hour rides each way to compete against the nearest schools. American popular culture of teenage music, dance, and movies is readily accessible via satellite and cable to young people in this remote Canadian setting. His exposure to the media version of the lives of American teenagers has convinced Paul that his daily life closely resembles that of American teenagers growing up in a rural area.

THE CANADIAN SCHOOL PRINCIPAL

The school principal in Canada has much in common with his/her American counterpart. Canada is the only other nation in this study that requires a formal preparation program for school administrators. These programs consist of advanced degree or certification programs at Canadian universities. The common preparation for a principalship in the various Canadian provinces is a master's degree in school administration or another related area, and additional courses leading to an administrative certificate. The typical career path for a school administrator is from assistant principal to principal, or from the principalship of a small school to the principalship at a larger school.

Separate preparation programs for school administrators emphasize the difference in job functions between principals and teachers and reinforce the concept, as in the United States, that teachers and principals belong to different professional groups. The existence of such administrative preparation programs in Canada has not negatively affected the sense of membership in a common profession among teachers and administrators, which continues to be the norm in Canadian schools.

Building administrators in Canadian schools are more likely to have teaching assignments than are their American counterparts. In smaller schools it is common for an assistant principal to maintain a half-time teaching schedule.[74] Even the principal may teach one or two classes each day in a small elementary school.[75] An elementary teacher from British Columbia reported that her administrators provide planning periods for teachers in her school by substituting two periods per week for each teacher. The assistant principal in this instance devotes about half of his or her time to direct teaching, while the principal teaches a lesser amount.[76] This particular district does not have the special subject teachers who in many American districts serve the dual function of providing specialized instruction to students, while allowing planning periods for teachers.

In both Manitoba and Saskatchewan provinces, principals' salaries relate directly to their positions on the standard teacher salary schedule. This teaching salary for a given principal is supplemented by allowances for administrative responsibilities and for supervising the teaching staff.[77] In 1991, principals in Saskatchewan received a supplement of $1,847 for administrative responsibilities, $529 per teacher for supervising up to ten teachers, and an additional $371 for each teacher between eleven and twenty. Additional supplements are given for supervising larger numbers of teachers. Under this formula a principal with twenty staff members who earns about $51,000 per year as a teacher would earn about $61,000 as a principal (all figures are in Canadian dollars).[78]

The link between administrator and teacher pay is so direct in many Canadian provinces and districts that teachers actually negotiate for the salary supplements that principals will receive. This phenomenon clearly diminishes the degree of hierarchical separation between administrators and teachers.[79] Salaries tied this directly to standard teacher salary scales make no provision for merit pay for principals, and thus there are no financial incentives for dynamic leadership at the school principal level. Canadian principals also typically enjoy tenure as teachers. In these respects the Canadian principals' professional situation resembles the European model, rather than the manager/worker model that is common, though not universal, in the United States.

The daily and annual work schedule for Canadian principals corresponds to that of American principals. Active after-school programs at most schools demand the presence of the principal until late afternoon. Evening activities include parent conferences, sporting events, and musical and other student performance programs. Principals work a longer school year than teachers, although they will schedule several weeks for vacation during the summer months.

Principals in Canada perform the same general functions as European principals and head teachers. They play a critical role in staff selection, student discipline, and school schedules and organization. They tend to make budgetary decisions in a collaborative fashion by considering the opinions of teachers and department heads. Formal evaluation of teachers' classroom performance is infrequent, occurring more frequently than is common in European schools, but less frequently than is the norm in the United States.

Canadian administrators have only an indirect influence on curriculum. Provincial-wide teacher committees write a curriculum, which is then published by the province. Special subject supervisors and advisors are provided by the provinces to consult with individual schools and teachers regarding curriculum implementation and revision.[80] Principals also represent the schools to the community, and respond to parental concerns.

Canadian building-level administrators interact with the local school superintendent rather than directly with a school board as is common in the European model. The school superintendent chooses candidates for the principalship and recommends them to the local school board for approval. Teachers generally do not play a role in principal selection.

The availability of support staff in Canadian schools parallels that found in American school systems. A secondary school of 800 students, for example, may have two assistant principals, two counselors, a nurse, a social worker, and various part-time resource teachers, psychologists, etc.[81] Smaller schools may have a principal, and a part-time assistant principal who will have major teaching responsibilities. Such schools will also share other support personnel such as counselors, librarians, and nurses with other schools in the local district. Support staffing patterns in Canadian schools more closely resemble the American pattern than they do the pattern in the other countries in this study.

Canadian principals appear to function in a collegial relationship with their teachers, as is common with the head teacher concept in Europe. There is little emphasis upon a supervisory and evaluative role since direct teacher classroom supervision is infrequent and often perfunctory. The link in the pay scales of principals and teachers forms an additional bond between Canadian principals and their teachers. The manager-employee relationship characteristic between principals and teachers in the United States is less pronounced in Canadian schools.

SCHOOL ADMINISTRATION AND FINANCE

The Canadian nation is governed through a federal system with strong provincial governments. The British North America Act of 1867 specifically assigns responsibility for education to the provinces. Each province has a cabinet-level minister of education. This official presides over a department of education that is responsible for both private and public education within the province.[82] Day-to-day school operations are managed at the local division or district level, corresponding to local school districts in the United States. The role of provincial governments in education is similar to, although greater than, the role that individual states typically play in the American educational system.

Specific educational responsibilities at the province level include: enforcement of regulations governing local school boards and teachers, financial and staff development support through grants and services, curriculum development, textbook approvals, teacher certification, and research and statistics.[83] Most provinces have regional offices to provide consultative services at the local level. In recent years there has been a trend toward decentralizing provincial systems, thereby granting more autonomy to the local districts.[84]

Boards of school directors, either elected or appointed, govern schools at the local district level. Each board employs a superintendent to administer the school district in compliance with school board policies. As in America, school boards tend to concentrate on management tasks relating to school facilities, teacher recruitment and assignment, pupil transportation, purchasing supplies, the preparation of budgets, and accounting for school revenues and expenses.[85] This description of local school governance in Canada applies equally well to the great majority of school districts in the United States.

Canada and the United States are the only countries in this study that feature elected school boards representative of the entire community, with no special provision for representation of teachers or parents. Thus Canadian schools, more than those of other countries, are likely to experience the controversies over curriculum, taxes, and teacher salaries that are commonplace on the American scene.[86] American school board meetings often provide a forum for debate among residents with diametrically opposed educational, moral, or cultural values. Canadian communities avoid many of these problems because of public support of religious schools. Most Canadian parents are able to secure publicly subsidized religious education for their children.[87]

The major difference between Canada and the United States regarding local school governance is the common Canadian practice of financing several types of local schools from public funds. Thus, within one geographic area there might be a nondenominational public school, a French-speaking Catholic school, and an English-speaking Protestant school. In some localities taxpayers may even designate the type of local school that should receive their taxes.[88]

Although there is some freedom to create local course options, schools at the local level must follow the provincial curriculum, rather than develop a local curriculum. Provincial curriculum guides allow for individual teacher discretion and are not excessively prescriptive.[89] Canadian teachers report a high level of adherence by teachers to the provincial curriculum guides, even though direct monitoring of compliance is minimal or missing.[90] An American exchange teacher, after spending one year in a Canadian school, confirmed the willingness of Canadian teachers to follow the curriculum guides developed by the provinces. She reported that this was true even though the typical Canadian teacher had no direct role in developing the curriculum, and therefore had no ownership of it.[91]

Local bargaining over teacher salaries represents another governance procedure shared by Canada and the United States, but not practiced by other nations in the study. During the past two decades many Canadian provinces have granted teachers the right to strike, the most recent being British Columbia.[92] Local bargaining in those provinces that require it has produced many cases of teacher bitterness and community hostility,[93] an all-too-familiar occurrence in school districts in the United States. Regardless of whether teacher salaries are set at the local or provincial level, teachers in both denominational and public schools are paid on the same salary scale.

Canadian schools receive financial support through provincial taxes distributed through various grants and subsidies. Although the model resembles the system found in the United States, the process as implemented in Canada results in a significantly more equitable pattern of school financing. Canadian schools have for many years received

generous financial support in comparison to schools in other industrialized countries.[94] Further, provinces distribute subsidies in a manner that
equalizes resources among districts to a greater extent than is common
in most states in America.

At one time, local taxes provided the largest share of school revenue
in Canada, but they now represent less than one-quarter of the total.
Provincial governments have been increasing their contributions to the
funding of education and are now the largest contributors.[95] There
remains, however, much variance among the provinces in the proportion
of support they provide for education. The provincial portion of financial
support ranges "from 84 percent in Prince Edward Island to 52 percent
in Manitoba; and the local share from 27 percent in Ontario to zero
percent in Prince Edward Island and New Brunswick."[96] Provincial
funding of schools can help to ameliorate differences in wealth among
districts within a province, but does not address difference in wealth,
and thus the ability to finance schools, among the provinces. The federal
government has begun to take a greater role in correcting the financial
inequities that invariably exist in a federal system of states.[97] By the
early 1980s the federal government was providing 9 percent of total
educational funding. Sixty-six percent of funding was from provincial
governments, 18 percent from local governments, and the remaining 7
percent from private sources.[98]

Within the provinces there is a trend toward legislation to distribute
provincial funding on a more equal basis. British Columbia recently
authorized greater provincial support for private schools and Manitoba
province is moving toward a process to equalize spending between rich
and poor areas of the province.[99] Canada has made and continues to
make education funding a major priority. Both increasing federal involvement and changes in subsidy formulas within individual provinces
reveal a national commitment to equal educational opportunities for all
students. The dynamic expansion in higher education over the past few
decades is a further example of this commitment. The United States
proudly proclaims its commitment to a common school to provide equal
educational opportunity for all. Canada is currently making greater
strides than the United States in achieving this shared goal.

SOCIAL AND CULTURAL INFLUENCES ON EDUCATION

Throughout this chapter we have seen the many similarities between
American and Canadian schools. The constant cultural cross-fertiliza-

tion between these two North American nations ensures a continued convergence of our two cultures in future years. The maritime provinces in the east reflect some of the unique cultural characteristics of our New England states. Citizens of British Columbia in the west follow a lifestyle common to people in our own Pacific Northwest. The central provinces of Quebec and Ontario relate most closely to our industrial heartland. The provinces of the Western plains share an agricultural-based economy and lifestyle with our Great Plains states. Geographic proximity and access to the same television stations and other media help to forge common values, interests, and concerns.

Both Canada and the United States operate schools that stress opportunity over achievement. Similar teenage subcultures produce the same adolescent emphasis on part-time jobs, use and support of automobiles, extracurricular activities, and early interest in dating and sexual activity. In Canada as in the United States, school performance is not of vital concern to the typical high school student. Fulbright Exchange teachers from Canada report that the incidence of dysfunctional families and single parent households in Canada is very similar to the situation in the United States.[100]

Social support systems to families and students in Canada, however, are clearly superior to those found in the United States. In the areas of health care and government support for children, Canada closely follows the model outlined for Denmark, England, and Germany. In Canada every family, regardless of income, receives a family allowance for each child each month.[101] The current amount of this allowance is $32.00 per month per child.[102] In addition, families of children in poverty receive welfare grants each month funded jointly by the federal government and the provinces. Canada also provides national health care, which is administered at the provincial level and funded jointly by the federal government and the individual provinces. Under this system everyone gets medical coverage.[103]

Although these social support systems are clear advantages for child health and welfare, they do exact a significant financial cost. The Canadian health insurance system, for example, is experiencing skyrocketing cost increases, time delays for services, and the introduction of co-pay plans to help defray the cost of the system. A teacher in Canada will find that nearly half of his or her salary will go to income taxes, mostly to finance health care and other social welfare costs.[104] The tax system in Canada, however, allows higher deductions from income for each dependent child.[105] On balance, Canada makes a significantly greater effort to provide financial support to families with children than does the United States.

Traditional antagonisms in Canada between English and French, Protestant and Catholic, have provided the catalyst for the evolution of publicly supported school systems that accommodate individual preferences of parents and communities. In various provinces of Canada we can find communities that decide upon the language of instruction and the religious denomination of their public school. We find communities that publicly support several schools offering different languages of instruction and different religious teachings. Other schools in the same community may be nondenominational schools. Educators in the United States are currently grappling with these issues under the rubric of "schools of choice." Canada appears to have devised a system that retains the ideal of publicly supported schooling while simultaneously satisfying special schooling preferences of parents and students.

Rapid expansion of access to Canadian higher education has been accompanied by several associated phenomena also common to the American experience. The abandonment of required school leaving examinations, along with a corresponding increase in college admission places, has led to the democratization of higher education. Limited access in the past, combined with rigorous entrance examinations, promoted a meritocracy in higher education. High school students were academically motivated by the knowledge that college admission was highly competitive and that their performance on the school leaving examinations would have a significant impact on their future career opportunities.

A teenage subculture with myriad distractions from schoolwork, a diminished need for students to demonstrate skills and knowledge on high school leaving exams, and easy access to college, may produce a decline in academic motivation among Canadian students. Canadian perceptions of declining academic achievement in the secondary schools could well be a reflection of the effects of the cultural influences now operating on Canadian adolescents.

High unemployment and an increasing supply of college graduates in Canada are making a college degree both more vital and less valuable. Canadian colleges and universities operate in a free market atmosphere, as do colleges in the United States. A constant need to recruit new students, however ill-prepared, drives colleges to embark upon marketing and recruiting campaigns worthy of fast-food franchises. Canada's experience mirrors that of the United States, offering a second example of a nation where relatively open access to higher education is accompanied by a decline in motivation and achievement by students at the secondary school level.

Canadian schools bear the closest resemblance to American schools among the six countries in this study. There are, however, several noteworthy differences. Canada allocates a larger portion of available resources to elementary and secondary schooling than does the United States. Canadian teachers enjoy somewhat higher wages, and thus higher status, than their American counterparts.[106] Provincial mechanisms for distributing educational support dollars produce a more equitable system of educational finance than exists in the United States. Child welfare is a higher concern in the Canadian society than in America, as evidenced by the family allowance grants for children and the presence of a universal health system that includes children.

In many respects Canada provides us with a mirror image of the strengths and weaknesses of America's educational system. There is significant public concern in Canada about the perceived decline in educational standards, even though the Canadians have invested heavily in their educational system. There is a growing trend toward reinstituting school leaving exams in several Canadian provinces, as well as a movement to require student assessments on a province-wide basis. This trend is reaching fruition in Canada more rapidly than similar initiatives in the United States.

Canada has created a satisfactory method for accommodating cultural and religious differences within the tax-supported public school system. Canadian provinces do a much better job than most states in America to guarantee financial equity among the districts within their control. The federal government also makes a greater effort than its American counterpart to compensate through educational funding for differences in wealth among the provinces. Canadian provincial and federal governments seem more willing than their American counterparts to take proactive steps to aggressively address educational problems in Canada.

The close cultural affinity between Canada and the United States guarantees that both nations will continue to share the same goals of high student achievement and open access to educational opportunities.

REFERENCES

1. 1990. *Encyclopedia Americana, Vol. 5.* Danbury, CT: Grolier Incorporated, pp. 313–314.

2. 1991. *The World Almanac.* New York, NY: Pharos Books, p. 695.
3. Holmes, B., ed. 1983. *International Handbook of Education Systems, Vol. 1,* Chichester: John Wiley & Sons (Europe and Canada), p. 111.
4. Holmes, B., ed., p. 110.
5. Kurian, G. T., ed. 1988. *World Education Encyclopedia, Vol. 1,* New York, NY: Facts on File Publications, p. 182.
6. Kurian, G. T., ed., p. 180.
7. 1990. *Encyclopedia Americana, Vol. 5,* p. 403.
8. Kurian, G. T., ed., pp. 180–181.
9. 1990. *Encyclopedia Americana, Vol. 5,* pp. 403–404.
10. Nelson, F. H. 1991. *International Comparisons of Public Spending on Education.* Washington, DC: American Federation of Teachers, p. 16.
11. Kurian, G. T., ed., pp. 181–182.
12. Holmes, B., ed., pp. 112–113.
13. Kurian, G. T., ed., p. 182.
14. Graham, F. Interview with author, February 1992.
15. Kurian, G. T., ed., p. 185.
16. Kurian, G. T., ed., p. 183.
17. Friend, E. Interview with author, February 1992.
18. Gammage, P. "Changing Ideologies and Provision in Western Canadian Primary Education," *Comparative Education,* 27(3):311.
19. Graham, F. and E. Friend. Interviews with author, February 1992.
20. Friend, E. Interview.
21. Graham, F. and E. Friend. Interviews.
22. Graham, F. and E. Friend. Interviews.
23. Holmes, B., ed., p. 103.
24. Kurian, G. T., ed., p. 183.
25. Kurian, G. T., ed., p. 182.
26. McKinnon, D. and L. Korol. Interviews with author, February 1992.
27. Holmes, B., ed., p. 114.
28. McKinnon, D. Interview with author, February 1992.
29. Graham, F. Interview.
30. Holmes, B., ed., p. 114.
31. 1990. *Encyclopedia Americana, Vol. 5,* p. 407.
32. McKinnon, D. Interview.
33. Korol, L. Interview with author, February 1992.
34. Kurian, G. T., ed., p. 184.
35. Kurian, G. T., ed., p. 184.
36. 1990. *Encyclopedia Americana, Vol. 5,* p. 408.
37. Kurian, G. T., ed., p. 185.
38. Kurian, G. T., ed., p. 185.
39. Holmes, B., ed., p. 115.
40. Friend, E., D. McKinnon, L. Korol, and F. Graham. Interviews with author, February 1992.
41. Kurian, G. T., ed., pp. 188, 190.

42. National Center for Education Statistics. 1991. *Digest of Education Statistics 1990.* Washington, DC: U.S. Government Printing Office, p. 380.

43. Friend, E. Interview.

44. Graham, F. Interview.

45. McKinnon, D. and L. Korol. Interviews.

46. Friend, E., D. McKinnon, L. Korol, and F. Graham. Interviews.

47. Nelson, F. H., p. 37.

48. Graham, F. Interview.

49. Friend, E. Interview.

50. McKinnon, D. Interview.

51. Korol, L. and F. Graham. Interviews with author, February 1992.

52. Filson, G. 1988. "Ontario Teachers' Deprofessionalism and Proletarianization," *Comparative Education Review,* 32(3):309.

53. Filson, G., 32(3):308−309.

54. Friend, E. Interview.

55. Korol, L. Interview.

56. Graham, F. Interview.

57. McKinnon, D. Interview.

58. Friend, E. Interview.

59. McKinnon, D. Interview.

60. Friend, E., D. McKinnon, L. Korol, and F. Graham. Interviews.

61. Friend, E., D. McKinnon, L. Korol, and F. Graham. Interviews.

62. Holmes, B., ed., p. 113.

63. Graham, F. and E. Friend. Interviews.

64. Friend, E., D. McKinnon, L. Korol, and F. Graham. Interviews.

65. Friend, E., D. McKinnon, L. Korol, and F. Graham. Interviews.

66. Graham, F. Interview.

67. Holmes, B., ed., p. 113.

68. Friend, E. Interview.

69. Graham, F. Interview.

70. McKinnon, D. Interview.

71. Korol, L. and F. Graham. Interviews.

72. Filson, G., 32(3):309−310.

73. Filson, G., 32(3):310.

74. McKinnon, D. Interview.

75. Davis, B. Interview with author, February 1992.

76. Friend, E. Interview.

77. Graham, F. and D. McKinnon. Interviews with author, February 1992.

78. Graham, F. Interview.

79. McKinnon, D. Interview.

80. Friend, E., D. McKinnon, L. Korol, and F. Graham. Interviews.

81. Korol, L. Interview.

82. 1990. *Encyclopedia Americana, Vol. 5,* p. 404.

83. Kurian, G. T., ed., p. 191.
84. Holmes, B., ed., p. 118.
85. Kurian, G. T., ed., p. 191.
86. McKinnon, D. Interview.
87. Glenn, C. L. 1989. *Choice of Schools in Six Nations.* Washington, DC: U.S. Dept. of Education, pp. 150–152.
88. Graham, F. Interview.
89. Graham, F., L. Korol, and D. McKinnon. Interviews with author, February 1992.
90. McKinnon, D. and L. Korol. Interviews.
91. Davis, B. Interview.
92. Friend, E. Interview.
93. Filson, G., 32(3):309.
94. Nelson, F. H., p. 16.
95. Holmes, B., ed., p. 118.
96. Kurian, G. T., ed., p. 192.
97. Holmes, B., ed., p. 119.
98. Kurian, G. T., ed., p. 191.
99. McKinnon, D. and E. Friend. Interviews with author, February 1992.
100. Friend, E., D. McKinnon, L. Korol, and F. Graham. Interviews.
101. 1990. *Encyclopedia Americana, Vol. 5,* p. 400.
102. Graham, F. Interview.
103. Henderson, N. 1992. "Budget Blues in Canada's Health Care System," *Kiplinger's Personal Finance Magazine,* 46(3):102.
104. Henderson, N., 46(3):102.
105. McKinnon, D. Interview.
106. Nelson, F. H., p. 31.

CHAPTER 7

Japan — A Culture Shapes Its Schools

THE JAPANESE CREATION myth offers the image of the newly formed Japanese islands, created in heaven and later dropped into the sea. The grandson of one of the Gods, Ninigi, later descends to the islands bearing symbols of power and authority. According to legend, Ninigi's great-grandson, after successfully completing a cross-country expedition, was awarded the title of emperor. This great-grandson then became the first of a long line of emperors. Thus, according to Japanese tradition, Japan represents the central location for divine intervention into human affairs. This creation myth with its emphasis on the uniqueness of the Japanese people is the source of the continuing Japanese concern about "what it means to be Japanese." [1]

For most of its history, Japan has been isolated from the main currents of both Western and Eastern civilizations. The first major external cultural influence on Japan occurred with the introduction of Chinese culture in the seventh century A.D. The Japanese developed their own culture, relatively free of external influence, until the arrival of Commodore Perry's American warships in 1853. [2]

The following century brought unprecedented changes to Japan, beginning with the Meiji Restoration in 1868 and culminating with Japan's defeat by the Americans to end the Second World War in 1945. During this period Japan adopted many of the educational and industrial methods of Europe and the United States, catapulting itself from an agrarian economy to a major industrial and military power. A similar transformation has occurred since 1945 as Japan has raised itself from the ashes of a devastating war to become a major world economic power. The educational system played a critical role in both of these transformations.

Japan has a population of 124 million people on a land mass the size of Montana. More than 50 percent of the population lives on 2 percent of the land. Ethnically, Japan is a homogeneous country with fewer than one million foreigners.[3] Japan's governing body is a bicameral legislature elected directly by the people. The head of government is the prime minister, who leads through a party-cabinet system. There is no dominant religious system in Japan. The moral and ethical framework of Japanese culture incorporates the national and communal cults of Shintoism, the public and private morality of Confucianism, and the metaphysical speculations of Buddhism.[4]

Japan's geographic isolation, scarce natural resources, and shortage of arable land have greatly influenced both education and culture. These influences explain the Japanese concern with survival in a hostile world, their consciousness of limited resources, their consequent commitment to the development of their human resources, and their belief that as a nation they are utterly unique.[5] Such cultural assumptions express themselves in several characteristic Japanese traits that are plainly evident in the educational system. These traits include *gambaru* (persistence), a strong identity with the group rather than the individual, and a deep respect for their cultural heritage and traditional ways of life.

HISTORY AND DEVELOPMENT OF JAPANESE EDUCATION

Major new educational influences first entered Japan with other aspects of Chinese culture in the mid-sixth century. The Japanese adapted the Chinese character system to their own written language, founded schools on the Chinese pattern, and began to teach the Confucian ethical system. By A.D. 700 they had adopted so many Chinese institutions that they became a part of the Chinese cultural sphere. Over the next several hundred years the Japanese adapted the Chinese system to their own needs, with many Chinese features remaining a permanent part of their system.[6]

The basic curriculum of the schools during these feudal ages consisted of the Confucian classics. Students were taught the cardinal virtues of filial piety, duty, loyalty, and benevolence. Young people were taught that they had an absolute duty to study, to repay their debt to Heaven and to their parents for being born. This traditional importance placed on educational achievement still shapes Japanese values in the twentieth century.[7]

The feudal system of the Tokugawa period (1600 – 1868) was replaced by the impetus for modernization characterized by the Meiji Restoration beginning in 1868. In 1871 a ministry of education was created and by

1886 an outline of a national framework for education was in place. The concept of private education alongside the public sector continued from the Tokugawa period. The 1870s featured extensive borrowing of educational processes from Europe and America, the building of many school facilities, and a greatly increasing number of children attending school on a regular basis.[8]

By the late 1880s the Ministry of Education had created a truly national system of education. The ministry now controlled all major aspects of education including textbook selection, establishing school hours and schedules, determining curriculum, preparing examinations, and selecting appropriate instructional methods.[9] By 1900 elementary education was universal in Japan. The early decades of this century saw a further development of an educational system that primarily served the needs of the state rather than the individual. The nationalistic indoctrination in the schools, including emperor worship, helped prepare the Japanese people and nation for the expansionist policies of the 1930s, leading to the Second World War in the Pacific.

The end of the war in 1945 brought about a transformation in Japanese education. The American occupation authorities imposed American democratic forms on all phases of Japanese government, including education. By 1950 the Japanese school system mirrored the organizational pattern of American schools. Elementary school extended from grades one to six, a middle level encompassed grades seven to nine, and a senior high school level served grades ten to twelve. In a more modest version of a similar trend in the United States, the Japanese university system expanded tremendously so that by the 1980s more than 30 percent of Japanese high school graduates attended some form of higher education.[10] Locally elected school boards were also a feature of Japanese schools in the early post-war years.

Although the form of the educational system remains similar to that of the United States, the substance is distinctively Japanese. Locally elected school boards were discontinued in the mid-1950s, to be replaced by appointed boards. The national Ministry of Education reasserted control over the entire educational system so that today Japan, unlike the United States, has a highly centralized system. Education is compulsory only through grade nine, although approximately 94 percent of Japanese students graduate from high school. There are parallel systems of private and public schools at the high school level, with the public schools being of higher status. Since high school attendance is not compulsory, students must seek to be accepted by the high school they wish to attend. Student competition is keen for admission to high schools with a good record for student acceptance into the top universities. About 30 percent of Japanese students are enrolled in vocational schools, but these programs are of lower status than the general academic high school programs (see Figure 7.1).

JAPANESE ELEMENTARY SCHOOLS

April 1st is the beginning of regular school for first grader Kenichi Watanabe. His parents and school officials have ensured that it will be a memorable day for him. "Parents and children, dressed to the hilt, converge on the schoolyard. Mothers wear their very best dresses, grandmothers come in kimono, and fathers wear the dark suits, white shirts, and polished black shoes which they may otherwise wear only to weddings and important company functions. The boys are in new dark suits with short pants and caps, the girls in new suits or party dresses and hats." [11]

The opening day ceremonies formally welcome the new students to the school community and reinforce in all of them the importance of education. The principal exhorts all students to work to their maximum capacity. Opening exercises are held in a partially enclosed schoolyard. This space is also used for morning assemblies, recess, and sports activities.

Schools are relatively spartan in appearance, generally constructed of concrete with two or three floors of classrooms. The school itself consists of long corridors with classrooms on one side and windows along the other. Wall surfaces are often in need of paint or plaster, but are substantially covered by student artwork and other projects. Classrooms themselves are plain, although usually lively and bright. Surprisingly, many elementary schools contain well equipped swimming pools, usually financed through fundraising activities by the PTA. [12]

Throughout his school years Kenichi will be influenced significantly by his mother. In the Japanese culture the mother is almost totally responsible for the education of her children. During the elementary years she will visit the school frequently to observe her child in class and to confer with the teacher. She will work closely with the child to complete homework assignments that begin in kindergarten and become increasingly elaborate and extensive each year. The mother typically creates an environment in the home that fosters educational achieve-

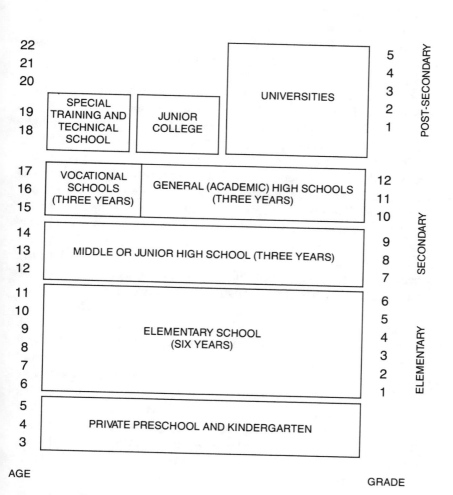

AGE

GRADE

Figure 7.1 Structure of the Japanese education system.

ment. Extreme involvement by some mothers gives meaning to the term *kyoiku mama,* or "educational mom" describing mothers who are excessively active, even by Japanese standards, in promoting the education of their children.[13]

Japanese children attend school for 240 days each year. School is in session for about forty six-day weeks each year, with half-day sessions on Saturday. As a first grade student Kenichi will attend school for only about four hours each day. Daily school hours increase gradually through the first few elementary years until fourth grade, when the student will be scheduled for the standard 1,015-hour school year.

Each of these hours actually represents a forty-five- to fifty-minute lesson. Thus the actual number of instructional hours per year is closer to 800, a number comparable to actual instructional time for American school students. First grade students in Japan receive only 850 lessons, which translates to slightly more than 600 clock-hours of instruction. Even junior high school students spend only about 800 hours per year under direct classroom instruction. Included in these class hours is one hour per week for moral education. Activities such as assemblies, club activities, and guidance also absorb one to two hours per week of the scheduled instructional time. While Japanese students attend school for sixty more days each year than Americans, their actual number of hours of academic instruction each year is comparable to that of American students.[14]

The legal minimum school year is 210 days, but most local school officials schedule an extra thirty days, a 240-day total, for school festivals, athletic meets, and ceremonies with nonacademic objectives, especially those encouraging cooperation and school spirit. Given that Saturday sessions last only a few hours, the actual number of equivalent full days of regular classroom academic instruction is about 195.[15]

The elementary school day in Japan begins at 8:30 A.M. and continues to about 2:30 P.M., except for the early primary grades where the day is somewhat shorter. Students have longer breaks between classes than American students and generally have a somewhat longer lunch period. The several hours each week devoted to special activities are not necessarily academic in nature. Elementary students, for example, may spend a few hours each week, for several months, practicing for the annual sports festival held at the school.[16]

Class sizes in Japanese elementary school average about forty. A teacher's primary expectation is that students will be engaged in their work, not that they will necessarily be quiet or docile. Most American teachers would find the decibel level in Japanese elementary classrooms unacceptable. These large class sizes imply expectations for pupil behavior and teacher role that would be foreign to American teachers and parents. As Joseph Tobin suggests, "The Japanese teacher delegates more authority to children than we find in American schools; intervenes less quickly in arguments; has lower expectations for the control of noise generated by the class; gives fewer verbal clues; organizes more structured group activities, such as morning exercise; and, finally, makes more use of peer group approval and control and less of the teacher's direct influence. In general, children are less often treated on a one-to-one basis, and more often as a group."[17]

This emphasis on the group is carried over to promotion policies and ability-grouping practices in Japanese elementary schools. Social promotion is the norm. To fail a grade or to skip a grade is unthinkable. Students are placed in mixed-ability groups in virtually all situations.[18] All classes in Japanese elementary schools are conducted in mixed-ability groups, with little special attention given to academically slow students or to the gifted student. In the upper elementary grades a teacher will often assign a brighter student to tutor one of his or her slower classmates.

By the upper years of elementary school the teacher will rely on group activities and projects as the primary instructional strategy. The class frequently divides into small groups of from four to six students known as *hans*. The leadership of each group rotates among its members with the designated leader called the *hancho*. These groups also perform various housekeeping duties in the classroom on a rotating basis.

Thus, Japanese children receive an early introduction to the concept of a work group, a circumstance that they will encounter throughout their adult lives.[19] These traditional work groups in Japanese schools bear a striking resemblance to the cooperative learning groups that are currently being encouraged in American elementary schools.

The curriculum in the elementary schools is determined by the national Ministry of Education, both in terms of content and time allotments. The major subjects at the elementary level are Japanese, social studies, mathematics, and science. There is a special emphasis on social studies, reflecting the importance of group cohesion in the Japanese culture. The required program also includes generous allocations of time for music, art, and physical education.[20]

The grading system at the secondary levels of Japanese schooling consists of numerical grades of 5, 4, 3, 2, and 1 (failing) or A, B, C, D,

E, and F (failing). Elementary schools are free to adopt any report card system that they wish, although a three-level grading system is most common. They may also eliminate report cards, a rarely exercised option.[21]

Elementary schools in Japan are comparatively free of the pressure and competitiveness that is characteristic of Japanese secondary schools. Children enjoy going to school and form very close bonds with their classmates, with whom they will associate closely throughout the six years of elementary school. The emphasis on group work allows students to interact frequently with one another and to take an active part in learning activities. Frequent short breaks contribute to a relaxed pace in the school day. During the first few years of school the school day itself is comparatively short. The lack of individual attention by the teacher is more than compensated for by the intensity of the involvement of the mother in the elementary child's school experience.

Moral education as one of the compulsory subjects in Japanese schools at every grade level. One hour each week is devoted to the development of ethical and moral reasoning so that students will be able to resolve moral dilemmas. The Japanese regard moral issues as essentially social or interpersonal problems, which cannot be resolved by strict rules or objective moral principles.

The content of the moral education at the elementary level might include such concepts as learning to bear hardship, listening to the opinions of others, admitting frankly to one's own faults, and behaving unselfishly. Students in the middle grades are taught to persist to the end with patience, and to live a life of moderation. High school students are urged to be steadfast and to accomplish goals undaunted by obstacles or failure. Older students are also taught to reflect upon their own behavior, to act with prudence, and to live an orderly life.[22]

The success of the Japanese schools and culture in nurturing basic literacy is evident by the end of the elementary school years. Superior results are achieved through an elementary system that is neither highly competitive nor stressful to students. It occurs in a context of very large classes, mixed-ability groups, and within a time allocation for academic instruction that is comparable to that provided to students in other countries.

Two comprehensive studies of math performance of fifth grade students in the United States and several Asian countries found that Japanese students performed best, while the performance of American students was uniformly poor. In only one of the Chicago schools sampled in the study were average scores as high as the *lowest* of the average scores for matched fifth grade classrooms in the Asian schools. [23]

Stevenson further notes "that these conclusions are not restricted to Chicago, for the results parallel those of a previous study in which we compared first and fifth graders in the Minneapolis metropolitan area — which has a more middle-class school population than Chicago — with their counterparts in [Japan and Taiwan]. . . . In both of these studies care was taken to construct tests based on textbooks actually used by students and to obtain representative samples of children in each city visited." [24]

At the elementary level, at least, Japanese academic excellence cannot be attributed to excessive pressure on students, highly disciplined and structured classrooms, or greater time allotments for academic instruction. We must look to other factors to explain the success of Japanese elementary schooling.

JAPANESE SECONDARY SCHOOLS

The junior high school years, grades seven to nine, are part of the compulsory school system, and sufficient public places are reserved for all students. Some students, even at this level, begin to attend the more exclusive and competitive private junior high schools, but the great majority remain in the public system. Kenichi, whom we earlier met as a first grade student, will reflect fondly on his elementary years as he enters the more demanding and competitive junior high school years.

These middle school years will be a time of testing for students as they begin the rigorous selection process that leads to the prestigious universities for the academic elite. Vocational training programs, or even early departure from school, await the less able or less motivated. Life begins to intensify and time begins to compress for students as they reach junior high school. More pressure is exerted on students to conform to cultural expectations, and there is less tolerance for childlike behavior. Students are expected to begin to act as young adults. [25]

The middle school years are the peak period for bullying, suicides, and violence against teachers. The Japanese press often reports such incidents in exaggerated and lurid detail. None of these problems in Japan remotely approaches the incidence of similar behaviors by students in the United States. Nevertheless, such incidents illustrate the heightened pressure on Japanese students as they move through junior high school.

All students in junior high schools study the same basic curriculum and continue to attend mixed-ability classes of forty or more students. A small portion of time, between 5 and 10 percent, involves non-academic subjects such as homemaking and industrial arts. Most students take English to meet their foreign language requirement. Basic subjects are studied at a challenging and rigorous level. Mathematics textbooks, for example, are more difficult than American math texts. Although Japanese and American curricula contain similar concepts and skills, they are introduced earlier in the Japanese curriculum. [26] Homework assignments will now require two or more hours each evening.

The school day will be similar in length to that of the upper elementary years. The day typically begins at 8:30 A.M. and ends by 2:30−3:00 P.M. Students attend six classes each day with brief breaks between classes and about forty-five minutes for lunch. There are certain club activities that all students are expected to join. These clubs meet weekly for one hour. Students usually select one club and remain in that activity throughout their junior high school years. There are also less formally organized club activities that meet every day after school and during vacation periods. Students often consider these activities as the most rewarding of their school experiences. [27]

By the eighth grade, ambitious Japanese students are beginning to prepare seriously for the high school entrance examinations given in March of ninth grade. Great numbers of students now begin to attend remedial and tutoring schools known as *juku*. These "cram schools" are devoted to preparing students to pass the entrance examinations for the high school that the student will attempt to enter. By the ninth grade, 86 percent of Japanese students have attended juku at some point. [28] Students attending the Hiroshima YMCA juku, for example, might devote two or three afternoons each week to juku lessons. [29]

High school attendance in Japan is not compulsory. Students are not assigned to a school by geographic area, as in the United States, but instead must apply for entrance to a given school. High schools are rank-ordered according to their academic standing in a community, with vocational schools being ranked at the bottom. Admission to a school is by examination and at the discretion of the school. Public high schools are generally the best academically in Japan, since they are government funded and there are a limited number of places available. This situation has created a market for private high schools, which generally attempt to offer an academic curriculum similar to that of the public schools.

These private schools generally attract students who could not gain admission to a preferred public high school.[30]

About 97 percent of graduates from lower secondary schools attend senior high school. Twenty-eight percent of these students attend private high schools. More than two-thirds of all high school students enroll in the general education course to prepare students for university study.[31] More than 94 percent of Japanese students graduate from high school.

Thirty percent of the students select a vocational program as they enter high school. Vocational training is commonly provided in specialized schools emphasizing industrial, commercial, or agricultural studies. Even the vocational schools reflect the Japanese belief in broad academic training by requiring that half of the vocational school courses be in academic subjects. By age eighteen, about 20 percent of the age group, having attended a vocational school, will proceed to short courses in private sector *special training schools.*[32]

The 70 percent of students pursuing a general education at academic public and private high schools are fully conscious of the importance in Japanese society of attending the *right* university. The Japanese attach great importance to the university that the student will attend, believing that the university attended will largely determine the life chances of the student. Many major corporations do indeed restrict their recruitment efforts to these select universities. This reality serves as a strong motivation for many students to exert great effort in their studies.[33]

Although virtually all Japanese academic high school students are affected by the competitive nature of college admission, only about 10 percent of students experience the extremely intense competition for admission to the most prestigious universities, which in Japan are the public universities. The remaining university-bound students encounter a lesser, but still significant pressure to achieve high academic standards.[34]

By high school age, over 90 percent of urban students are attending juku school to enhance their chances for admission to a university. Homework will typically require three or four hours each day, with five or six hours required for the most academically ambitious students. All high schools teach the same ministry of education-approved curriculum, although the more academically elite high schools implement the curriculum at a higher level of rigor.

The regular public school system is very egalitarian. However, the necessity to attend privately funded juku schools to gain a competitive advantage places a heavy financial burden on some Japanese families.

Currently over 30 percent of high school graduates in Japan attend some form of higher education. An additional 20 percent attend specialized short courses in vocational areas offered by private businesses. Fewer than 10 percent of the population fail to complete high school. Japan educates more students, at a higher level of academic achievement, than any other nation in the world.

THE JUKU SCHOOL

The juku is a unique institution among the countries profiled in this study. Although primarily known in the West as large "cram schools" for the high school and university entrance exams, these schools actually vary greatly in size and purpose. Eighty-six percent of junior high school students and over 90 percent of high school students attend a juku at some time.

Juku schools may be small one-teacher establishments operated out of the home of the teacher and serving from five to fifteen students. Small-scale jukus operate as private businesses with one or more branches, and focus directly on preparing students to take examinations for the local universities. There are large-scale jukus that operate on a national level, with branches in cities throughout Japan.[35]

Juku schools may be remedial, or may offer accelerated work to prepare students for the entrance examinations. They may closely follow the school curriculum or emphasize the preparation for college entrance exams.[36] Juku fees, as well as other educational costs borne directly by parents of a typical junior high school student, averaged $1,000 per year in 1988, according to the Japanese Ministry of Education. Parents of high school students expend about $2,000 per year for a public school student and twice that amount for a private school student toward juku and other education costs.[37]

In the case of the juku operated by the Hiroshima YMCA, students attend classes after regular school hours two or three times weekly, for a total of five to ten hours per week. Class sizes are twenty-five or less, with students grouped by their performance on achievement tests. The student studies with a class that will be challenging and rigorous enough to prepare the student for the entrance exams to specific high schools and universities. Homework assignments of several hours each week are a typical part of the juku experience.[38]

Jukus employ certified teachers who directly instruct students on a teaching schedule similar to that of regular public school teachers. Their hours of work, however, may be from 2:00 P.M. to 9:00 P.M., to accommodate the after-school nature of the classes. Salary levels for juku teachers are comparable to those of public school teachers, although the fringe benefit and pension system are inferior to public-sector teachers. The bigger juku chains may offer higher teacher salaries than the public schools as a means of attracting the best teachers to the juku schools. [39]

The public system's commitment to mixed-ability grouping and a common curriculum for all students has created a market for juku schools to provide the accelerated instruction and ability-grouped classes not available in the public schools. The competitive nature of the entrance examination system further drives parents and students to gain a competitive edge through juku attendance. "As the juku system has prevailed, the school's major role as an agency of cognitive training has become curtailed. Thus, the legitimacy of public school education has been somewhat undermined in contemporary Japan." [40] In a society that has, by any measure, created a school system that is both egalitarian and highly effective, parents remain willing to incur great expense to provide special advantages for their children.

Many Japanese are unhappy with the stress on students known as *examination hell,* and with the time, energy, and resources that families must devote to the juku schools. Nevertheless, parents continue to send children to juku schools, fearful that without this extra schooling, their student will fail the entrance exam to his or her chosen school, and thus seriously jeopardize the chances for later career and economic success.

PRIVATE EDUCATION IN JAPAN

More than 97 percent of Japanese students attend public schools from first through ninth grade. The small numbers of private schools that exist at these levels serve religious minorities, principally Catholics and other Christian groups. This situation changes dramatically for students at the high school and university levels. The government controls the number of publicly financed places for students at the noncompulsory high school level. This creates keen competition for places in the lower tuition public schools, making these schools the academic and status elite in the Japanese system. [41]

Private high schools and universities satisfy the demand for academic high schools and college-level programs that cannot be met through the public system. The government provides partial funding for private schools to supply places for students beyond the carefully regulated public supply. This policy has allowed Japan to maintain selective and elite public education, with public schools occupying the highest places in the educational hierarchy. This system favors upper income groups who can afford the special juku tutoring to gain admission to the elite public secondary schools. Failing that, such families can afford the tuition to send their students to comparable private schools.[42]

Private schools serve much of the student population in the noncompulsory segments of the Japanese education system. Seventy-three percent of kindergarten children attend private preschools. Twenty-eight percent of the high school students attend private schools. At the college and university level, private schools enroll 76 percent of the students. Ninety-one percent of junior college students attend private schools.[43]

HIGHER EDUCATION IN JAPAN

In 1980 there were 446 universities in Japan, of which more than 300 were private. The higher prestige public universities numbered about 120, ninety being national universities and thirty being local universities. A small number of the public national universities, such as Tokyo, Kyoto, Osaka, and Nagoya, are of the highest status.[44] It is this caliber of university that major corporations and government agencies favor in selecting new employees. The low tuition at these public universities, compared with private schools, offers another incentive for students to compete for admission to them.

Criteria for university admission include previous scholastic records and performance on the entrance achievement examination. The exam results are the most important criterion. Applicants to a public university must take a general achievement examination early in January covering the areas of Japanese, social studies, mathematics, science, and foreign language. The scores from this first round of tests help students to determine which national universities are likely to accept them. Using these test results, the student then applies to a particular university and registers for a second round of tests, specific to that university, to be given two months later. The student's performance on this second test determines whether or not the student is admitted to his or her chosen university.

Only one-fourth of the college-bound student population gains admission to the prestigious public universities. The remaining three-fourths of the students attend private universities. Some students who fail to gain admission to an elite university will not settle for attendance at a private school. They retake the test the following year, using the intervening time to study full-time for the retest. Some students continue in this fashion for several years. Secondary school graduates who spend one or more years studying full-time for entrance examinations are called *ronin* (masterless samurai).[45]

Each private college and university administers its own entrance examination, which varies in difficulty according to the status and academic rigor of the school. Most students apply to private universities since entrance requirements are generally, though not always, lower than those of public universities. Also, some students are not willing to make the extraordinary effort necessary to attend the most prestigious schools.

The entrance examination system creates a hierarchy of secondary schools, ranked according to the success of their students in passing the entrance exams to the best universities. The quest to have students admitted to the most prestigious universities creates the demand for cram schools, private tutors, and test preparation publications. As much as 10 percent of all educational expenditures in Japan are spent for these purposes.[46]

Higher education is an area where even the Japanese acknowledge the superiority of American schools. Akito Arima, president of prestigious Tokyo University, speaking at Philadelphia's Drexel University in 1992, noted that the United States has more high quality universities, accessible to a broader range of students, than are found in Japan.[47]

THE JAPANESE TEACHER—A TRUE PROFESSIONAL

A professional can be defined as one who possesses a specialized body of knowledge, is respected for that knowledge and skill by the larger society, has autonomy in performing his or her work, and is subject to peer review and sanctions. The teacher in Japan possesses all of these attributes, while the American teacher fares poorly when measured against the same criteria. Of all the nations in this survey, Japanese teachers have attained the highest level of professional respect and practice.

Teaching is a much sought after occupation in Japan. There are as many as five to six applicants for each available teaching position in

Japan.[48] Teachers at the elementary level usually attend the national teachers' colleges, while secondary school teachers are generally graduates of the universities.[49]

Elementary teachers may provide instruction in all subjects while secondary teachers offer instruction in one or two specific subjects. Teacher candidates must take a recruitment examination to receive a teaching certificate from the prefecture to which they have applied. Certificates granted by one prefecture are accepted in all forty-seven prefectures and are valid for life.[50] The recruitment examinations are difficult and a teacher candidate will invest much time and effort to prepare for them.[51]

As a true professional, the Japanese teacher assigns the highest priority to his or her teaching responsibilities. Japanese teachers typically arrive at school by 7:30 A.M. and remain until 6:00 P.M. They work a 240-day school year, including half-day Saturday sessions. Teachers also typically report to school on fifty to sixty of their vacation days. Thus, teaching in Japan is a twelve-month occupation and teachers are forbidden to do any other paid work.[52]

Although Japanese teachers spend twenty hours more each week at school than their American counterparts,[53] they spend far fewer hours providing direct classroom instruction. A typical Japanese teacher will spend fifteen hours each week in classroom instruction. An American teacher will spend approximately twenty-five hours each five-day week in directly teaching and supervising students.[54] The Japanese teacher uses these many hours of extra school time to perform a myriad of additional obligations that an American teacher, because of time and energy constraints, performs in a perfunctory fashion or not at all.

Japanese teachers have a role that is much broader than that of teachers in other countries surveyed. They share far more in the administration and program planning of their schools. In the nonacademic area they have responsibilities for students' use of vacation time, and students' behavior and appearance both on and off campus.[55]

The Japanese commitment to group interaction is quite evident in the daily life of a teacher. Japanese teachers are far more involved in the governance of their schools than are American teachers. School and teacher schedules, student assignments, and most other school matters are decided at daily and weekly teacher meetings. The meetings are held each morning for about five minutes as well as once per week after school for about one hour. The teachers chair these meetings on a rotating basis.[56]

Japanese schools each have one large room where each teacher has a desk. Here teachers devote their noninstructional time to grading papers, preparing lessons, and discussing teaching techniques. Teachers use this space for faculty or department meetings to resolve both administrative and instructional issues. Much of the nonteaching time available to Japanese teachers during the school week is devoted to these group meetings.

There are regular meetings planned by the principal to allow experienced professionals to advise and guide their younger colleagues. Meetings are organized among groups of teachers to discuss teaching techniques and to devise lesson plans and handouts.[57] Such sharing among teachers is more feasible in a system operating with a standardized curriculum, where all teachers at a grade level are teaching the same material at about the same time.

A group of teachers might devise a lesson plan that will be presented to a class by one of the teachers, while the rest of the teachers in the group observe the class. The group meets later to critique the lesson and to offer suggestions for improvement. Sometimes teachers from other schools are invited to visit, rate the lessons taught, and select the teacher with the best lesson for special recognition.[58]

What is the effect in the classroom of this attention to lesson construction, the honing of teaching skills, and the free flow of ideas and strategies among teachers? To begin with, Asian teachers appear to be filled with zest and enthusiasm. Lessons are presented with great energy and the teachers succeed in engaging students in the lessons, in spite of average classes of about forty students. Asian teachers can draw on the great energy levels required because of their relatively light teaching schedule compared to American teachers. Japanese teachers have considerably more available time during the day to prepare lessons, grade papers, work with individual students, and perform other job-related tasks.[59]

Conventional wisdom in the United States criticizes Japanese teachers for relying on rote memorization and teacher lectures as teaching techniques, thus inhibiting student creativity and problem-solving skills. This characterization may have some validity at the upper secondary and university levels, but it does not accurately portray classrooms at the elementary and junior high school levels.

Lessons at these levels emphasize problem solving rather than rote mastery of facts and procedures. The teacher is a discussion leader who tries to stimulate students to explain and evaluate solutions to problems.

In whole-class discussions and through working in their small groups, Japanese students are active participants in the learning process. Teachers design the lessons to fill a forty-five to fifty-minute period with sustained attention and the development of a concept or skill. Each lesson has an introduction, a conclusion, and a unifying theme. [60]

The economic status of teachers in Japan matches their high social status. In 1984, teachers earned 1.77 times the average salary of a manufacturing worker in Japan. This differential far exceeds that for teachers in any other country in this survey. On an international comparison of teacher salaries, however, Japanese teachers earn just 95 percent as much as American teachers (in 1984). [61] To ensure a steady supply of suitable teachers in Japan, a law was enacted in 1973 setting teacher salaries at a higher level than that of other national public service personnel. [62]

Prior to World War II teachers in Japan were considered to be *obedient servants of the state*. A Japanese union for teachers, known as *Nikkyoso*, was formed at the end of the war. This union is socialistic in political orientation and has for forty years vigorously opposed most of the initiatives of the conservative Ministry of Education. Japanese teachers do not have the right to bargain collectively or to strike. [63]

There have been two noteworthy clashes between the union and the Ministry of Education. In 1958 the Ministry of Education imposed a nationwide compulsory Teachers' Efficiency Rating Plan. Under the plan, principals were to rate each teacher yearly on a detailed rating scale devised by the Ministry of Education. The union vigorously opposed this initiative by staging walkouts, strikes, demonstrations, and even hunger strikes in forty-two of the forty-seven prefectures.

A protracted ten-year battle ensued, which greatly weakened the union but also ensured that no school board would dare to use the ratings for salary or personnel determinations. As a result of this painful experience, the government has not pursued the question of teacher evaluation. [64]

In April 1974 the Nikkyoso teacher union called a one-day strike to press for restoration of their right to strike and to gain large wage increases. The strike involved 330,000 teachers and caused classes for 12 million students to be suspended. This strike was heavily criticized by the general public, and many teachers, as being unsuitable to the teaching profession. [65] During the past two decades the appeal of the unions has declined, particularly among younger teachers, so that now only about two-thirds of the teachers belong to one of the major teacher unions. [66]

Teachers in Japan have neither the right to strike nor the right to negotiate directly with the Ministry of Education regarding salaries. Instead, a national personnel authority makes recommendations to the cabinet, the ruling party in the government, regarding salary scales necessary to keep teacher salaries competitive with those of private industry. The cabinet may accept, modify, or ignore these recommendations. The cabinet does, however, ultimately set a national wage scale for public employees.

This national scale becomes a guideline for local and prefectural salary agreements throughout the country, thus ensuring that there is relatively little difference in teacher salaries in various parts of Japan.[67] Teachers in the upper secondary schools earn a higher salary than lower secondary school teachers, who have a higher scale than elementary teachers.[68] Japan has the highest proportion of male teachers of any country in this study, with 56 percent of teachers being male. In the United States, only 29 percent of teachers are male.[69]

There are several aspects of a Japanese teacher's lifestyle that make teaching an attractive alternative to corporate life in Japan. Unlike corporate workers, teachers can live out their professional lives in one region and not be forced to uproot their families for frequent transfers.[70] Also, Japanese teachers are not expected to engage in long evenings of business-related socializing that are so much a part of the Japanese corporate culture. Finally, the teacher in Japan enjoys a greater degree of autonomy than many other professions permit.[71]

THE JAPANESE STUDENT

Cultural influences on students and their education manifest themselves most clearly in the case of Japan. The Japanese mother, beginning in the child's earliest years, will develop and mold the behaviors, attitudes, and characteristics that the child will need to succeed in school and later adult society. In traditional Japanese society the predominant link in a family is vertical—between parent and child, in contrast to an increasing tendency in Western societies to accord primacy to the relationship between the spouses, rather than parent and child. This Confucian ideal is strongly supported by Japanese women according to recent opinion polls showing that 76 percent of women believe that their first responsibility is to their children.[72]

In comparing Japan to America, Kiefer identifies three major differences between the two cultures. ''(1) The Japanese middle-class mother is more solely responsible for children's education than the American; (2) the Japanese mother-child (especially mother-son) tie is more intensive than the American; (3) the Japanese individual is bound by the family for life and learns to consider the effect of all his actions on the family. The American child makes more distinctions between family-controlled areas and those outside the family." [73]

Mothers in Japan guide their children away from negative behaviors and toward positive behavior. They accomplish this through mild disapproval rather than through harsh disciplinary measures. To Western observers, child-rearing practices in Japan appear to be laissez-faire, or even permissive. It may be that the closer emotional bond between mother and child in Japan allows the mother to exercise a more powerful influence over her child than is common in the West.

By age six, most Japanese children have attended private nursery schools and kindergartens and are ready to participate fully in the group orientation of the Japanese elementary school. Even at this young age, Japanese children assume greater responsibility for themselves and for members of their small group within the classroom than is found in Western schools.

Teachers often do not even attempt to find children who are late for lunch or class activities. Young children can be seen searching for missing classmates, reminding one another of upcoming activities, and summoning their classmates for a school activity. Teachers create opportunities for students to exercise group leadership and to share in group responsibilities. [74]

A child attending school in Japan experiences a varied and rich curriculum, including an emphasis on moral education and special activities. The breadth of the curriculum reflects a Japanese commitment to a comprehensive goal of developing *ningen* (human beings). The development of the *whole person* implies a school curriculum that emphasizes art, music, and physical education, as well as the traditional basic skills.

Teachers consider their responsibilities to extend to student guidance, personal habits, and on- and off-campus student behavior. The prominent role that moral education and special activities—such as assemblies, sports festivals, cultural ceremonies, and club activities—play in the school schedule speaks to the importance assigned by the Japanese to the development of *ningen*. A high percentage of the additional time provided by the 240-day school year is invested in these nonacademic activities. [75]

In America we think of education primarily in terms of cognitive development and academic achievement. A review of the goals of the America 2000 education plan, with their exclusive emphasis on academic dimensions, is testimony to this narrow conception of schooling.[76] Americans tend to concentrate on technical explanations for achievement differences, such as "time on task" or "time in school." A more productive approach might be to accept a basic cultural explanation for the differences. The Japanese simply think about education differently than we do.[77]

Group identity is maintained in Japanese classrooms by total mixed-ability grouping and virtually 100 percent promotion rates from grade to grade. The students remain in one classroom for the full day, except for special subjects such as industrial arts, science, or physical education. This common classroom system continues through the secondary school years, where the teachers move from room to room and the students remain in their own classroom for most of the day.[78]

Communal responsibility and service to others are taught through the Japanese practice of four or five students from a class, on a rotating basis, serving hot lunches to their fellow classmates in the classroom. Cummings reports that:

> This lunch routine contains several moral messages: no work, not even the dirty work of cleaning, is too low for a student; all should share equally in common tasks; the maintenance of the school is everyone's responsibility. To underline these messages, on certain days each year the entire school body from the youngest student to the principal put on their dirty clothes and spend a couple of hours in a comprehensive cleaning of the school building and grounds.[79]

Since students clean the schools on a regular basis, Japanese schools do not generally employ janitors, except for needed maintenance personnel to perform certain jobs requiring technical knowledge or skills. School uniforms are standard attire for secondary students in Japan, while they are less common for elementary students. A visitor to a Japanese school will often encounter rows of cubbyholes near the entrance, where arriving students put their shoes upon entering the school. They then change into slippers or sneakers to wear during the school day. An exhibit case in the main hall of the school may also display samples of the food items that will be available for lunch later in the day.

It is commonly accepted that schools have supervisory rights over students' behavior beyond school hours. One purpose of uniforms is so that the student's school can be readily identified by members of the general public. Public misbehavior by students is reported to the school as well as to parents.[80] Elementary and secondary schools enforce strict behavior codes, both inside and outside of school. These codes prescribe where and when students may go by themselves, who may accompany them, and how they should dress.[81]

A Japanese exchange student from Tokyo reports that public displays of affection between boys and girls, and public intoxication from drugs or alcohol found among some American teenagers, rarely occur in Japan. Such behaviors are reported to both the parents and the teachers. This student further indicated that alcohol and drug abuse are far less a problem among teenagers in Japan than in the United States.[82]

Few Japanese teenagers hold part-time jobs. Those who do, tend to be vocational school students who are not studying for university entrance exams. Also, Japanese businesses prefer employees to be eighteen or older. In many cases the school that a student attends will have a rule against outside employment. Citizens in Japan must be eighteen to apply for a driver's license. Very few young people have access to cars and in many cases school rules prohibit students from driving cars, or motorbikes, to school.[83]

Japanese high school students usually reserve Sunday for recreation and socializing. They congregate in shopping districts of the big cities to go window shopping, eat ice cream, and walk with their friends. On such occasions the students may dress in ways forbidden during the regular school week, and may engage in street dancing in places such as Tokyo's Harajuku area. Many Japanese young people routinely read huge comic books, which they devour in great numbers. During the school week, students may spend an hour or so each day watching television. They do not generally have much interaction with other family members.[84]

By American standards, Japanese children seem slow to reach adolescence. Japan, in fact, does not have a word for teenager. Students of high school age are still referred to as children. The Japanese culture does not attach special significance to the ages from thirteen to nineteen and does not consider children of this age to have any special problems to confront.[85]

Life for the Japanese students revolves around the school. The entire culture appears mobilized to reinforce the importance and primacy of education in the life of its youth. The family, the school, and the wider community cooperate closely in a shared responsibility for educating the next generation of citizens. The distractions of jobs, sports, cars, sexual activity, and drug and alcohol use, so prominent in the lives of America's students, are virtually absent in the Japanese culture.

Sato awoke with a start, thinking about his uniform cap. At yesterday's preschool uniform inspection he had to raise his hand in humiliation and admit that he had forgotten his cap. As a ninth grade student, in his last year at the junior high school, he was berated by his teacher for his laxness and irresponsibility. Today he would remember his cap. He ate breakfast quickly, and by 8:00 A.M. his twenty-minute bike ride to school was well under way. His bookbag was strapped to his back, as the dress code required, and his black blazer with black pants fluttered gently as he rode through the cool breezes of early morning. All of his male friends, dressed exactly like him, as well as the girls in their navy blue blazers and matching skirts, arrived at the soccer field at about the same time for the daily inspection.

The inspection completed, Sato and his forty classmates entered their classroom, where they would spend most of the next seven hours as a variety of teachers came to instruct them in various subjects. Sato, a gifted student academically, was becoming frustrated by the slow pace set by his teacher in covering academic material. As Sato and his classmates grew older, the teachers found it increasingly difficult to teach a standard curriculum to all students, especially in a mixed-ability class with forty students. Sato needed to rely on juku school to provide him with the level of academic rigor necessary for him to score well on the high school entrance exam, which he would be taking in a few months.

Today it was Sato's turn, along with four classmates, to bring the hot platters of luncheon food from the cafeteria to the classroom. While they were on this errand other students in the class rearranged the classroom furniture into a series of dining tables. A brief moment of silence before the meal signaled the end of the noisy preparations, and the beginning of mealtime. The class homeroom teacher, Mr. Samoto, ate his lunch with the class, all the while observing the students to see that they were eating their meal in the prescribed way, following proper Japanese etiquette.

Afternoon classes continued until 2:30 P.M. when Sato and his classmates changed into their work clothes, their fourth clothing change of the day, to participate in the weekly cleaning of the school. Even their teacher could be seen scrubbing the desks in this communal cleaning activity. Sato and his classmates did not consider this activity to be

(continued)

drudgery, however, since their boisterous chatter and good-humored teasing lent a playful tone to the event.

By 3:30 P.M. Sato was visiting the soccer field for the third time today, this time to play soccer. A few hours after his early morning visit for dress code inspection, Sato and more than a hundred of his classmates spent an hour practicing a close-order marching drill to be presented at the sports festival scheduled at the school in two weeks. He found the endless practices tiresome, and yet these events, attended by parents, were important days for the school and its students.

Sato returned home at 6:00 P.M. and ate dinner with his mother and younger sister. His father, who worked 100 miles away in Tokyo, would not arrive home until 11:00 P.M. Since Sato would soon be taking the high school entrance exam, his mother did everything possible to provide a comfortable, quiet environment for him to do his homework and study. Thus Sato spent no time with his sister or mother during the evening hours. Later in the evening he and two friends walked together to a neighborhood juku school for an 8:30 P.M. exam-preparation class. Even though he was tired at the end of a long day, Sato enjoyed his juku classes since he found the material more academically challenging than most of his regular school work.

By 10:30 P.M. Sato was back in his bedroom where he spent an additional hour on homework. Sato finally took a half hour for his own enjoyment. He laid back in bed and listened to the newest CD album by his favorite American rock group. The lyrics to the songs spoke of men and women overwhelmed by love and passion, a situation that he had certainly never experienced. Drifting off to sleep, he reflected ruefully that, although almost fifteen, he had never even held hands with a girl, much less kissed one.

THE SCHOOL PRINCIPAL IN JAPAN

The aspiring school principal in Japan follows a well-defined route of professional experiences before being appointed to a principalship. School principals are generally older, experienced educators, with an average age of fifty-five and about twenty-five years in education.[86] For the first ten to fifteen years of their careers future principals are posted in several different schools, often in less desirable rural or urban areas, to receive a broad experience and to prove their dedication. These individuals often leave their families behind while posted in the less desirable locations. Eventually, they are appointed a principal, having demonstrated the qualities valued in every Japanese organization: ability, self-sacrifice, and dedicated patience.[87]

There are no formal graduate-level administrative preparation programs as there are in Canada and the United States. Candidates for a principalship must attain a higher level of teaching certification than is required of regular classroom teachers. Promotion to the principalship requires candidates to pass promotional examinations and complete specific training programs.[88]

The Japanese principal has broad decision-making authority within the school, power that is, nonetheless, constrained by the group orientation of the teachers. The daily short meetings of teaching faculties and the longer meetings each week or month ensure that there is much teacher involvement and discussion before any significant decision is made.[89]

American administrators are trained to take a management approach to their teachers, with an emphasis on close supervision and control of practice. The Japanese teacher, however, views his/her function as protecting teachers from external pressures and managing the school in a manner that will allow teachers the greatest latitude in performing their duties.[90] The principal views his/her main duty as providing advice and guidance to teachers, rather than supervising directly, and formally evaluating their work.[91]

American teachers rate their principals higher on leadership qualities than Japanese teachers rate their principals. Conversely, Japanese teachers report higher levels of collegial relationships among teachers than American teachers find in their own schools. Japanese teachers also feel that they have a greater role in setting school policy, that they receive more help from their colleagues, and that their success is more dependent on their own efforts and abilities.[92]

Japanese principals do not formally evaluate their teachers in any meaningful sense. The educational system is still conscious of the fiasco of the teacher rating scales in the 1960s, and there is no desire to reopen these old wounds. In the 1970s the Ministry of Education created a position of *head teacher* to assist the principal with administrative tasks in the schools. Even this initiative was greeted with strong opposition from the teachers' unions, and was viewed as an attempt by the Ministry of Education to restrict teacher autonomy. By the late 1970s most prefectures had created this position despite union opposition.[93]

Japanese schools typically have a vice-principal to assist the principal in the performance of his or her duties. The site administrators usually organize workshops for new teachers so that experienced teachers can share their knowledge with their inexperienced colleagues. New teachers in Japan must spend the equivalent of twenty days during their first year engaging in training activities. Master teachers, who have been given a year's leave of absence from the classroom to assist their new colleagues, direct these training sessions.[94]

Each prefecture employs teacher-consultants, who visit the schools to provide instructional and curriculum guidance and supervision to both new and experienced teachers.[95] The intensive and continuous discussions among teachers of a given subject or grade level provide an additional method of improving instruction through peer pressure and collaboration.[96] Although the principal has little direct responsibility for teacher supervision and instructional improvement, these vital functions are achieved through the additional mechanisms previously discussed.

Japanese principals are routinely transferred from one school to another on a four-year schedule. Many prefectures also mandate the transfer of teachers every six or seven years.[97] Both of these practices contribute to a cross-fertilization of ideas and strategies to improve instruction. Decisions regarding teacher dismissal and transfer are made at the level of the prefectural superintendent, and not by the school principal.[98]

The principalship in Japan is a position of honor and respect. The principal has sufficient assistance to ensure that the important functions of teacher supervision, instructional quality, and organizational efficiency are attained. In Japan, secondary school principals are far less likely than their American counterparts to spend their time conducting drug busts in the lavatories, handling student protests in the cafeteria, or attempting to control an unruly crowd at a Friday night basketball game.

The role of the principal in Japanese schools corresponds closely to that of a head teacher in the European school systems profiled earlier. Of the five foreign countries surveyed in this study, only Canada defines a role for its administrators that closely resembles the American model.

EDUCATIONAL GOVERNANCE

Japan exercises the most centralized control of education of any country in the survey. With a population of 124 million people, half the population of the United States, all important educational policy issues are set by the national Ministry of Education. The minister of education holds cabinet rank and is among the most influential public officials in the Japanese government. At the end of World War II the occupation forces attempted to decentralize the Japanese educational system, but these efforts were resisted and the national Ministry of Education quickly reasserted its dominance once the U.S. occupation ended in 1952.[99]

The Ministry of Education exercises strict control over the curriculum by publishing courses of study for every subject, and by dictating the amount of time to be allocated to each subject. Local officials select textbooks from a published list of acceptable titles prepared by the national Ministry of Education. The ministry also allocates financial aid to prefectures and municipalities and provides prefectural and municipal school boards with advice and guidance.[100]

There are forty-seven prefectures in Japan that provide regional administrative units for all governmental functions, including education. The prefectural governor, with the concurrence of the prefectural assembly, appoints five members to the prefectural school board. These board members serve for four years and select a prefectural superintendent, who must be approved by the national Ministry of Education.

The major duties of the prefectural board and superintendent are to administer prefectural educational establishments, to supervise and give financial assistance to municipal boards of education, to issue certificates to teachers, to receive reports from municipal boards, and to require educational improvements as needed. They also appoint, dismiss, and pay the salaries of teachers in schools established and operated by the municipalities.[101]

Each of the more than 3,200 municipalities has a local school board of three to five members appointed by the mayors, with the approval of their respective councils. One of the board members also serves as the local superintendent. The budgets of these local boards are controlled by the prefectures and the local municipalities. Both municipal and prefectural school boards are administrative arms of the national government, rather than vehicles for providing local control for education as in the United States. For the first decade after the war, school boards were directly elected by the local citizens in an attempt by the Americans to decentralize Japanese education. This law was changed in 1956 amidst much controversy, so that today school boards are appointed, rather than directly elected.[102] While the Japanese government is in most respects among the most democratic in the world, the Japanese people have rejected the democratic forms of local school governance imposed by the Americans after the war and have reverted to a centralized, bureaucratically controlled system.[103]

There is irony in the fact that a historically authoritarian society such as Japan has achieved a higher level of educational equity, at least through the first nine years of compulsory schooling, than American educational reformers have dreamed possible for our country. The Japanese believe that the goal of equal educational opportunity requires uniform academic standards established through a national curriculum, textbooks that are selected from an approved list, and national guidelines on teaching techniques for use by teachers. Such an approach provides some assurance that every child will have an equal opportunity to learn.[104]

This situation changes, however, when students enter the highly competitive realm of upper secondary school and the university qualifying examinations. As is true of the United States, Japan has a school system that tends to replicate the existing status and class distinctions in Japanese society.[105] Residential patterns in the United States play much the same role as the examination system in Japan in determining who receives the best educational opportunities.

Public schools have a virtual monopoly on education through the nine years of compulsory schooling. Significant uniformity is assured in the public school sector by equal funding throughout the country, by residential patterns not primarily determined by income or occupation, by national control of curriculum and textbooks, and by an unusual degree of cultural homogeneity.[106]

Japan finances its public education system primarily through prefectural funds. These funds are derived from direct taxation of the population of the prefecture as well as funds transferred from the national government to each prefecture. Poor prefectures receive more national funds per capita than do the richer prefectures.[107] Close to half of the funds for elementary and secondary education come from the national government, with approximately one-fourth coming from the prefectural government and one-fourth raised by local municipal taxes. The national government pays half the cost of teacher salaries while the prefectural government pays the other half.[108] Local municipalities have no responsibility to pay for teacher salaries. This method of financing teacher pay allows Japanese municipalities to avoid the public acrimony over teacher pay that is so much a fixture of the local education scene in the United States.

Critics of American education often cite international cost comparisons for public education to assert that Japan is able to produce a highly educated citizenry at a lower cost than the United States. This cost advantage is often attributed to the very large class sizes in Japan. Both of these assertions bear closer scrutiny. The assumption that Japanese schools save vast sums of money on staffing because of large class size is simply incorrect. Although the Japanese teacher has very large classes, he or she also has relatively few student contact hours compared to American teachers. Thus the actual student-to-teacher ratio in Japan is similar to that in the United States. In 1987 there were 20.7 students per teacher in Japan compared to 18.4 students per teacher in the United States.[109]

The major reason for lower public educational expenditures in Japan versus the United States is that full public support for education in Japan ends after ninth grade. There are not enough public school places in Japan to accommodate all high school students. Even those students admitted to these highly competitive public school places must pay part of their educational costs. Twenty-eight percent of Japanese high school students attend private high school where there is a small state subsidy, but where the major cost burden falls to the parents. Additionally, the almost universal practice of students attending juku tutoring schools is an educational cost borne solely by the parents. Thus the private contribution to upper secondary school education in Japan, through tuition and fee payments by parents, far exceeds the direct contribution of American parents of high school students toward educational costs.

A major distortion in comparing international educational expenditures occurs when data on higher education costs are included in the comparisons. Since the United States supports a comparatively high proportion of students in higher education, this factor alone substantially raises the level of public spending on education in the United States compared to other countries. Reagan and Bush administration officials, as well as other critics of American elementary and secondary schooling, consistently used data that includes our large expenditures on higher education to demonstrate that America spends more than almost every other country on education.

A second source of distortion is the fact that the United States has a relatively large school-age population compared to most other industrialized countries. This fact will also raise the proportion of national income dedicated to education. By adjusting for the relative size of each country's K–12 enrollment, a recent sixteen-country comparison of educational spending shows that the United States spends less on precollege education than all but two of the countries in the study. The data from this study indicates that in 1985 Japan spent 4.8 percent of the gross domestic product on K−12 education compared to 4.1 percent of the gross domestic product in the United States.[110]

The successes of the Japanese educational system have not produced self-satisfaction or complacency among the Japanese. While foreign observers are quick to praise Japanese schools, the Japanese themselves are highly critical of their education system. The Japanese National Council of Educational Reform captures the intensity of this internal criticism in its conclusion that ''Japanese education currently suffers from a 'grave state of desolation' caused by pathological conditions of society and schools.''[111] Interestingly enough, the council's concerns relate to perceived failings in the area of moral education more than in the academic areas. The Japanese media are critical of centralized control, standardized educational practice, and the adverse effects of competitive college entrance examinations.[112] The generally conservative nature of Japanese society, however, as well as the unquestioned academic success of the Japanese schools, renders the chances for significant reform remote at best.

SOCIAL AND CULTURAL INFLUENCES ON EDUCATION

A critical distinction between Japanese and American society is the group orientation of the Japanese versus the individualism of the Americans. This group identity among the Japanese manifests itself in great loyalty toward the family, and a sense that the actions of each member of the family reflect on the family as a whole. This commitment induces Japanese students to work hard for the sake of their family reputations as much as for their own benefit.

The Japanese mother's orientation is primarily toward the rearing and educating of her children, rather than toward her own career or personal fulfillment, as is often true with the American mother. The Japanese husband remains willing to work from early morning to late at night as the primary, if not sole breadwinner for his family. This attitude contrasts with that of both American men and women that the woman will be a partner in providing an income for the family.

The primary emotional tie for the Japanese woman is her children, rather than her husband. An American parent is more likely to subordinate the parent-child relationship to the demands of the spousal relationship. The Japanese lack of emphasis on husband-wife relationships may partially account for the extremely low divorce rate in Japan in comparison to the United States. A recent survey of teachers from several countries, including Japan and the United States, showed that ten times as many American teachers surveyed were divorced as were Japanese survey participants.[113]

Japanese students mature in a culture where elders are respected, if not venerated. Three-generation households are still commonplace in Japan. The youth subculture in Japan is but a pale imitation of the strength and influence of the teenage subculture in the United States. Japanese adolescents accept greater academic accountability than their American peers, but are given less social freedom than American teenagers. Not surprisingly, Japan's problems with teenage pregnancy, drug and alcohol abuse among youth, and delinquency, are minuscule compared to those of the United States.

We have seen that Japanese society is organized in a manner that restricts social and economic benefits to the educated elite. There are few roads to success other than through school achievement. The individual Japanese commitment to the importance of education is reflected in the willingness of students to endure the process of "examination hell," and the willingness of parents to make great financial sacrifices to send their children to juku cram school, and to private high school when necessary.

The mother, especially, evaluates her own worth through the academic achievements of her children. The mother of an elementary child will spend many hours each week providing individual tutoring to her child. She will cooperate very closely with the school to enhance the education of her child. She will leave the work force before the birth of the child to devote herself to her duties as a mother. As a high school student, the child is relieved of household chores to concentrate his or her efforts on school. The mother will often prepare separate meals for her high school student late into the evening to accommodate a study schedule.

The general society provides for the health and welfare needs of virtually all citizens. We have already detailed the method employed by the government to ensure educational equity for all citizens. Universal health care is available, primarily through generous private company programs, but also by government sources when needed. The mixed system of private and government health and welfare benefits includes unemployment compensation, work injury compensation, disability, sickness, maternity, and old age benefits. Health conditions in Japan are among the best in the world. Life expectancy currently stands at seventy-three for men and seventy-eight for women.[114]

The disparities between rich and poor are narrower in Japan than in the United States. The pay differentials in a Japanese company between the average worker and the CEO are far less than is typical in an American company. The lack of ethnic diversity in Japan reinforces an intolerance for nonconforming behavior. This adherence to group norms molds the Japanese child into an acceptance of the importance of education that is preached both in the home and in the larger society.

The Japanese social and cultural realities described previously may strike an American reader as neither desirable nor possible for the United States. There can be little question, however, that family and social structure in Japan provide a stable and supportive environment for childhood growth and development. The family and societal influences on the Japanese child contribute powerfully to the success that the Japanese educational system continues to enjoy.

The Japanese take education seriously. This accounts for the paradoxical fact that the Japanese are highly critical of their schools and are seeking to further improve them, while their educational achievements are greatly admired by the outside world. Americans most often attribute high Japanese academic achievement to the 240-day school year and to a stereotype of a Japanese classroom featuring rigid control and emphasizing drill-and-practice instructional methods. We have seen that the Japanese actually spend about the same number of hours each year on academic subjects as do American students. Also, the Japanese classroom, at the elementary level at least, relies heavily on active group involvement by students in an atmosphere that is noisier and less teacher dominated than that found in most American schools.

We must look to the Japanese culture to understand the unique quality of their schools. Japanese mothers exert a far stronger positive influence on their child's education than American mothers or fathers typically do on their children. A competitive examination system for admission to the best high schools and universities introduces an academic seriousness in Japanese young people that is simply not necessary in the United States, where students are assigned to high schools based on residential patterns and where most colleges follow a virtual open admissions policy.

In Japan educational attainment almost always bears a direct relationship to future occupational and social status. In the United States educational attainment is perceived as but one of several viable paths to social and economic success. Many American students, as well as many of their parents, simply do not view a good education as critically important to the student's future.

Japanese students, teachers, and parents are extremely dedicated to work at the level necessary to achieve academic excellence. The Japanese government exerts strong leadership by ensuring that educational goals are established, monitored, and met. School funding practices ensure that equitable educational opportunities are available to virtually every Japanese student, regardless of the wealth of his/her parents. While it would be foolhardy to attempt to graft the Japanese educational system onto an American culture that is fundamentally different from that of Japan, many of the practices in Japanese education could be profitably adapted to our American system.

REFERENCES

1. White, M. 1987. *The Japanese Educational Challenge.* New York, NY: The Free Press, p. 15.
2. 1991. *Encyclopedia Americana, Vol. 15.* Danbury, CT: Grolier Incorporated, p. 729.
3. 1985. *The International Encyclopedia of Education, Vol. 5.* Oxford: Pergamon Press, p. 2766.
4. 1968. *Encyclopedia Britannica, Vol. 12.* Chicago, IL: William Benton, Publisher, p. 882.
5. White, M., pp. 11–16.
6. Anderson, R. S. 1981. "Japanese Education," *Comparative Educational Systems,* E. Ignas and R. J. Corsini, eds., Itasca, IL: F.E. Peacock, Publishers, p. 237.
7. Anderson, R. S., p. 237.
8. Rubinger, R. 1989. "Continuity and Change in Mid-Nineteenth Century Japanese Education," *Japanese Schooling,* J. J. Shields, Jr., ed., University Park, PA: The Pennsylvania State University Press, pp. 224–228.
9. Rubinger, R., p. 232.
10. August, R. L. 1992. "Education," *Japan: A Country Study,* R. E. Dolan and R. L. Worden, eds., Washington, DC: Department of the Army, p. 150.
11. White, M., p. 111.
12. White, M., p. 67.
13. Stevenson, H. W. 1989. "The Asian Advantage: The Case of Mathematics," *Japanese Schooling,* J. J. Shields, Jr., ed., University Park, PA: The Pennsylvania State University Press, pp. 88–89.
14. White, M., pp. 68–69.
15. August, R. L., p. 142.
16. Yamada, C. Interview with author, March 1992.

17. White, M., p. 68.
18. Singleton, J. 1989. "Gamburu: A Japanese Cultural Theory of Learning," *Japanese Schooling*, J. J. Shields, Jr., ed., University Park, PA: The Pennsylvania State University Press, pp. 12−13.
19. White, M., pp. 114−115.
20. Anderson, R. S., pp. 250−251.
21. Anderson, R. S., pp. 256−257.
22. White, M., p. 17.
23. Stevenson, H. W., p. 85.
24. Stevenson, H. W., p. 86.
25. Anderson, R. S., p. 276.
26. Stevenson, H. W., p. 92.
27. Iwama, H. F. 1989. "Japan's Group Orientation in Secondary Schools," *Japanese Schooling*, J. J. Shields, Jr., ed., University Park, PA: The Pennsylvania State University Press, p. 81.
28. White, M., p. 77.
29. Yamada, C. Interview.
30. Benjamin, G. R. and E. James. 1989. "Public and Private Schools and Educational Opportunity in Japan," *Japanese Schooling*, J. J. Shields, Jr., ed., University Park, PA: The Pennsylvania State University Press, pp. 153−157.
31. 1985. *The International Encyclopedia of Education, Vol. 5*, pp. 2767−2768.
32. McCormick, K. 1988. "Vocationalism and the Japanese Educational System," *Comparative Education*, 24(1):38.
33. 1991. *Encyclopedia Americana, Vol. 15*, p. 731.
34. White, M., p. 142.
35. Yamada, C. Interview.
36. White, M., p. 77.
37. August, R. L., pp. 146, 148.
38. Yamada, C. Interview.
39. Yamada, C. Interview.
40. Fujita, H. 1989. "A Crisis of Legitimacy in Japanese Education," *Japanese Schooling*, J. J. Shields, Jr., ed., University Park, PA: The Pennsylvania State University Press, p. 137.
41. Shields, J. J., Jr., ed. 1989. *Japanese Schooling*. University Park, PA: The Pennsylvania State University Press, p. 103.
42. Shields, J. J., Jr., ed., pp. 103−104.
43. Kurian, G. T., ed. 1988. *World Education Encyclopedia, Vol. 2*. New York, NY: Facts on File Publications, p. 702.
44. Holmes, B., ed. 1984. *International Handbook of Educational Systems, Vol. 2*. Chichester: John Wiley & Sons, p. 230.
45. Kurian, G. T., ed., p. 708.
46. Kurian, G. T., ed., p. 708.
47. Arima, A. Speech given at Drexel University, Philadelphia, PA, spring 1992.
48. August, R. L., p. 139.

49. August, R. L., p. 712.
50. Holmes, B., ed., p. 233.
51. Yamada, C. Interview.
52. Sato, N. and M. W. McLaughlin. 1992. "Context Matters: Teaching in Japan and the United States," *Phi Delta Kappan,* 73(5):362.
53. Sato, N. and M. W. McLaughlin, 73(5):360.
54. White, M., p. 87.
55. Sato, N. and M. W. McLaughlin, 73(5):360.
56. Iwama, H. F., p. 76.
57. Stigler, J. W. and H. W. Stevenson. 1991. "How Asian Teachers Polish Each Lesson to Perfection," *American Educator,* 15(1):46.
58. Stigler, J. W. and H. W. Stevenson, 15(1):46.
59. Stevenson, H. W., pp. 94–95.
60. Stigler, J. W. and H. W. Stevenson, 15(1):14.
61. Nelson, F. H. 1991. *International Comparisons of Public Spending on Education.* Washington, DC: American Federation of Teachers, p. 37.
62. Holmes, B., ed., p. 246.
63. Ota, H. 1989. "Political Teacher Unionism in Japan," *Japanese Schooling,* J. J. Shields, Jr., ed., University Park, PA: The Pennsylvania State University Press, pp. 243–245.
64. Anderson, R. S., p. 267.
65. Ota, H., p. 249.
66. Kurian, G. T., ed., p. 712.
67. Ota, H., pp. 247–248.
68. Kurian, G. T., ed., p. 712.
69. Nelson, F. H., p. 38.
70. Yamada, C. Interview.
71. White, M., p. 84.
72. White, M., p. 34.
73. Imamura, A. E. 1989. "Interdependence of Family and Education: Reactions of Foreign Wives of Japanese to the School System," *Japanese Schooling,* J. J. Shields, Jr., ed., University Park, PA: The Pennsylvania State University Press, p. 17.
74. Lewis, C. C. 1989. "Cooperation and Control in Japanese Nursery Schools," *Japanese Schooling,* J. J. Shields, Jr., ed., University Park, PA: The Pennsylvania State University Press, p. 37.
75. Sato, N. and M. W. McLaughlin, 73(5):361.
76. Sato, N. and M. W. McLaughlin, 73(5):360.
77. Singleton, J., p. 14.
78. Iwama, H. F., p. 79.
79. Iwama, H. F., pp. 80–81.
80. Ito, Y. Interview with author, March 1992.
81. Fujita, H., p. 134.
82. Ito, Y. Interview.
83. Yamada, C. Interview.

84. White, M., pp. 153–154.
85. White, M., p. 151.
86. Anderson, R. S., p. 264.
87. White, M., p. 87.
88. 1985. *The International Encyclopedia of Education, Vol. 5*, p. 2770.
89. Iwama, H. F., p. 76.
90. Sato, N. and M. W. McLaughlin, 73(5):361.
91. Anderson, R. S., p. 264.
92. Sato, N. and M. W. McLaughlin, 73(5):360.
93. Anderson, R. S., pp. 264–265.
94. Stigler, J. W. and H. W. Stevenson, 15(1):46.
95. Anderson, R. S., p. 265.
96. White, M., p. 86.
97. Sato, N. and M. W. McLaughlin, 73(5):364.
98. Holmes, B., ed., p. 234.
99. Kurian, G. T., ed., p. 710.
100. 1985. *The International Encyclopedia of Education, Vol. 5*, p. 2769.
101. Holmes, B., ed., pp. 233–234.
102. Kurian, G. T., ed., p. 710.
103. Duke, B. C. 1989. "Variations on Democratic Education: Divergent Patterns in Japan and the United States," *Japanese Schooling*, J. J. Shields, Jr., ed., University Park, PA: The Pennsylvania State University Press, p. 267.
104. Duke, B. C., p. 267.
105. Shields, J. J., Jr., ed., p. 102.
106. Benjamin, G. R. and E. James, pp. 152–153.
107. Benjamin, G. R. and E. James, p. 156.
108. Kurian, G. T., ed., p. 711.
109. Nelson, F. H., p. 33.
110. Rasell, M. E. and L. Mishel. 1990. *Shortchanging Education: How U.S. Spending on Grades K–12 Lags behind Other Industrial Nations*. Washington, DC: Economy Policy Institute, pp. 1–5.
111. Shimahara, N. K. 1989. "Japanese Education Reforms in the 1980s: A Political Commitment," *Japanese Schooling*, J. J. Shields, Jr., ed., University Park, PA: The Pennsylvania State University Press, pp. 272–273.
112. Shields, J. J., Jr., ed., p. 222.
113. Poppleton, P. 1990. "The Survey Data," *Comparative Education*, 26(2/3):184.
114. 1985. *Encyclopedia Britannica, 15th Edition*. Chicago, IL: University of Chicago, 5:498–499.

CHAPTER 8

Comparing Schools in Six Cultures

THE FULBRIGHT EXCHANGE YEAR IN RETROSPECT

ANNAPOLIS, MARYLAND, APRIL 10, 1992 — The noontime tourist crowd watched as the midshipmen at the U.S. Naval Academy, marching to the cadence of drumbeats, participated in the daily tradition of formation in the courtyard of Bancroft Hall. Among the crowd were fifteen Fulbright Exchange teachers attending a spring regional conference to discuss and analyze their experiences as teachers in American schools during the 1991 – 1992 school year.

The teachers from Germany, Cyprus, and France, who had shared their initial impressions about America at the Baltimore conference seven months earlier, bantered among themselves within the larger tourist crowd. Her dark eyes flashing, the woman from Cyprus spoke with emotion of the parental indifference she had encountered. Heda from Germany spoke approvingly of the "informal and friendly relationship that had developed between her and her high school students." The Frenchman, with an air of bemusement, marveled "at the extent to which American teachers are expected to be both coach and camp counselor to their high school students."

Earlier that day, the Fulbright teachers were given a VIP tour of the Naval Academy, designed to showcase the very best of American education, in terms of programs, facilities, equipment, and students. The morning began with an initial briefing for the Fulbright teachers, describing a rigorous and effective educational program provided at the Naval Academy for a highly motivated and well-prepared student body.

During a walk through the campus, or yard as it is known, the visiting teachers encountered public school graduates from every region of the country who were well-disciplined, hardworking, and vigorous in both mind and body. The smell of freshly cut grass, the immaculate cleanliness of the buildings, and the small craft sailing along the harbor, each reinforced the impression that the Naval Academy represents an especially good example of the best in American education.

At mealtimes, as well as at formal meetings during the two-day conference, the Fulbright teachers exchanged experiences and impressions of their year in American schools. At the final session of the two-day meeting, Ms. Ilo-Mai Harding, senior program officer from the Fulbright Exchange, led the group in a formal attempt to summarize their impressions of American schools, teachers, students, and the educational system in general. Winifred Flanagan and Maurice Feldman, both associated with the Fulbright program, assisted her in this process.

The assembled teachers drew on experiences as diverse as a Dutch teacher working in rural West Virginia to a teacher from Senegal reporting on a year spent at an affluent public school district on the Philadelphia Main Line. Other teachers present were natives of England, Scotland, Germany, Cyprus, France, and Hungary. This varied group of teachers, reporting on their experiences in very diverse schools, nonetheless reported many similar experiences with the American educational system.

Comments on their experiences quickly divided themselves among professional impressions relating to their teaching assignments, and personal impressions regarding the American lifestyle. Peter, from Holland, learned to enjoy country and western music, since that was the only music he could find on his car radio as he traveled the hilly, rural roads of West Virginia. There was a consensus that Americans are very open, friendly, and positive in their interpersonal relations. Many Fulbright teachers commented favorably on the high level of competent and friendly service provided by American businesses and governmental agencies. The convenience of shopping at American supermarkets at any hour and the multitude of choices in American retail stores were universally admired. One woman teacher from Scotland commented that "you never need to know what time it is in America because stores are open virtually all the time." Ease of travel, the great size of the country, and the multitude of tourist attractions were also cited by many Fulbright teachers.

When the discussion turned to America's schools, the tenor of the testimony was mixed. The following generalizations about American education were affirmed by a clear majority of the fifteen Fulbright teachers as they reflected on their year in American schools.

Access to Education

(*1*) The American ideal of providing open access to education to all of its citizens is greatly admired. The American commitment to allowing second and third chances to students to prove themselves academically also received favorable comment.

(2) The degree of access to higher education in the United States, offering yet further chances for late-bloomers to succeed academically, was noted with approval.

(3) This American commitment to equal educational opportunity is fatally undermined by an overdependence on local funding of schools, creating tremendous disparities in the available financial resources among school districts.

The American Teaching Profession

(4) American teachers have more freedom to decide on their curriculum than do teachers in other countries. This is viewed as both a positive and a negative. As a teacher from Scotland noted, ''Teachers in America are free to be as good, or as bad, as they wish.'' The presence of a national curriculum and set standards in other countries serves as both a guide and a goal for teachers in planning their instruction.

(5) Teachers in America have heavy work loads compared to teachers in most other countries. There are few breaks during the day and teachers are assigned to more teaching time and more supervisory duties than in other nations. A teacher from Germany remarked that in light of the heavy teaching schedule of American teachers, she was absolutely astonished that many teachers hold second jobs in addition to teaching.

(6) Teachers in American schools are more isolated from one another than teachers in other countries. This is a result of very full teaching schedules with few breaks and short lunch periods. American teachers simply have fewer opportunities to meet for either social or professional purposes than do their colleagues abroad.

(7) Teachers in the United States are supervised by their principals more closely and more frequently than is common elsewhere.

(8) Exchange teachers endorsed the comment from a teacher from France that the American definition of a teacher seems to include elements of a camp counselor and an entertainer, role expectations that were new to his experience.

(9) American teachers are often put on the defensive by students and parents. It seems that in conflict situations the onus is always on the teacher rather than on the student.

(*10*) American teachers do not enjoy high status in our society and are generally not valued by the wider community.

American Students

(*11*) Students in America are generally more concerned with teacher-assigned grades than students in other nations. This occurs because there are generally no exams or standards external to the classroom by which student achievement is measured. Thus the grades given by the classroom teacher are usually the sole criteria for measuring student academic success.

(*12*) American students have many more distractions from studies than in most other countries. American students drive cars, hold jobs, and in general follow a much more adult lifestyle than do students in other nations. A middle-aged secondary teacher from England remarked that, "If I had all the distractions of American students, I wouldn't study either."

(*13*) Students and parents from affluent school districts are often complacent. These students have little motivation to excel academically, or to use education as a route to a better life. The Senegalese teacher remarked that, "My American school was all body [good facilities and many instructional materials] but no soul, while my school in Senegal had little body but a lot of soul [student enthusiasm and commitment]."

(*14*) American students are less willing to do homework or other out-of-class assignments than their counterparts in many other countries. This may be related to the many distractions available to American students.

(*15*) While American students are expected to follow an adult lifestyle outside of the school setting, students in schools are very dependent on teachers for guidance and direction in the most trivial aspects of academic work.

Daily School Life

(*16*) The level of informality in the relationships between teachers and students was generally applauded.

(*17*) The availability of extensive extracurricular programs for students, although criticized for their excesses, was generally viewed as a positive aspect of America's schools.

(*18*) Many teachers noted that both student absences and classroom interruptions undermine the continuity and concentration necessary to academic achievement. American schools seem to tolerate far more interruptions to the teaching process than is common elsewhere.

(*19*) The daily school schedule and the school calendar are demotivators for both students and teachers. Classes scheduled at the same time every day, many classes in succession with no breaks, and long periods of time between vacation periods, all conspire to drain energy and enthusiasm for academic work.

(*20*) American students believe they need only learn material from test to test, with no expectation that they should permanently retain knowledge and skills. External exam systems in foreign countries foster the concept of cumulative learning in those countries.

Political Organization of American Schools

(*21*) Local control of schools creates political pressures on school boards, administrators, and even teachers, to relax academic standards in the face of parental pressures to award students higher grades than they have earned.

(*22*) School boards and local communities have neither the expertise nor the political will to establish curriculum standards that promote high academic performance.

(*23*) Parents exert undue pressure on teachers in the United States to inflate student grades and accept mediocre standards of performance.

Societal Influences on Schooling

(*24*) Other countries have a shorter school day for younger elementary students. Foreign schools are less involved in performing social agency functions than their counterparts in the United States. A teacher from Germany noted that in her rural area of Germany "it is still likely that the mother of a young student will be at home when the child returns from school in early afternoon." This differs from her observations in her local American community, where more women are in the work force full time.

(*25*) Schools are a reflection of their society. School policies and practices from one country cannot simply be transplanted from one culture to another.

These judgments of the Fulbright Exchange teachers concern themselves primarily with their experiences living the day-to-day lives of

American teachers. Comparisons among the countries surveyed in this book are made in a more formalized manner later in this chapter. Comparisons are also made on aspects of the various educational systems that were not part of the daily experience of the exchange teachers and, therefore, were not discussed as topics at the spring regional meeting in Annapolis. There is, however, a remarkable correspondence between the individual impressions of these exchange teachers regarding American schools, and the more formalized findings from examining the educational systems of the six survey countries.

Our odyssey through the schools in six cultures reveals important differences, even among the major industrial and economic powers, in school effectiveness and student achievement. Our six-nation survey demonstrates that the notion of school effectiveness must be considered in terms of the goals that a nation expresses for itself, the culture in which the schools operate, and the social and economic milieu in each country.

School quality is clearly the product of an equation that includes explicit school policies and practices, cultural realities relating to child-rearing practices and the valuing of education, and political decisions regarding allocation of financial resources invested in schools. No single element in this equation can account adequately for differences among nations on any dimension of schooling, including comparative student achievement on tests of basic skills.

In this chapter we will compare the schools of six nations on a number of individual points, realizing that the whole is indeed greater than the sum of its parts. This process will identify many practices and beliefs of other nations that could be adapted in American schools, contributing to the radical restructuring of our schools that we so desperately need. We will also note that other nations have borrowed freely from the American ideal and model for public schooling, and that these nations continue to emulate positive aspects of our own schooling practices.

TEACHERS IN SIX NATIONS

The status of teachers in the six nations surveyed varies dramatically. There is a direct correlation between the level of professionalism that teachers enjoy and the quality of the schools in each country. In this section we will explore the worklife, compensation level, education, and socioeconomic status of teachers in each survey nation. This inquiry clearly demonstrates that teachers in several of the countries can claim true professional status, while those from other countries must be considered as workers or, at best, semi-professional (see summary in Table 8.1).

The number of hours weekly that teachers directly instruct and supervise students, provides a measure of the society's judgment regarding the nature and complexity of the teaching act. American teachers typically instruct classes or supervise playgrounds, study halls, and cafeterias, for between twenty-five and thirty clock-hours each week. This schedule might include teaching twenty-five to thirty different lessons, either to one group of elementary students, or to five or six different classes of secondary students.

As a practical reality, such a schedule limits the teacher to ten to fifteen minutes of preparation time for each lesson. Another ten to twenty minutes per class may be allotted for evaluating student classwork and homework. Even these minimal time allocations represent a work week of more than forty hours. Many teachers also make major time commitments to coaching. Various surveys over the years have shown that between 20 and 40 percent of teachers work at part-time jobs for pay during the school year.[1] It is fair to say that about one-third of American teachers hold second jobs during the school year. For most of these teachers with extensive out-of-school responsibilities, time constraints dictate that lesson plans and student assessment will be both superficial and minimally effective. This staggering teaching schedule and related activities undermine the notion that teaching is a serious intellectual activity.

Teachers in both England and Canada provide direct instruction to their students for a similar number of clock-hours as do American teachers. The pace of their teaching day is made somewhat less frenetic, however, by longer lunch periods than are typically found in America. English teachers also enjoy the tradition of a mid-morning break for tea or coffee. English and Canadian schools also distribute responsibilities for extracurricular activities more equitably among staff members, are less likely to provide supplemental contracts for these activities, and generally do not emphasize them to the extent found in American schools. English and Canadian teachers are also far less likely than their American counterparts to engage in part-time employment in addition to their teaching duties.

Teachers in Denmark and Germany, particularly in secondary schools, experience a work schedule similar to that of American college teachers. In Denmark the government specifies the number of lessons to be taught

Table 8.1 *Teacher Dimension.*

	Canada	Denmark	England	Germany	Japan	U.S.A
Teachers holding part-time jobs	Only a small proportion of Canadian teachers hold second jobs.	A small number of teachers work outside of their school responsibilities.	English teachers do not generally have second jobs.	Not only do teachers in Germany seldom hold second jobs, in some areas they are forbidden to have outside employment.	Japanese teachers seldom hold second jobs and are often forbidden to do so.	As many as one-third of U.S. teachers work at a second job during the school year.
Teacher unions and salary negotiations	Teachers have the right to strike in some areas and not others. In some provinces teacher salaries are set at the province level while in other areas they are negotiated locally.	Salaries are set at the national level. Unions exist but are not militant. Salaries are paid from national funds.	There is a national salary scale established, not negotiated, at the national level. The right to strike has been revoked in England.	Salaries are set at the federal level and paid at the state level. Unions exist but are generally not militant.	Salary guidelines are set nationally and generally modified only slightly at the prefectural level. The Japanese teacher union has on occasion been extremely militant. There is no right to strike.	Generally teacher salaries are negotiated and financed at the local level. There is statewide bargaining in some states. Teacher strikes are allowed in some states but not in others.

236

Table 8.1 (continued).

	Canada	Denmark	England	Germany	Japan	U.S.A
Teacher empowerment issues	Management-worker model found in American schools is also common model in Canada.	Teachers serve on school boards and operate schools on a collegial basis with a head teacher.	Teachers are concerned that new requirements will make the head teacher more of a manager than a colleague.	Collegial relationships are the rule between head teacher and the staff. There is usually much staff involvement in decisions.	Almost all decisions in Japanese schools are made by the faculty. There are daily short staff meetings and longer meetings weekly.	The principal has a more managerial role than is true in other countries. Principals do usually involve teachers, however.
Teacher workload (hours per week)	Twenty to twenty-five hours plus supervisory duties	Fifteen to twenty hours with no supervisory duties	Twenty to twenty-five hours plus supervisory duties	Fifteen to twenty hours with no supervisory duties	Fifteen to twenty hours with no supervisory duties	Twenty-two to twenty-seven hours with extensive supervisory responsibilities
Average teacher salaries (in U.S. dollars)	29,667 (1984)	21,834 (1982)	17,409 (1984)	21,031 (1982)	20,884 (1984)	19,270 (1982) 22,019 (1984)
Ratio of teacher/worker salaries in same country	1.40 (1984) (Teacher earns 1.4 times as much as a factory worker.)	1.28 (1982)	1.20 (1984)	1.12 (1982)	1.77 (1984)	0.94 (1982) 1.00 (1984)

(continued)

237

Table 8.1 (continued).

	Canada	Denmark	England	Germany	Japan	U.S.A
Supply of qualified secondary teachers in academic subjects	Good	Excellent	Fair to Good	Excellent	Excellent	Fair
Academic quality of candidates in teacher prep programs	High salaries attract fairly qualified candidates.	Rigorous secondary and university programs produce well-qualified teachers.	Rigorous secondary and university training with poor salaries lead to fairly well-qualified teachers.	Rigorous training and high status of teaching produce a well-qualified corps of teachers.	There are five to six applicants for each teacher position. Teacher quality is excellent.	Future teachers are among the least academically able of American college students. Low pay and status create supply and demand problems.

by teachers at each grade level. Teachers of subjects requiring a large amount of evaluation of student work, such as English, are given reduced teaching schedules. Danish elementary school teachers teach twenty-four lessons each week, requiring eighteen clock-hours of instruction. Secondary teachers teach eighteen to twenty-two lessons each week, representing about fifteen clock-hours per week of instructional time. Teachers in Germany instruct twenty-five to twenty-seven lessons each week, representing about twenty clock-hours of instruction.

Secondary teachers in Denmark and Germany do not perform supervisory duties such as study hall, bus duty, or cafeteria duty. They are required to be at school only for their scheduled classes and may otherwise come and go as they please. Most teachers return home early in the afternoon to prepare classes and grade papers for the next day's lessons. In spite of their lighter class schedule and shorter workday than American teachers, Danish and German teachers seldom hold second jobs. In at least some regions of Germany, a teacher must obtain permission from a supervisor to hold a second job. After-school extracurricular and athletic programs are minimal in both Germany and Denmark. Such functions are typically sponsored either privately or by the local municipality. Thus teacher time and energy in these countries are not diverted from their academic mission, an all too common occurrence in the United States.

Japanese teachers also spend relatively few hours each week providing direct instruction. Although teachers in Japan are assigned to only about fifteen clock-hours of direct teaching each week, they spend many hours in faculty and department meetings. Schools in Japan depend on a great deal of teacher involvement in decision making. Also, teachers devote much time and energy toward jointly planning lessons, discussing teaching strategies, and refining their teaching skills. Japanese teachers spend ten to eleven hours at school each day, work a 240-day school year, and generally appear at work about half of their vacation time. They perform few supervisory duties, and have limited involvement with extracurricular programs.

Japan and the United States represent the two extremes in terms of quality of worklife for teachers. Japanese teachers operate in a collegial and professional environment with ample time to prepare lessons and to improve their teaching skills. They are not preoccupied with supervisory duties nor with coaching duties that are extraneous to their educational mission. Although their classes are very large, this is more than compensated for by the fact that they have a much lighter teaching load than

American teachers, and their school day proceeds at a much more humane pace. Teachers in Denmark and Germany enjoy a worklife that is similarly professionalized and productive.

The workday of the American teacher proceeds at a frenetic pace and with bone-crushing intensity. American teachers have little time to meet with colleagues to resolve school problems or to improve teaching practices. They are often poorly educated for their tasks and do not have sufficient time to prepare effective lessons, or to critically evaluate student work. These factors occur in the context of a student body that is the most diverse, and among the least academically equipped, of the six nations surveyed.

Comparisons of teacher training, as well as supply and demand for teachers, again place the United States and Japan at opposite ends of the spectrum. Studies repeatedly indicate that students in American teacher training programs are among the least able academically of all college students. Comparisons of IQ scores of teachers in the 1960s and teachers in the 1980s indicate that in the 1980s teachers were far more likely to score in the lower range on IQ tests than were their counterparts in the 1960s. A national sample of college graduates who took the Armed Forces Qualifying Test confirmed that lower-IQ graduates were more than twice as likely to choose a career in education than were those graduates with higher IQ scores.[2]

In addition, there is a chronic shortage of certified teachers in the rigorous academic subjects such as science and math. Japan, conversely, has five to six applicants for each vacant teaching position. Teaching is a high status occupation in Japan, with one-fourth of all university graduates receiving qualifications as teachers.

The shortage of qualified teachers in certain subject areas is a greater problem in American schools than in other nations. A recent report indicates that 20 percent of American teachers are teaching subjects that they feel unqualified to teach.[3] A second study, reporting even more alarming numbers is summarized in Table 8.2. This report provides data on the percentage of teachers in each country who, by their own testimony, believe that they have the proper qualifications to teach all of their assigned subjects.[4] The percentage of American teachers certified to teach their assigned subjects is higher than the figures shown in the table, an indication that teachers make a distinction between being *certified* and being *qualified*. With this caveat in mind, it is clear that American teachers are much less comfortable with their teaching assignments than are their colleagues in other nations.

The data in Table 8.2 indicate clearly that other nations in this survey

Table 8.2 *Percentage of Teachers in Each Country Who Feel They Are Qualified to Teach All of Their Assigned Subjects.*

	England	Japan	Germany	United States
Language arts	84	98	83	44
Foreign languages	87	95	99	40
Hist./govt./econ.	92	95	60	46
Mathematics	81	77	89	42
Physical science	80	95	91	47
Fine arts/music	90	72	93	58
Physical ed./health	97	24	97	36

Source: Poppleton, P. 1990. "The Survey Data," *Comparative Education*, 26(2/3):187 (with permission from Carfax Publishing Company).

are better able to provide their secondary school students with academically qualified teachers. Denmark, Germany, and Japan pay their secondary teachers on a higher scale than elementary teachers, a further incentive for academically qualified persons in those countries to pursue a teaching career.

Educational requirements for elementary teachers are similar in all countries surveyed. Common practice is for elementary teachers to attend a teacher's college or a university for three or four years, followed by a student teaching experience varying in length from a few weeks in Japan, to a year or more in Germany. The major difference between the academic training of future teachers in the United States compared with other countries is the quality of their secondary school education. American elementary teachers are the product of American comprehensive high schools where they were most likely to be B-level students, pursuing a minimally challenging general academic program.

Their counterparts from other nations typically have pursued a more academically challenging secondary school program. Elementary teachers in Denmark are graduates of the academic Gymnasium, or an equivalent HF program, and have successfully passed the challenging Studentereksamen or HF exam. German elementary teachers have successfully passed the Abitur, which entitled them to attend higher education. English elementary teachers graduate from sixth form with a GCSE A-level passing grade in at least two subjects.[5] Japanese elementary teachers graduate from the academically challenging secondary schools in Japan. Only in Canada does the level of precollege academic training for future teachers correspond to that of the United States. The academic rigor of secondary schooling experiences for elementary teachers from most other countries surveyed makes these teachers better equipped academically to pursue rigorous college-level work. Not surprisingly, these teachers ultimately become better-educated classroom teachers than their American counterparts.

Compensation levels for teachers vary greatly among the countries in this survey. Several countries, notably the United States, Canada, and England, pay both elementary and secondary teachers on the same salary scale. Japan, Denmark, and Germany pay their secondary teachers from 10 to 25 percent more than elementary teachers with similar years of service. Salary scales are essentially established at the national level in Denmark, Germany, Japan, and England. Some Canadian provinces establish provincial salary scales while most provinces allow local districts to set salary schedules. Salary schedules for teachers are adopted by local school districts in most sections of the United States.

International comparisons of teacher salaries are notoriously suspect because of currency fluctuations, imprecise data, different methods for calculating average salaries, and the necessity of using data for different years for different countries. Nevertheless, a 1988 study,[6] using the concept of Purchasing Power Parity, developed a comparison of teacher salaries for the countries included in this survey.

The Purchasing Power Parity concept was developed by the international Organization for Economic Cooperation and Development (OECD) as a method of making valid comparisons among countries regarding their relative standard of living. The Purchasing Power Parity (PPP) measure serves as an international cost-of-living index. Identical salaries based on the PPP currency conversions represent an identical standard of living. The results from this 1988 study using the PPP conversions are shown in Table 8.3.

Other data from this study, again using the PPP concept, compare the

Table 8.3 *Teacher Salaries.*

Country	In U.S. Dollars	Ratio to U.S. Salaries
United States (1982)	19,270	1.00
United States (1984)	22,019	1.00
Canada (1984)	29,667	1.35
United Kingdom (1984)	17,409	0.79
Germany (1982)	21,031	1.09
Denmark (1982)	21,834	1.13
Japan (1984)	20,884	0.95

Source: Nelson, F. H. 1991. *International Comparisons of Public Spending on Education.* Washington, DC: American Federation of Teachers, p. 37.

1985 salaries of urban elementary teachers in selected major cities within fifteen countries. This study again shows English teachers as the most poorly paid and Canadian teachers as the best paid among the six countries surveyed in this book. Since the comparison of 1985 salaries considered elementary teachers only, American teachers ranked second to Canadian teachers in average salary.[7] If salaries of secondary teachers had been considered in the 1985 study, Japan, Denmark, and Germany would have ranked higher, since they pay their secondary teachers on a significantly higher scale than their elementary teachers.

Although comparative salary levels have undoubtedly changed somewhat since the data were collected, a few valid generalizations can still be made. Canadian teachers earn significantly more than teachers from other countries surveyed. English teachers earn significantly less than teachers in the other countries. Teachers from the United States, Germany, Denmark, and Japan enjoy roughly comparable salary levels.

This picture changes when one examines teacher salaries from each country in relation to other salaries within each economy. By this measure American teachers earn the least while Japanese teachers earn the most. A 1988 study by the National Center for Educational Statistics provides information comparing teacher salaries in each country to the salaries earned by average manufacturing workers in the same economy.[8] This comparison provides a reasonable measure of the economic status of teachers within their own economy. All comparisons are in terms of the national currency for each country.

Table 8.4 shows that American teachers were gaining financial ground on other American workers during the mid-1980s. Even so, American teachers do not fare well in their economy relative to other workers, compared to the economic status of foreign teachers within their own economies. The low esteem accorded teaching in the United States is reflected in the relative salaries earned by teachers in our economy. While it is true that teachers in England, Canada, Germany, and Denmark work about two weeks longer than American teachers each year, in some of these nations the teacher workday is somewhat shorter than that of an American teacher. In Japan, however, teachers work many more days than American teachers, and also work longer hours each day than American teachers.

Merit pay, a much recommended reform by American school critics, is not practiced in any of the survey nations. Other than during their probationary period, teachers in the survey countries are only minimally observed and evaluated by supervisors. The level of teacher supervision

Table 8.4

Country	Average Teacher Salary	Average Manufacturing Worker Salary	Ratio Teacher to Worker Salary
United States (1982)	19,270	20,486	0.94 (dollars)
United States (1984)	22,019	22,018	1.00 (dollars)
United States (1988)	28,071	24,376	1.15 (dollars)
Canada (1984)	35,126	25,045	1.40 (Can. $)
United Kingdom (1984)	9,401	7,832	1.20 (pounds)
Germany (1982)	49,235	43,930	1.12 (marks)
Denmark (1982)	186,422	146,186	1.28 (kroner)
Japan (1984)	4,695	2,647	1.77 (yen)

Source: Nelson, F. H. 1991. *International Comparisons of Public Spending on Education.* Washington, DC: American Federation of Teachers, p. 37.

is scheduled to increase dramatically in England under the provisions of the Education Act of 1988. We have seen that the Japanese government's attempt to closely supervise and evaluate teachers in the 1950s created a breach of faith between Japanese teachers and their Ministry of Education that has yet to be fully healed.

Teacher unionism represents another explanation in the minds of some school critics for the poor performance of America's schools. Here again, a look at the situation in the other survey countries reveals that teacher unionism is not unique to the United States, but in fact is the norm for teachers in industrialized countries. There appears to be little relationship between the quality of schools and the influence of teacher unions in the survey countries.

STUDENTS IN SIX NATIONS

A student's native country represents a powerful environmental influence on his or her attitude toward, and experiences with, formal education. The underlying culture of each nation both supports and constrains the nature of the schooling that a child receives. Although schooling certainly matters, enthusiasm for the notion that schooling is the primary influence on a child's life must be tempered by the fact that a student spends less than 20 percent of his or her waking hours each year in a school environment. Given that formal schooling is not generally introduced until age four or five, a typical ten-year-old will have spent only 10 percent of his or her lifetime directly under the school's influence.

The age at which students begin compulsory schooling varies among the six countries. American students begin kindergarten at age five. While kindergarten is often not compulsory, virtually all American students do attend kindergarten as five-year-olds. Japan follows a pattern similar to the United States with private nursery schools for very young students and noncompulsory kindergarten, attended by almost all students, for five-year-old children. Compulsory schooling in Japan begins with first grade at age six. In Canada many provinces provide publicly funded kindergartens for five-year-olds, while others provide public funding beginning with first grade. In any event, the pattern of kindergarten for five-year-old students and first grade for six-year-old students also pertains to Canada.

Compulsory schooling in England begins at age five with a reception year, corresponding to kindergarten in other nations. In both Germany and Denmark kindergartens are voluntary and privately funded. Compulsory schooling at the first grade level begins at age six in Germany and age seven in Denmark. Thus Denmark has the latest starting age among the countries surveyed. Also, kindergarten is privately funded in Germany, Denmark, and Japan, while it is typically a part of the publicly funded system in England, the United States, and Canada.

The primary school years for American children differ in one important respect from the experience of their foreign peers. Whereas American children in the first few grades attend school for six or more hours each day, younger students in the other survey countries typically attend school for about four hours each day, or even less in some instances. In Denmark, students in the first three grades attend school for about three hours each day, while German students of the same age attend for four hours. In both countries, students return home for lunch, or attend a day care center if no one is at home. A first grade student in Japan attends school for about four hours each day. The school day gradually lengthens each year until by fourth grade the Japanese student is attending school for the standard six-hour day.

Elementary school students in England and Canada experience a school day that is marginally shorter than that of American students. Thus we find that the nations with the best student academic performance (Japan, Germany, and Denmark) have a relatively short school day for their primary school children. The length of the student school year is often cited as a contributing factor in the poor performance of American students on international achievement tests. The 180-day school year is fairly standard throughout the United States, while Germany, England, Canada, and Denmark each have school years ranging from 190 to 226 days. Japan has a 240-day school year, including forty half-day Saturday sessions. The Ministry of Education has recently issued guidelines to allow students one free Saturday per month. Interestingly, guidelines were then issued regarding how students should spend their time on this free Saturday.

Although other nations in this survey have a longer school year than the United States, the American school day is typically longer. Students in other nations also enjoy more frequent breaks in the school day and longer lunch periods than do American students. Also, time for moral education in Japan, the act of daily worship in England, and formal religious instruction in Denmark, Germany, and Canada, each serve to decrease the time available for classroom instruction in traditional academic subjects.

Elementary students in other nations participate in more frequent nonacademic experiences than do American students. Japan, for example, provides several hours each week for special activities, such as preparing for schoolwide sports festivals or participation in club activities. German elementary students typically participate in frequent day-long excursions or field trips to cultural and historical sites. A careful comparison of actual instructional time for students in the six nations surveyed contradicts the assertion that American students receive fewer hours of direct academic instruction than do their counterparts in other nations. Even Japanese students, with their 240-day school year, actually spend about as much classroom time as their American peers on purely academic pursuits.

Among the nations in the survey, only Canada schedules its academic year and vacation periods in a way similar to the traditional American pattern. The other survey countries schedule a summer vacation of about six weeks, two weeks or so at both Christmas and Easter (except in Japan, which does not schedule vacations to conform to Christian holidays), and a week each in the middle of the fall and spring terms. These shorter, but more frequent, vacation periods break up the school routine and serve to refresh and invigorate both teachers and students. The shorter summer vacation period also minimizes the opportunity for students to forget previously learned knowledge and skills, thus reducing the time required for review.

Out-of-school homework requirements for elementary students vary greatly among the nations surveyed. England and Canada follow the American practice of requiring little homework for elementary school students. Denmark, Germany, and Japan make greater use of homework assignments, requiring perhaps thirty minutes of homework in the first few grades and from one to two hours of homework by fifth or sixth grade. Since classes in all of these countries are of mixed ability, all students receive the same type of homework assignments. American students in the upper elementary grades experience differing homework requirements depending upon the ability level of their class and/or the academic rigor of the particular school that they attend. Academically able students in a middle-class suburban school, for example, will have far more homework assigned than a poor child in a ghetto school.

In summary, there is little data to suggest that the American school year and school day are too short, or that too much school time is spent on nonacademic matters in American elementary schools. On the contrary, primary school students in the other survey nations have a shorter school day, with more frequent breaks from strictly academic activities, than do their American counterparts. Elementary schools in other cultures make a special effort to educate their young students in a caring, nurturing and stress-free environment. American elementary schools, despite our attempts to offer a child-centered environment, are typically more task oriented and more rigorously structured than the elementary schools of the other survey countries.

The difference in the demands and expectations placed on American secondary school students compared to their foreign peers is dramatic. Canada is the only other country that places as few demands, expectations, and academic pressures on its secondary school students as the United States. Secondary school students in the United States must satisfy only the most minimal standards set by their classroom teachers to amass sufficient credits to graduate from high school. A high school diploma is often a sufficient credential to gain admission to a college or university. Subtle, or not so subtle, parental pressure at the local school district level ensures that teacher expectations of students will remain ''reasonable.'' This reasonableness standard implies a recognition by the teacher that academic studies should not interfere with the student's social life, extracurricular participation, or part-time job.

Secondary school age students in most of the other survey countries face rigorous academic challenges beginning as early as seventh or eighth grade. By age twelve or thirteen, students in Germany and Denmark must determine whether they will seek admission to the academic high schools, or will pursue a technical or vocational education. By age fifteen, English students need to perform well on their school leaving examination to qualify for attendance at the sixth form schools which prepare them for later university admission. In many Canadian provinces, examinations are being reinstated to ensure that a high school diploma represents a definable standard of achievement.

Japanese students experience the most extreme pressures in preparing for an academic high school. Students in Japan must take competitive exams in ninth grade to determine which high schools they will be able to attend. Schools in each region are rated according to academic excellence, with acceptance at certain high schools offering a better chance for later acceptance at a prestigious university. In their senior year of high school, Japanese students must again take competitive exams to win placement at a university. In Japan the national public universities are the most prestigious and also the least costly. Therefore, the competition for the limited places available is intense.

We have noted that over 90 percent of Japanese students attend juku schools for five to ten hours each week to prepare for these competitive entrance examinations. The student is relieved of all household chores during the year or two preceding the examination, and the mother makes a special effort to accommodate meal schedules to her student's study schedule. Japanese students do not have driver's licenses and Japanese employers usually do not employ students under the age of eighteen. Japanese high school students involved in the intense competition for admission to the top public universities may spend five or six hours each day on homework for regular classes as well as juku school.

Academic high school students in Denmark, Germany, and England invest considerable effort in mastering the material necessary to pass required university admission tests in their countries. English students generally take the General Certificate of Education Advanced Level (GCE A-level) in two or three subjects to apply for university admission. These national tests determine whether or not a student will be selected for a university of his or her choice, or even whether the student will be admitted to any university.

In Germany, students must earn the Abitur at the end of Gymnasium to qualify for admission to a university. The Abitur consists of a written test in two main subjects and one optional subject. There is also an oral exam in one optional subject. Required subjects to be tested include German, a modern foreign language, and either mathematics or a natural science.

Danish students must successfully pass a combination of ten written and oral tests during their final two years at the Gymnasium. Students must score satisfactorily on these tests, collectively known as the Studentereksamen, before being considered for admission to a university. Both Germany and Denmark now have more students meeting the Abitur and Studentereksamen requirements than there are places available at the universities. This has created an intense competition among students to receive the higher scores on these university admission tests.

Canada and the United States essentially offer an open admissions policy to higher education. Both countries provide a multitude of two-year community colleges and a variety of private colleges that accommodate even poorly prepared high school graduates. Although most U.S. colleges require students to submit scores on the SAT (Scholastic Aptitude Tests) or the ACT (American College Testing Program Assessment), only the more selective private and public universities use these scores as meaningful screening devices. A telling statistic on the extent to which many American students are ill-prepared to enter college is the astounding fact that fewer than half of the students who enter a bachelor's degree program directly after high school earn a degree within a six-year period. Significantly fewer college-bound seniors earn a bachelor's degree within the traditional four-year period. [9]

The ease of entry into American higher education, as well as the lack of generally accepted entrance examinations, conspires to lull the typical teenager into a state of complacency regarding his or her level of academic achievement. There is simply little external motivation for a student to attempt to excel academically. Also, academic credentials are more directly related to financial and social status in countries such as England, Germany, and Denmark than they are in the United States. Americans, both students and their parents, do not perceive academic excellence as critical to their future success and security.

In most countries studied, students pursuing vocational and technical paths also experience greater pressure to succeed academically than do their American counterparts. German vocational students must participate in challenging apprenticeship programs consisting of both a school and industry component. These students must pass a standard test of knowledge in their chosen trade or technical field before being formally admitted to practice that occupation. Similarly high performance standards are set for vocational programs in Denmark and Japan. In these three countries, students maintain some formal contact with the schools until age eighteen.

Vocational training programs are less well developed in England than in the previously mentioned countries, where a significant number of English students continue to leave school at age sixteen to enter directly into the work force. Although the percentage of sixteen- to eighteen-year-old English students participating in vocational training has risen rapidly in the past decade, there is still a strong tradition in England for students to enter the work force at age sixteen.[10]

Canada and the United States retain a large proportion of their student body until high school graduation at age eighteen. Vocational and technical training for noncollege-bound students is more loosely structured than in Germany, Denmark, and Japan. However, a large number of students graduate from high school with neither a rigorous academic education nor a strong vocational background. Many of these students have received a very meager general education and are equipped to perform only menial or semi-skilled jobs.

Average students in American high schools are not challenged by the academic requirements, nor are they motivated by specific standards to be achieved in connection with preparation for defined vocational or technical career goals. Most such students have little more than a generalized desire to achieve the meager standards necessary to be granted a high school diploma.

Student discipline is a perennial topic of intense interest to American educators. This matter is of some interest to the foreign teachers involved in the Fulbright Exchange Program, but does not appear to be a high-priority concern to them. Elementary classrooms in all countries tend to be somewhat noisy and filled with youthful activity and enthusiasm. Teachers interviewed for this survey report that classes in Denmark, England, and even Japan might seem excessively noisy by American standards. Teachers from other countries in the study reported relatively few serious disciplinary problems at their home schools. There were some indications that the German Hauptschulen, schooling the least academically able German middle school children, may have some problems with discipline. References to discipline problems in immigrant areas of both England and Germany were also cited by teachers from these countries. There were no reports, however, of entire schools out of control because of excessively rowdy or even criminally motivated students, as is true in too many American schools.

Foreign students are not as closely supervised by adults as are American high school and middle school students. Foreign teachers were generally unfamiliar with hall and bus supervision, cafeteria and study hall supervision, or the need to provide students with lavatory passes to visit the restroom. The American penchant for litigation has imbued the American teacher and administrator with an obsessive need to know where every student is at every moment. We attempt to guarantee that every student is being supervised continuously by an adult, who is exercising due diligence to protect the student's health and safety. This mentality simply does not exist in the other countries surveyed for this study.

Foreign schools consciously build short breaks, and other opportunities for students to move about the school, into the fabric of the school day. A more balanced attitude toward supervising students also lends a less institutional tone to the school, allowing students and staff to interact in a more relaxed manner. The foreign practice of students working together as a single group for much of the school day also builds group cohesiveness, lessening the chances of disruptions among and between students.

Teachers in foreign schools are more likely to instruct the same groups of students for several years, thus promoting a long-term teacher-student relationship. All these factors help create a school climate that fosters mutual respect and understanding among both students and staff. Such long-term relationships can seldom form in the more atomized and individualistic school-life experiences of both American teachers and American students. More attention to the details of daily school life in the United States, compared to common practices in other countries, may well reveal approaches that could decrease the level of student discipline problems in American schools (see summary in Table 8.5).

PRINCIPALS AND HEAD TEACHERS

Schools in each country surveyed are led by managers and administrators known as either principals or head teachers. In the European model of governance these leaders are known as head teachers and, as the name implies, they are considered to be a part of the teaching profession. The term, principal, carrying a more managerial connotation, is used in the school systems of the United States, Canada, and Japan. The use of this term in Japan is a carryover from the American occupation period, although the actual role of the Japanese school principal more closely follows the European head teacher model.

The most direct managerial and supervisory role of the principal in relation to teachers is found in the United States. American principals do not belong to the same professional organizations as teachers, are considered management rather than labor in states that have collective bargaining for teachers, and generally exercise direct supervision and evaluation authority over their teachers. American principals are far more likely to formally evaluate the work of their teachers than are administrators from any other nation surveyed.

The role distinctions between principals and teachers in the American

Table 8.5 *Student Dimension.*

	Canada	Denmark	England	Germany	Japan	U.S.A.
Starting age for students in publicly funded schools	Kindergarten at age five in many provinces, first grade at age six in others.	Kindergarten privately funded. First grade at age seven.	Kindergarten at age five, first grade at age six.	Kindergarten privately funded. Compulsory first grade at age six.	Kindergarten privately funded. Compulsory first grade at age six.	Kindergarten at age five, required first grade at age six.
Daily hours of attendance for primary school students	Five- to six-hour school day	Three- to four-hour school day. Students leave school by lunchtime or early afternoon.	Five- to six-hour school day	School day of four to five hours. Students leave school by lunchtime or early afternoon.	Four hours per day for first grade. Six hours per day after third grade.	Five to six hours each day
Length of school year	190 – 200 days depending on province. No Saturday classes.	200 days. No Saturday classes.	190 days. No Saturday classes.	Varies from 195 – 226 days. Some states schedule half-day Saturday sessions.	240-day school year, including 40 half-day Saturday classes.	180-day school year, no Saturday classes.
Scheduling of vacation periods	Twelve-week summer vacation. Other holiday periods similar to United States.	Six-week summer vacation, two weeks at Christmas and Easter, one week each in middle of fall and spring terms.	Similar to Denmark	Similar to Denmark	Six weeks in summer with other one- to two-week vacation periods scheduled during the school year.	Twelve-week summer vacation with one to two weeks scheduled at Christmas and Easter.

Table 8.5 (continued).

	Canada	Denmark	England	Germany	Japan	U.S.A.
Homework requirements	Minimal requirements at elementary level, usually one hour or less at secondary level, more for high achievers.	Thirty to sixty minutes per night in early grades, one to two hours in upper elementary grades. Several hours at secondary. level.	Minimal requirements at elementary level, usually one hour or less at secondary level, more for high achievers.	Thirty to sixty minutes per night in early grades, one to two hours in upper elementary grades. Several hours at secondary level.	Thirty to sixty minutes per night in early grades, one to two hours in upper elementary grades. Several hours at secondary level.	Minimal requirements at elementary level, usually one hour or less at secondary level, more for high achievers.
Student employment patterns	Many students have part-time jobs. Number of hours of work each week tends to be moderate.	Some students hold part-time jobs, although this is not as common as in the United States.	Relatively few English students hold part-time jobs.	Few students hold part-time jobs in Germany.	Japanese students seldom, if ever, hold part-time jobs.	More than one-third of U.S.A. teenagers have part-time jobs. Many work twenty to thirty hours each week.
Minimum age to receive a driver's license	Sixteen in most provinces, fifteen in some	Eighteen years of age	Eighteen years of age	Eighteen years of age	Eighteen years of age	Sixteen years of age
Degree of romantic attachments, sexual activity, teenage pregnancy, etc.	Similar to situation in the U.S.A., although perhaps to a lesser extent.	Rates of teenage sexual activity and births to unmarried mothers are very high.	Similar to situation in the U.S.A. Births to unmarried mothers approaches high U.S.A. rate.	Emphasis on group activities. Lower sexual involvement by teenagers, low rate of births to unmarried mothers.	Intense romantic attachments among Japanese adolescents are rare.	High rates of teenage sexual activity with attendant complications such as disease, pregnancy, abortion, single mothers and fatherless children.

school hierarchy are further emphasized by the specialized training that American administrators receive as a prerequisite for administrative positions. School administration in the United States is viewed as a separate profession from teaching, a distinction that is not made elsewhere. While school administrators in other countries typically carry at least a small teaching schedule, it is unusual for American principals or assistant principals to teach classes on a regular basis.

Canada also has formal graduate-level administrative training programs for future principals. Other countries in the survey rely on inservice workshops or on-the-job training to transmit administrative skills to new administrators. New school administrators are chosen from among the ranks of successful teachers in all nations studied. Japanese principals typically have about twenty-five years of teaching experience before being appointed as a principal. Fifteen years of teaching experience are required before being appointed as a head teacher in England.

American principals appear to have the most frenetic worklife of the school administrators from the six nations surveyed. They usually have a much heavier work load in student discipline, are more directly involved in the supervision and evaluation of teachers, and, at the secondary level, have far more responsibilities in the areas of athletics and other extracurricular activities. The politicized nature of many local school districts in the United States creates a special burden for American principals in dealing effectively with superintendents, school board members, influential parents, and others in the community.

The American concerns with student rights and due process have complicated the role of the principal in recent decades. A significant portion of administrative time is consumed in investigating complaints and grievances by teachers, students, and parents. Disciplinary and academic decisions which in other countries are seen as the clear prerogatives of teachers and principals, must be debated, defended, and justified by the American administrator. The ready access of a local superintendent and school board provides disgruntled parents and students with an appeal mechanism that further consumes the energies of the harried administrator.

In most of the foreign countries surveyed, the principal or head teacher, is viewed as the local representative of the regional or national educational system. He or she is appointed by the regional authorities and is charged with the responsibility to monitor the implementation of national curriculum and other educational regulations at the local school level.

School administrators in all countries surveyed administer certain school functions in a similar manner. In every country surveyed, administrators are responsible for devising the daily school schedule for students and teachers, and in all cases they rely heavily on teacher input before constructing the schedule. Administrators universally involve teachers in decisions regarding allocations of instructional budgets within the school.

The fact that administrators in other countries do not formally observe and evaluate their teachers helps to maintain a collegial relationship between teachers and administrators in these countries. American principals attempt to establish this same type of collegial relationship, although formal evaluations of teachers and role expectations for the principal by school boards and parents tend to hamper collegial working relationships in the United States. Administrators in all countries surveyed seem to have only a peripheral involvement in questions of curriculum, instruction, and textbook selection. These matters are either mandated from above, or are considered to be the prerogative of the classroom teacher.

Administrators in other cultures have a narrower range of duties and tasks than do American principals. Foreign administrators have a lighter work schedule with far less involvement in student discipline and control issues. American principals have significantly more responsibilities for after-school and evening activities than their colleagues in Germany, Denmark, and Japan, and somewhat fewer obligations in these areas than administrators in England and Canada.

Administrators in other countries work a slightly longer school day and school year than the typical teacher. The extensions of the day and the year appear to be far more significant for American principals, however, than for administrators from the other countries. Other nations make no provision for merit pay for administrators, and in some instances administrative pay is tied directly to the teacher pay scale. Other nations seem to view administrators as local managers of a national enterprise, whose role is to monitor and enforce educational regulations at the school level.

The American concept of the principal as an instructional leader, often preached but seldom seen, does not appear to be an expectation of administrators in the other survey countries. The instructional supervisory activities that American principals are expected to carry out through classroom observations and teacher evaluations are, in the other countries, the province of regional or national subject and instructional specialists who periodically visit teachers in the schools.

The recent changes in the English school system may cause a major role change for the English head teacher. Parental choice, local budgets, and more powerful school boards may modify the role of the English head teacher to a model closely resembling that of the American principal. The role of school administrators in the other countries surveyed will likely remain unchanged for the foreseeable future. The more centralized control of education in the other nations leads to a more bureaucratic role for school administrators than in the United States, where a greater number of policy decisions are made at the local level.

By international standards, American school administrators must fulfill role expectations that are both broader and more complex than those of their counterparts in other nations. The much-maligned American school administrators may be receiving unfair criticism for their inability to perform to everyone's satisfaction in an exceedingly complex and difficult job.

CURRICULUM AND NATIONAL TESTING ACROSS CULTURES

A significant distinction between American educators and those of all other countries surveyed concerns the American distaste for centralized curriculum mandates and planning. The mantra of local control is invoked by American teachers, administrators, and school board members in response to suggestions that curriculum should be determined at the national or even state level. Even within local school districts, classroom teachers consider a formal written local curriculum to be a mixed blessing at best.

States that do attempt to impose strict curriculum standards typically face bitter opposition from teacher unions, administrative groups, and state school board associations. In those rare instances where meaningful curriculum regulations are enacted, they are often undermined or even ignored at the local level. Few states have sufficient staff available at the state department of education to monitor effectively the implementation of curriculum regulations. Individual states are in the peculiar position of mandating that students attend school for 1,000 hours per year for thirteen years, and yet they are expected to show little interest in what actually occurs during those 13,000 hours.

Our society's cavalier attitude toward the daily activities of more than forty million students and several million teachers precludes the idea of setting educational standards and measuring achievement levels of either students or schools. Such measures as do exist, chiefly standardized achievement tests, provide relative achievement data only, are voluntary on the part of individual school districts, and are subject to manipulation by the test preparation companies and the school districts. State-mandated student achievement assessments have been implemented in many states, but their effects have been mixed at best. The one measure that the popular culture does cite, SAT scores, is a poor vehicle for evaluating the effectiveness of the schools.

Every other nation in this survey seriously addresses the issues of overall educational assessment and individual student achievement. The need for such assessments is accepted as obvious by foreign educators and laymen alike. Canada's educational system is the most similar to that of the United States, with a long tradition of provincial governance and local control by school boards and superintendents. Even there, however, most provinces have strong curriculum regulations that are monitored at the local level by provincial curriculum and subject specialists who visit schools on a regular basis. Canadian teachers accept the provincial curricula as binding upon them and make a conscientious effort to faithfully implement the curriculum in their daily lessons. [11]

Curriculum development in Germany occurs in each of the sixteen German states. Close coordination in curriculum matters among these states is achieved through a Standing Conference of the Ministers of Education of the Bundeslander (KMK). This coordination over the years has promoted uniform standards throughout Germany with respect to teaching content and final qualifications for various careers and occupations. The broad goals and guidelines established by this and other federal bodies provides the framework for more specific curriculum standards and objectives produced by the Ministry of Education and Culture in each German state. German Fulbright teachers interviewed for this book were very comfortable with the idea that they should faithfully teach the curriculum established by their particular state. [12]

Denmark, since it is a small nation, has little difficulty in maintaining a national curriculum for its schools. There are broad national curriculum goals that must be followed, as well as more specific curriculum guidelines for each course that are voluntary in nature. Most local school governing bodies adopt these voluntary curriculum guidelines for their schools. The national government enforces regulations regarding maximum class sizes (twenty-eight) and the specific courses to be taught at each grade level. Since virtually all classes are of mixed-ability groups, these national regulations ensure that every Danish student has a virtually identical educational experience up to at least age fourteen.

Japan, with a population of 124 million, exercises a national control over curriculum that equals, if not surpasses, that found in Denmark. The Japanese Ministry of Education publishes curriculum guides for every subject, including time allocations for each course. Educational officials from the forty-seven prefectures are directly responsible for monitoring the curriculum for the upper secondary schools and closely collaborate with municipal officials to monitor the curriculum in elementary and junior high schools. Local school officials must select textbooks from an approved list authorized by the Ministry of Education.

This strict centralized control over the curriculum, the time allocations for each subject, textbook selection, teaching certification requirements, and equity in educational financing, provide an equality of educational opportunity that America has not remotely approached. The fact that more than 97 percent of Japanese students attend public school through grade nine, in mixed-ability class groups, provides an educational experience for Japanese students that is both universal and of high quality.

In recent years, England has been moving rapidly toward the level of national control of curriculum found in Japan and Denmark. This radical departure from the previous laissez-faire approach to curriculum is a measure of the extent of public dissatisfaction with the English educational system. The Education Act of 1988 requires that a national curriculum be developed in ten subject areas. Time allocations for topics within the curricula are also to be part of the curriculum guidelines. Teachers in England are disenchanted with the reality that they have largely been excluded from the curriculum development process, and yet there is a consensus that more standardized curriculum regulations are a positive development. The English perceive the national curriculum as a means to provide true educational entitlement—the concept that every student in England should have the same educational opportunity.

Americans appear to have a unique concern about establishing national curriculum standards. Our traditions of local school governance and distrust of big government have trapped us in a time warp with respect to educational governance. Other nations have met the challenges of global competition by raising educational practice and policy to the level of a national concern and responsibility. In the United States, the daily substance of schooling is too often determined by the political whims of whatever group of local citizens can exert the greatest political pressure on the local school board. This provincialism usually blinds people to the educational needs of students in the same county, much less in the nation as a whole.

Closely linked to the question of a national or regional curriculum is the issue of external examination of student achievement. Here again the United States, and Canada to a lesser extent, deviate markedly from the practice in other survey countries. England is currently moving toward a national student assessment program in conjunction with the newly formulated curriculum standards.

Beginning in 1991, English schools were required to administer assessment tests to all students ages seven, eleven, fourteen, and sixteen. These tests are given in the ten subjects required in the national curriculum. The assessments are expected to allow students to demonstrate their knowledge through practical demonstrations, portfolios, and essay questions. There is a determination in England to avoid the short answer, multiple-choice assessment characteristics of American standardized tests. A second purpose for the testing is to provide parents with comparative achievement data, by school, to assist them in choosing a school for their students. By 1994 virtually all English students will be required to take the General Certificate of Secondary Education (GCSE) exam in the areas of English, mathematics, and science. These sixteen-year-old students will also be assessed in technology, a modern foreign language, and either history or geography.

Students in Germany must pass a series of tests known as the Abitur to qualify for admission to a university. Each German state administers its own abitur program, although requirements are closely coordinated by agreements among the sixteen states. Currently about 30 percent of an age cohort is enrolled in the upper years of a Gymnasium to prepare for these tests. Vocational students in Germany must pass one of the 400 or more qualifying tests designated for the major technical and vocational occupations available to German students. Even students leaving full-time schooling from the Hauptschule at the end of ninth grade typically earn a school leaving certificate, based on test results. The close cooperation between German schools and apprenticeship programs operated by private industry ensure that students are held to performance standards suitable for a given occupation.

The external examination system in Denmark is similar to that of Germany. Here students take a series of tests known as the Studentereksamen to qualify for admission to a university. The lack of sufficient places at the universities to meet the demand from qualified applicants has led to a competition for higher grades on these tests among Danish youth. Although this developing competitive element is viewed with concern by Danish educators, the competition does serve as a motivator to higher student performance. All Danish Gymnasium students must also prepare a major written report, known as the *Danskopgaven,* as one of their graduation requirements.

About 35 to 40 percent of Danish secondary school students attend the academic Gymnasium during their final years of school.[13] Most of the remaining students participate in part-time schooling and vocational training programs for one or more years after completing tenth grade at the Folkeskole. As in Germany, these apprenticeship programs are coordinated with Danish industry and are characterized by high standards for student performance. Vocational students who later wish to re-enter an academic education program may pursue higher preparation examination courses. Somewhat older students attend these two-year programs. They include rigorous academic work and the same final examinations and major written paper required of Gymnasium students. These programs offer a second chance and a second avenue for gaining admission to the university.

The competitive examination system in Japan begins with the process of applying for high school admission as a ninth grade student. Since high school is not compulsory in Japan, students must apply for admission to a suitable high school in their geographic region. Competitive examinations are given by the high schools as a means of selecting students. The most prestigious academic high schools can boast of a high-caliber student body and a high admission rate to the elite universities. Virtually all students at middle school age begin attending supplemental juku schools to help prepare them to succeed on the high school admission examinations.

This same competitive examination system applies, with even more intensity, when high school students apply for admission to a university. The elite public universities feature very restrictive admission standards and very low tuition, relative to private universities. Japanese high school seniors take a general achievement exam early in January. Scores on this test help students determine which universities are likely to accept them, and therefore which universities they should apply to for the second round of testing in early spring. Each college and university administers its own admissions test, which varies in difficulty according to the exclusiveness and academic rigor of the university.

This "examination hell" is much criticized in the West and among the Japanese people themselves. The system does, however, produce an overall high level of student achievement in Japanese schools. About 70 percent of Japanese students attend academic high schools that provide the rigorous curriculum necessary to prepare students for the college entrance examinations. It bears repeating that more than 90 percent of Japanese students complete high school in an educational environment where even the vocational school students devote half their time to academic subjects. Over 30 percent of Japanese students attend some form of higher education.

College admission in Canada, until recent times, was determined largely by student performance on school leaving examinations. These examinations have been discontinued so that college admission is now determined by high school grades and aptitude tests, the same criteria used throughout the United States. Canada, like the United States, has the capacity to absorb virtually all applicants to college, and therefore the competitive pressures for college admission found in other countries are largely absent. As in America, university admission is highly competitive in only a few schools. Canadian high school students can approach their college years with the same nonchalance and complacency found in their American cousins. The proportion of students attending college in Canada closely parallels that of the United States.

Several Canadian provinces are moving away from the American model of relying solely on high school grades and aptitude tests as measures of student achievement and suitability for college-level work. Various types of school leaving examinations and mandatory student assessments have been reintroduced in provinces such as Manitoba, Saskatchewan, and Ontario. These moves toward student assessment measures reflect an increasing concern in Canada regarding educational quality.

The same reservations about a national curriculum in the United States apply to the issue of national student assessments and school leaving examinations. For twenty years the National Assessment of Educational Progress has been taking very tentative steps toward providing national achievement data and establishing standards for student performance. Only the confidential and anonymous nature of this data has made it politically possible to make even this modest attempt to gather national student performance data. The sorry state of academic performance of American students that is revealed by this data ensures that more comprehensive assessments will be vehemently opposed.

A similar lack of enthusiasm applies with respect to formulating national goals and standards for student achievement. The six goals for the year 2000, established in 1990 at a national governors' conference, are far too general to provide guidance and direction to America's educational effort. Even these modest first steps are of interest primarily to policymakers and academics, and have not penetrated the consciousness of the average American citizen, or even the typical American teacher. While citizens are dissatisfied with public schools in general, they continue to be satisfied with the schools in their own community. In a nation with a very parochial view of education, there is insufficient public concern to insist on accountability either for individual students or the educational system as a whole. A summary of curriculum and instruction practices in the six survey nations is shown in Table 8.6.

SCHOOL LIFE ACROSS SIX CULTURES

In previous chapters we have seen snapshots of classroom life from the perspectives of both teachers and students. In this chapter, comparisons are made regarding instructional strategies and techniques that seem to characterize schools in the nations surveyed. Since we will be comparing daily school activities in several million classrooms, there will be countless exceptions to the generalizations that will be offered.

A striking difference between American schools and others is that the mission of foreign schools is more focused on the development of academic knowledge and skills. A consensus exists in other cultures that there is a definite body of knowledge and skills that students should learn, that such knowledge and skills are easily identifiable, and that students should be held accountable for learning them. Such attitudes among educators abroad explain the ready acceptance of national curricula and external testing programs in other advanced industrial nations. The absence of such a consensus in America makes such ideas highly controversial in this country.

Many American teachers see their principal mission as meeting the social and emotional needs of their students, rather than their intellectual needs. Others concentrate student energies on developing learning processes rather than on accumulating and manipulating concrete knowledge and skills. Only a minority of teachers would define their mission as the transmission of our cultural and intellectual heritage to the next generation. Schools of education often indoctrinate their future teachers in the necessity for a child-centered curriculum, one in which

Table 8.6 *Curriculum and Instruction.*

	Canada	Denmark	England	Germany	Japan	U.S.A.
Procedure to establish school curriculum	Detailed curriculum set by province and implemented by local schools.	Broad goals and detailed objectives set by national government.	New education law requires nationwide curriculum for first time.	Broad educational goals set at federal level. Each state develops detailed curricula to be used by schools.	Detailed educational goals and curricula set at national level for use in all schools in Japan.	Some states provide detailed curricula while most issue broad education goals. Districts generally have major role in developing curricula.
Student assessment practices at various governmental levels	Most provinces require student assessment tests at several grade levels.	National standardized assessments are not required.	New law requires assessment of all students at three grade levels.	National standardized assessments are not required.	National standardized assessments are not required.	Many states require assessment of all students at several grade levels. There are no national requirements.

(continued)

Table 8.6 (continued).

	Canada	Denmark	England	Germany	Japan	U.S.A.
School leaving exams and/or qualifying exams for higher levels of schooling	A few provinces require exams to graduate from high school. There are no formal entrance exams for college.	Applicants to a university must pass a series of ten oral and written exams known as the Studenterek-samen to apply for limited places at a university.	Students must take the general certificate of education advanced level in two or three subjects to enter a university.	University applicants must pass the Abitur which consists of two main subjects and one optional area to qualify for limited university places.	Japanese students must perform well in entrance exams for highly selective schools at both the high school and university levels.	There are no national exams for college admission, other than the SAT, which is an aptitude test. A high school diploma will ensure admission to most colleges.
Average class sizes	Twenty to thirty students per class	Fifteen to twenty students per class	Twenty to thirty students per class	Twenty to thirty students per class	Forty students per class	Twenty to thirty students per class
Grouping for instruction	Mixed-ability groups are the norm until student reaches about tenth grade.	Mixed-ability groups are the norm until ninth or tenth year of the Folkeskole. Assignment to secondary schools is by academic achievement.	Mixed-ability grouping through six years of elementary school. Grouping both by school and within a school begins with first form (seventh grade).	Mixed-ability grouping through first six years of schooling. Students then divided into one of three school types according to achievement and ability.	Mixed-ability grouping throughout nine years of compulsory schooling. High school assignment is determined by results of entrance exams.	Grouping in American schools usually begins, for some subjects, in the middle elementary grades. Academic tracking is the norm by seventh or eighth grade.

Table 8.6 (*continued*).

	Canada	Denmark	England	Germany	Japan	U.S.A.
Textbook selection	Textbooks are selected at the individual school or district level.	Textbooks are used sparingly in Denmark, but are selected by the individual schools when needed.	Textbooks in England must be selected from the approved list that is developed at the national level.	Textbooks are used sparingly in Germany, but may be selected at the individual school level from a state-approved list.	Textbooks must be selected from those included on the nationally approved list.	Some states have an approved textbook list from which individual schools must choose. Generally, textbook selection is a local option in the U.S.A.

"it is the teacher's job to interest the students, not the students' responsibility to buckle down and learn."[14]

The concern of American educators for student self-esteem, socialization, and motivation is based on the grim social realities facing many American children in the 1990s. Schools in other countries can concern themselves less with these issues because the general society in these countries appears to be more responsive to the emotional, physical, and material needs of children than is American society. This distinction becomes painfully obvious when comparing social and cultural supports for children in other nations with the situation in the United States.

While perhaps understandable, this American preoccupation with the emotional health of students breeds indifference to, and sometimes hostility toward, academic excellence by students. When one considers that American colleges largely follow an open admissions policy, and that future teachers are among the weakest students academically at these colleges, it is not surprising that rigorous intellectual development is not a priority in most American schools and classrooms.

Teachers in Japan, Denmark, Germany, and England are the product of rigorous academic programs at the secondary school level, and have met strict academic standards for admission to a university to pursue training as a teacher. These teachers accord primacy to the academic mission of their schools and willingly follow a rigorous national or regional curriculum. They expect and accept that their students will participate in various formal assessments, school leaving exams, and university qualifying exams based on these curricula.

Fulbright Exchange teachers marvel at the number of interruptions to classroom instructional time tolerated in American schools. PA system announcements, student messengers from the office, students entering and leaving regular classes for special education, gifted, or remedial classes, and shortened class periods to accommodate sports and other assemblies—each contribute to a sense that concentrated academic work is not the priority in American schools.

The notion that an American teacher can prepare three to five intellectually challenging and instructionally appropriate lessons each day, with perhaps ten to fifteen minutes to prepare each lesson, is patently absurd. Such minimal time in a teacher's schedule for planning virtually ensures that a typical lesson will be both slipshod in construction and superficial in content. The minimal amount of homework assigned to the average American student guarantees that he or she will neither reflect on today's lessons nor be prepared for tomorrow's lessons.

Teachers in Japan, Denmark, and Germany have much lighter teaching schedules than American teachers, and much more time available for individual or group planning. The Japanese utilize this group planning opportunity to refine their lessons and to devise new methods and techniques to improve their teaching. Students in these cultures are assigned more homework than American students and experience fewer distractions from the general culture. Thus both teachers and students in these nations are better able to maximize academic learning in the classroom situation.

Average class sizes in each country surveyed, except Japan, were between twenty and thirty students. Schools in Denmark, however, operate many classes averaging only fifteen to twenty students. Japanese class sections typically have about forty students. This number is acceptable in Japan because there is no expectation that the teacher will provide individualized instruction to students. It is the student's responsibility to keep abreast of his or her class work.

The concern among American teachers about classroom discipline problems may be partially explained by the organization and pace of the school day in American schools. Most other countries in the survey have a somewhat shorter school day, particularly at the primary school level. Other nations have longer lunch periods for their students and teachers than are common in America. In Germany and Denmark both teachers and students may return home for lunch by about 1:00 P.M., when their scheduled school day is completed.

Foreign schools normally schedule fifteen- to twenty-minute school-wide breaks in mid-morning. Some schools also allow ten to fifteen minutes between each class, providing students with a short break from the academic routine. The class interruptions in American schools, and the more frequent classroom student misbehavior, may simply reflect coping mechanisms for dealing with a school schedule that requires too many consecutive hours of sitting in a classroom. Foreign schools have more school days each year than America does. These school days are generally shorter, however, with more short breaks each day in the academic routine.

The United States has fewer, but longer and more intense school days than the other countries surveyed. Actual academic instruction time in all of the countries surveyed is remarkably similar. Other countries tend to pace their school day in a more humane manner, thus improving the learning environment by reducing student fatigue, boredom, and restlessness. The comparative data on this issue indicates that exposing

American students to more of the same kind of school days that they now experience would exacerbate rather than resolve our educational problems.

Elementary school classrooms in the foreign countries surveyed seem more likely to emphasize project work and other group activities than do American elementary classrooms. This emphasis on group work is particularly pronounced in England and Japan. The noise and activity levels in these classrooms are greater than in a typical American elementary class. Elementary classes abroad are heterogeneously grouped, with little concern for formal written evaluation of student performance in the early elementary years. Even in Japan and Germany there is little evidence of academic pressure being exerted on elementary school children.

American elementary classes are more dependent on textbooks and worksheets than are schools in most other countries. Individual American students spend much time alone at their desks filling out worksheets for math and reading, and practicing their writing skills. Formal grades are often assigned to students in the early elementary years. Ability-grouped classes in reading and math often begin as early as third or fourth grade. American children as young as six or seven are often required to take district- or state-mandated student achievement tests.

The secondary school experience for American students also differs from that of their foreign counterparts. Secondary schools in other countries tend to schedule the same group of students together for most of the school day, and even for several school years. Teachers frequently instruct the same groups of students over a period of several years. The external exam system provides students and their teachers with a common focus for their joint efforts. A level of camaraderie often develops among students in foreign schools that is not possible in the typical American high school.

American high school students each have an individual computer-generated schedule. They have different classmates for each class of the day. They typically will have a given teacher for only one subject for only one year. The student usually has only three or four minutes to move from one class to the next class in a new location, with different classmates, and a different teacher. The student will have no sense of group identity and thus will be isolated in his or her academic pursuits.

Fulbright Exchange teachers often speak of the passivity of American students. Such an attitude may be expected in an environment where each subject is disconnected from others, where there is no sense of group cohesion or purpose, and where the instruction is often uninspired due to a lack of sufficient preparation by either the teacher or the students. American students, unlike their foreign counterparts, do not see a direct relationship between academic achievement and future social and financial security. Their attention is not directed toward mastery of academic content in preparation for external examinations. Finally, school is not the center of their lives in a teenage subculture featuring access to automobiles, part-time jobs, early romantic attachments, and the distractions of the mass media.

Student attitudes toward their teachers may be affected by the manner in which student achievement is measured in different cultures. American schools, lacking stringent curricula and external achievement testing, rely almost exclusively on the classroom teacher to determine the level of student performance. In this environment the student may view the teacher as his or her adversary, and even an obstacle to future plans. Simultaneously, subtle political pressures on teachers may incline them to dilute academic standards rather than confront irate parents, students, or school officials.

A different dynamic operates in a nation that has a required curriculum with a stringent external exam system to measure student achievement. In this environment, the student is not as likely to perceive teacher classroom requirements as unreasonable. The parent cannot complain that the teacher should give an easier exam or grade more liberally. Instead of viewing the teacher as an adversary, the teacher is seen as a coach, mentor, and guide. The teacher and the members of the class are engaged in a joint enterprise to prepare the students to take the external examination. Both teachers and students have a fixed goal to achieve that will be measured by an outside objective standard. Such an educational setting promotes a relationship between students and teacher based on respect and common purpose.

Other nations appear to place a greater personal burden of responsibility on their secondary students for their success or failure than we do in America. It is the student who must meet the standard in foreign countries. Responsibility for failure is primarily placed on the students, and only secondarily on the teacher. In the United States the failure of the student is usually blamed on the teacher. Common complaints against American teachers are that their tests are too hard, they didn't teach the material correctly, or they are insensitive or unkind to the student. The all-too-common scandal of school officials falsifying student achievement results on district or state standardized tests attests to the fact that poor student performance will be seen as a reflection on the teachers, not the students.[15]

REFERENCES

1. Roffel, J. A. and L. R. Groff. 1990. "Shedding Light on the Dark Side of Teacher Moonlighting," *Educational Evaluation and Policy Analysis,* 12(3):405.
2. Murname, R. J., J. D. Singer, J. B. Willett, J. J. Kample, and R. J. Olsen. 1991. *Who Will Teach?* Cambridge, MA: Harvard University Press, pp. 35–36.
3. National Center for Education Statistics. 1991. *Digest of Education Statistics 1990.* Washington, DC: U.S. Government Printing Office, p. 79.
4. Poppleton, P. 1990. "The Survey Data," *Comparative Education,* 26(2/3):187.
5. Archer, E. G. and B. T. Peck. 1992. *The Teaching Profession in Europe.* Glasgow: Jordanhill College of Education, pp. 83, 109, 354.
6. Nelson, F. H. 1991. *International Comparisons of Public Spending on Education.* Washington, DC: American Federation of Teachers, p. 37.
7. Barro, S. M. and L. Suter. 1988. *International Comparisons of Teachers' Salaries: An Exploratory Study.* Washington, DC: National Center for Educational Studies, pp. 24–25.
8. Nelson, F. H., p. 37.
9. National Center for Education Statistics, pp. 280–281.
10. 1992. *The London Times Education Supplement* (May 29):12.
11. McKinnon, D., F. Graham, and B. Davis. Interviews with author, February 1992.
12. Koelling, U., D. Pohl, and S. Riel-Kermann. Interviews with author, October 1991.
13. Ministry of Education, Denmark. 1988. *The Folkeskole.* Copenhagen: Ministry of Education, p. 9.
14. Leo, J. 1992. "The Sorry Teaching of Teachers," *U.S. News and World Report* (April 27):28.
15. 1992. "Schools for Scandal," *U.S. News and World Report* (April 27):67–72.

CHAPTER 9

Cultural and Societal Influences on the Schools

IN THE LAST chapter we compared the daily operation of the schools and the school lives of students and staff members in the six survey nations. In this chapter we will compare elements in the culture, government, and social structure of each nation that, although external to the schools themselves, exert a powerful influence on school quality and student achievement.

EQUALITY OF EDUCATIONAL OPPORTUNITY

The aspect of American schooling most emulated abroad is the American *ideal* that free, publicly supported, equal educational opportunities should be available to all, regardless of wealth, social class, race, religion, or gender. The United States was the nation that most closely approximated this ideal by the end of the Second World War. Ironically, as the other survey nations consciously attempted to match the American commitment to educational equality, American school students, primarily as a result of residential patterns, were themselves being educated in a system that was becoming less equal and less equitable.

We have seen that Canadian provinces have sought to provide equal educational opportunities to all students and have, in large measure, succeeded in this effort. Japan, adopting a model imposed by the American occupation forces after World War II, now provides universal, free public education, with a standard curriculum and course time allotments, to over 97 percent of students in grades one through nine. Acceptance at more desirable secondary schools and universities in Japan is based almost solely on achievement, rather than the wealth of the parents or the particular elementary or middle school that the child attends.

Denmark and Germany have long provided a quality education for their academic elite. Their vocational programs, although world renowned for their effectiveness, are often criticized for assigning students to nonacademic tracks at too early an age. Both countries have taken effective steps to allow students to make career decisions at a later age, and to pursue alternative routes to later entrance to higher education institutions as young adults. Parents now play a greater role in both countries in determining the academic tracks their children will pursue. Danish and German students are assured equal educational opportunities through effective national or regional systems that provide equal financial resources, through almost total mixed-ability grouping at least until the middle school years, and through a standard curriculum throughout Denmark and in each of the German states.

The ideal of educational equity is farthest from realization in England. Here residential patterns, as well as the continuing influence of social class, combine to retard the progress that has occurred elsewhere. The radical educational reforms currently under way in England are designed to move England rapidly in the direction of educational equity. The new national curriculum and student assessment programs address the English concept of *entitlement,* a commitment to the idea that every student in England will have a common school experience within the limits of governmental policy.

In summary, the five other countries in this survey have made and are making continuing strides toward creating democratic, meritocratic, and equitable educational systems. The United States, meanwhile, is moving rapidly in the opposite direction.

SCHOOL FINANCING AND EDUCATIONAL EQUITY

A major cause of the widening gulf in educational opportunities available to American students is our system of school financing. No other country surveyed allows such a degree of disparity in resources to exist among schools as is found in the United States. Denmark, Japan, and England have national systems of education that provide a mechanism for infusing schools in poorer parts of the country with funds collected from more affluent areas. Japan provides 50 percent of school funding at the national level, 25 percent at the prefectural level, and 25 percent from local sources.

English schools receive about 80 percent of their funding from national sources and 20 percent from local sources. In Denmark, local government finances relatively inexpensive aspects of education such as teaching materials, supplies, equipment, and facilities. The major portion of educational costs, relating to teacher and other staff salaries, is supported at the national level. Each of these three countries totally supports teacher salaries from either regional or national funds, thus eliminating the need to make teacher salaries a matter of controversy when local tax rates are set.

Canada, Germany, and the United States are governed through a federal system in which major responsibilities for the schools reside with the Länder in Germany, the provinces in Canada, and the states in America. By the 1980s the Canadian federal government was providing 9 percent of educational funding, the provinces provided 66 percent, 18 percent was raised locally, and 7 percent was from private sources. The sixteen German states bear the major responsibility for school funding in Germany. Only a small part of expenses is met by the federal government or by local municipalities.

School funding in the United States is primarily a shared responsibility between state and local government. In 1988, states provided 50 percent of public school funding, localities provided 44 percent, and the federal government contributed 6 percent.[1] This state-level financing system in the United States results in some states spending almost three times as much per pupil as other states. In 1988, for example, Mississippi spent only $2,500 per pupil while New York state spent approximately $7,200 per pupil.[2] Even within states, some districts spend more than twice as much per pupil as other districts in the same state, or even the same county. The basic injustice of this system was plainly evident to the Fulbright Exchange teachers visiting the United States during the 1991 – 1992 school year.

A telling example of the fate of proposals to fund schools equitably can be found in the recent saga of school funding reform in the state of New Jersey. In 1990 Jim Florio, a Democrat, was elected governor, and promptly convinced the legislature to enact the largest increase in state taxes in New Jersey history. A major rationale for the need for new taxes was to satisfy a judicial ruling that a new state subsidy formula needed to be devised to create more equitable school funding, particularly between the affluent suburbs and poverty-ridden cities such as Newark and Camden.

Two years later the Democratic majority was voted out of the legislature, and was replaced with a new Republican majority, determined to roll back the tax increases. Within months tax rates were lowered and the new aid to urban schools was sharply curtailed. Not content with this achievement, the majority Republicans sought to amend the state constitution to remove the requirement that the state provide a "thorough and efficient" education. If successful, this constitutional gambit would prevent the judiciary from mandating a more equitable school funding system for New Jersey and allow the people's representatives to continue to ignore the educational needs of the urban and rural poor.[3] (See the summary of educational funding patterns in the six survey nations in Table 9.1.)

LOCAL SCHOOL GOVERNANCE

The unique American reliance on local funding for schools is undoubtedly related to the cherished American ideal of local control of schools. Among the nations surveyed, only Canada has a local school board with functions that resemble those of an American school board. The fact that Canada has found a way to publicly support religious schools, and provides a larger share of school financing at the provincial level, provides fewer issues for public controversy over local school board operations than is common in the United States.

We have seen that Japan firmly rejected the concept of locally elected school boards that had been imposed on it after World War II. Japan returned policymaking on school matters to the national level, with local decision making on school issues limited to selecting textbooks from an approved list and recommending the appointment of teachers to the prefectural authorities. The five-member school boards are appointed by the mayor rather than directly elected.[4] There is little need for a strong local board of education in a nation where funding is provided nationally and regionally, and all significant decisions relating to curriculum, instruction, and teacher selection are reserved to national and prefectural authorities.

Schools in both Denmark and Germany have school boards composed of parents, teachers, sometimes students, and perhaps one or two municipal officials. These boards primarily represent the interests of those directly involved in the school and, except for a single municipal official, are not representative of the entire local community, as is the practice in the United States. Here again we have schools where decisions on curriculum and courses of study are made at the national or regional level, with only minor decision-making powers devolving to

Table 9.1 *School Governance and Finance.*

	Canada	Denmark	England	Germany	Japan	U.S.A.
Political control of education	Small federal role, strong provincial role, and moderate local control.	Strong national direction and control with regional control at county and municipal levels.	Dramatic move toward strong national control and smaller role for LEAs under 1988 education law.	Significant federal coordination, with real power with German states.	Strong national control of all important aspects of education.	Small national role, states have potential for strong role but tradition of local control is still the norm.
Role of local school boards	Similar to U.S.A. model, although with fewer powers over taxation and curriculum authority.	Boards of local schools composed of parents, teachers, and students. Major financial and curriculum decisions are made by regional or national governments.	Boards of local schools composed of parents and teachers. These boards have some control over operating processes of schools, although major power is at national level.	Local parent councils have little power. Teachers not involved in governance. Most major decisions are made at regional level of state education system.	Local boards of parents operate in a manner similar to U.S. PTO groups. Power is reserved at the national and prefectural levels.	Local boards consist of community members and some parents. Major decisions on budgets, salaries, curriculum, and tax levels are made by local boards.

(continued)

Table 9.1 *(continued).*

	Canada	Denmark	England	Germany	Japan	U.S.A.
Financing of the schools	While financial support varies among the provinces, on average, 9 percent of funds are raised at the federal level, 66 percent by the provinces, 18 percent by local school districts, and 7 percent by private funding.	All major costs such as salaries are paid by the national government. Local funds support items such as texts and supplies.	Eighty percent of school costs are paid from national funds while 20 percent of expenses are met by local taxes.	The German states bear the major costs of education, including monies for teacher salaries. Small amounts are contributed by the federal and local government.	The national government pays 50 percent of educational costs in Japan, 25 percent is paid by the prefecture level, and 25 percent by local taxes.	Fifty percent of funding is provided by state government, 44 percent by local taxes, and 6 percent by federal sources. Heavy reliance on local property taxes.

Table 9.1 (*continued*).

	Canada	Denmark	England	Germany	Japan	U.S.A.
Educational equity	Funding system provides for equity within a province. There is significant disparity of resources among the provinces. Provincial curriculum guides promote equity within each province.	National financing within this small nation provides for an equitable distribution of school funding. National curriculum promotes equal education.	Majority funding from national level provides a good degree of equity, although residential patterns affect socioeconomic level of school population. New common curriculum will promote equal education.	Major funding at state level provides equity within a German state, but there is disparity in educational resources among the sixteen states. Coordinated educational goals among the states also promote equality.	National and prefectural funding provide for equitable financing of public schools in Japan. Common curriculum also promotes equal education.	Great disparity among states regarding ability to raise funds for education. High dependence on local funding also creates great disparities within states, and even within counties.

(continued)

277

Table 9.1 (continued).

	Canada	Denmark	England	Germany	Japan	U.S.A.
Use of public funds for private and denominational schools	Assuming they follow provincial curriculum and other regulations, private and denominational schools are funded on same basis as public schools in most provinces.	Denmark pays 85 percent of the costs to operate non-public schools. Even so, only 10 percent of parents choose private schools. Religious instruction is given in the public schools.	English maintained and voluntary schools receive public funds for private and denominational schools. Religious act of worship is required by law in all English schools.	Support for private education varies among German states, although most states generously support nonpublic schools. Religion is taught in public schools.	Ninety-seven percent of Japanese students attend public schools for the first nine grades. Private high schools, attended by 25 percent of the students, receive some state support. Moral instruction is provided in the public schools.	Public support for private schools in the U.S.A. is generally limited to areas such as busing, health services, or textbooks. Religion is carefully excluded from public schools and there is a continuing argument over funding for private schools.

the school. School funding is largely a concern of a higher level of government and even personnel decisions are heavily influenced by regional educational officials.

English school boards, as a result of the Education Act of 1988, are now similar in form and function to those described for Denmark and Germany. The parental choice movement will tend to weaken the connection between geography and school attendance. Thus English schools will cease to be community schools in the same sense as schools are in a typical American town or city. The minimal role for local school boards in these countries also eliminates the need for local superintendents and other district office personnel. The presence of such officials in America is made necessary by the extent of policy issues, political decisions, personnel, and tax decisions that the American system assigns to local school boards. Only Canada has district-level superintendents and other administrators comparable to American district school officials.

The deficiency of local school governance in the United States was the subject of a recent highly critical report on American school boards released by the Twentieth Century Fund. The report found school boards to be "consumed by trivial administrative decisions rather than setting educational policy." [5] The report noted that the present system of school governance, which is unique in the world, was established between 1859 and 1900, when the country was largely rural and school districts were far smaller and less complex. The study cited a recent survey of West Virginia school boards that found that only 3 percent of school board decisions focused primarily on educational policy. [6]

Local school boards too often fall victim to petty local politics, resulting in the election of individuals with neither an interest in, nor an understanding of education. Individual board members are often the captives of special interest groups, and interpret all policy decisions in terms of how the policy will affect their particular narrow focus and concern. Volatile issues requiring local board attention include teacher negotiations, property tax increases, and controversial curriculum issues such as sex education and the teaching of values. Such a scenario ensures that school board meetings will often be the occasion for contentious wrangling, rather than for resolution of important educational issues through the deliberations of a representative legislative body.

Local school boards, as currently constituted, are incapable of setting and executing policies on serious educational issues. We have seen that the role of the federal government in education is minimal, and that many state departments of education are ineffectual. The United States suffers from a power vacuum in educational policymaking and implementation that effectively prevents meaningful educational reform. (See the summary of local governance procedures among the six survey nations in Table 9.1.)

COLLEGE AND UNIVERSITY EDUCATION

All nations surveyed provide national and regional support to their colleges and universities. Canada and the United States provide the most open systems of college admission, with a majority of high school graduates in both countries beginning a college program at either a four-year institution or a two-year community or junior college (see Table 9.2). In both countries, admission to college is based on high school grades and standardized aptitude tests, although the practical reality is that virtually any high school graduate can gain admission to some type of post-high school education.

American students of limited means will often attend state universities or two-year community colleges as a method of obtaining a relatively inexpensive college education. Both state universities and community colleges are heavily subsidized by public funds. High tuition rates at private universities and colleges are met by aid packages including loans, work study opportunities, and scholarship grants. Parents and students

Table 9.2 *Proportion of Students in Survey Countries Attending Second and Third Level Educational Institutions.*

Country	Year	Second Level[1]	Third Level[2]
United States	1987	92%	65%
Federal Republic of Germany	1988	85%	32%
Canada	1989	93%	66%
Denmark	1987	84%	30%
Japan	1989	96%	31%
England	1986	79%	22%

[1]Second level enrollment includes general education as well as technical and vocational education. This level generally corresponds to secondary education in the United States. In Germany and Denmark a high proportion of students attend school only part time during their last few years of secondary school. In England, many students finish secondary school at age sixteen while some of the students who remain in school until age eighteen do so on a part-time basis.

[2]Third level enrollment includes college and university enrollment, and technical and vocational education beyond the high school level. There is some variation in reporting among countries.

Sources: 1991. *UNESCO Yearbook,* Paris; National Center for Education Statistics. 1991. *Digest of Education Statistics 1990,* Washington, DC: U.S. Government Printing Office.

are also expected to meet a significant portion of the costs. Meeting the financial obligations for college is a major financial drain on the resources of parents, while high student loan obligations leave many young college graduates with a significant amount of debt as they begin their working careers.

Scholastic achievement levels of American college students are hampered by their poor secondary school academic preparation, lack of effective study habits, and low overall motivation for study. The low rate of program completion by American college students has been previously noted. There are also no formal structures to match college preparation programs to the needs of the general society. Consequently, too many students are pursuing too narrow a range of majors to reflect the employment needs of the society. American students are particularly reluctant to pursue demanding courses of studies in the sciences and mathematics. Only 7 percent of American degree holders earn their degrees in the areas of biology, physical and earth sciences, mathematics, and statistics. An additional 8 percent earn degrees in medicine, nursing, and related fields.[7]

The money and other resources available for research at America's premier universities makes them the best in the world for graduate education. Foreign students often represent a significant proportion of students in math and science advanced-degree programs in American universities. Such prestigious research universities often divert resources from the general undergraduate programs toward the more prestigious research programs at the graduate level.

Many universities in Canada began as private religious institutions. They have become more secular as they have accepted an increasing amount of federal and provincial funding in recent years. Canada provides a greater level of governmental support for higher education than does the United States, so that tuition in Canadian universities, including private schools, is comparable to tuition at American public universities. Canada emulates the American model of providing higher education opportunities to virtually all who can benefit from them.

Higher education in Japan bears a superficial resemblance to the American system. A limited proportion of Japanese high school graduates, about 30 percent, attend some form of higher education (see Table 9.2). Japanese higher education features a mix of four-year private and public universities and two-year community colleges. The government provides financial support to both public and private universities, with a higher subsidy available to public institutions.

In Japan the national public universities are the most prestigious. The low tuition, the practice by large corporations of recruiting from these schools, and the competitive entrance examination system, all play a role in creating an elite status for the public university graduate. Private universities tend to have a lesser prestige, although several of them are considered the equal of the national universities.[8] This is the reverse of the situation in the United States, where private universities such as Harvard and Princeton are the most prestigious, with a smaller number of public universities being considered on a par with the best private schools.

Two-year community colleges in Japan have the least prestige, with 90 percent of the students being female and pursuing programs in home economics, child care, or nursery school teaching. Japanese women who attend the better universities and pursue the more traditionally male professions are still stigmatized in the Japanese culture.[9] Many young women will not attend a top university for fear that such a choice will hurt their future chances for a good husband.

Japanese students work extremely hard to gain admission to a university and begin their college careers with high levels of academic knowledge and skills. Acceptance at a well-respected university virtually guarantees that a student will eventually graduate and be offered a job at a large corporation. Once accepted at a university, therefore, most Japanese students approach their college studies in a relaxed manner. The academic climate at college in Japan does not match the level of intensity in high school, nor does it match the academic intensity found at most American colleges.

The traditional route to higher education in Denmark was to gain admission to an academic Gymnasium and to pass the qualifying tests for university admission. As recently as the 1950s, only 5 – 10 percent of students would attend the Gymnasium and enroll at the university. In recent years Danish parents have demonstrated an increasing commitment to enrolling their children in a university preparation program at a Gymnasium. Currently from 25 – 30 percent of an age cohort graduates from a Gymnasium and passes the qualifying exam for the university. There are not sufficient places at the university to accommodate those eligible, however, so one-third of those qualified are not admitted.

A second source of applicants for university admission is the Higher Preparation programs, which provide Danish students and young adults with a second chance to receive the educational background necessary to pass the university qualifying exams. This opportunity for a second chance refutes the criticism that Danish students are locked out of an academic career at too early an age, and that the system does not accommodate late-bloomers. There has been a definite effort in Denmark to democratize higher education and to provide wider educational opportunities to all citizens.

In addition to the universities, there are other higher education institutions preparing students for specific professions such as nursing or elementary teaching. Including enrollments at these institutions, Denmark currently enrolls about 30 percent of an age cohort in some form of higher education (see Table 9.2). While this is only half the proportion found in the United States, it represents a significant expansion of higher education opportunities for Danish citizens. Denmark also provides excellent vocational training programs for the 50 percent of the student body who complete their full-time schooling after tenth grade. The Danish government pays the full tuition for Danish university students, as well as a small monthly living allowance.

Recent German experiences in higher education parallel those of Denmark. A strong vocational and technical training system has for many years supplied the German economy with a highly skilled work force. University attendance was for many years restricted to a small elite, 5 – 10 percent of the population who gained admission to a Gymnasium and passed the Abitur, qualifying them for university admission. Irrevocable academic placement decisions were previously made for students as early as fourth grade. These decisions were made unilaterally by the teacher and school with little concern for the opinions of parents or students.

This traditional educational system has been greatly democratized over the past generation. Parents and students are now actively involved in educational placement decisions. An increasing number of parents insist that their students pursue an academic education at the Gymnasium, with the expectation that they will be able to gain admission to a university. The university qualifying exams, known as the Abitur, have been made somewhat less rigorous, although they still represent a significant challenge to the prospective university student. Additional higher educational institutions have been created to supplement the limited places available at the traditional universities.

As in Denmark, the proportion of the student population attending the Gymnasium in Germany has increased from 5 – 10 percent to about 25 percent. There are some complaints that academic standards have been lowered, and there are now more students possessing the abitur qualifications than can be admitted to the universities. Germany, like Denmark, has instituted an allocation system for admitting students to various university programs. University tuition is paid by the various German states, while living expenses are the responsibility of the student. Currently about one-third of German college-age citizens attend some form of higher education (see Table 9.2). As with Denmark, this proportion represents a dramatic increase compared with the recent past.

The academic path to higher education in England corresponds to the Danish and German models. The English sixth form is similar in function to the Danish and German Gymnasiums. The university qualifying exam in England, the General Certificate of Education Advanced Level (GCE A-level), fulfills the same gatekeeping function as the Abitur in Germany and the Studentereksamen in Denmark. Additional colleges and universities have been created in England in recent decades to satisfy the increasing demands for higher education. Thus, some of the same dynamics for democratizing education seen in Germany and Denmark have also been experienced in England. University tuition in England is paid through local education authority grants, with living expenses being the responsibility of the students. Educational loans for English students are beginning to replace some of the former outright tuition grants for university study.

The high number of English students quitting school at age sixteen, the chronic economic weakness of England, and the demotivating effects of the English class system, have led to a higher education system that serves fewer of its citizens than any other country in this survey. About 20–25 percent of an age cohort attends some form of higher education in England.

The rigor of the academic programs required in other nations for students, coupled with university entrance exam requirements, produces a college-age student body with significantly higher knowledge and skill levels than are found in the typical American college student. Although no nation other than Canada approaches the United States in the percentage of students attending college, all nations surveyed have made great strides in this direction over the past several decades. The United States offers the widest accessibility to a college education, but also imposes a much higher direct financial burden on parents and students than is found in the other survey countries.

PRIVATE EDUCATION IN THE SURVEY NATIONS

Phrases such as *schools of choice, separation of church and state,* and *tuition vouchers* stir much controversy in America. We have been engaged in a century-long debate regarding the proper relationship between private education and public financial support and control. The constant heated debate in this country regarding private education contrasts sharply with the accommodating and apparently satisfactory manner in which all other countries surveyed approach this issue. In short, the United States clearly has the most restrictive practices regarding public support for private schools of any of the six countries surveyed.

Nonpublic schools in the United States must depend almost totally on student tuition and gifts from patrons to meet operating expenses. Many states do, however, provide some peripheral assistance in areas such as transportation, textbook purchases, and health services. Although technically subject to state laws regarding curriculum requirements, there is generally little or no monitoring of private schools by state or local educational agencies. Nonpublic schools in America are viewed essentially as private enterprises, warranting neither financial support nor monitoring by public school governmental agencies.

Generally speaking, the other countries in this study consider the education of every child to be a matter of direct concern to the larger society. Thus private schools in these countries are subject to the same curriculum requirements as public schools. Most nations employ inspectors or utilize other mechanisms to ensure that the public interest in education is being served by nonpublic schools. Each country has devised a unique mechanism for providing some level of public financial support for the operation of nonpublic schools.

The Japanese government's relationship with nonpublic schools is the least complex of the survey nations. During the compulsory schooling years, grades one through nine, 97 percent of the students attend the well-regarded public schools. The remaining 3 percent attend religious private schools that receive little, if any, state support. High school is not compulsory in Japan, and there are not a sufficient number of public places available to accommodate all students who wish to attend high school. The state provides a significant subsidy to private high schools, whether religiously affiliated or not, since they enroll students who cannot be accepted at the generally more prestigious public schools. These private high schools must meet all the curriculum and course time requirements that apply to the public school sector.

Public support for nonpublic schools in Germany varies among the sixteen states that form the German republic. Religious instruction is provided in the public schools in Germany, so there is little need for parents to select private schools for religious reasons. Only about 5 percent of German children attend private schools. Some states provide as much as 95 percent of the tuition cost to attend religious and other private schools, some provide a small subsidy, and a few provide no subsidy. Private schools must meet the curriculum and other requirements of the public schools, although adherence to these requirements is not always closely monitored.

Denmark also provides religious instruction as part of its public school curriculum. In Denmark, 85 percent of tuition costs to attend private school are provided by the government. Private schools must follow all Danish curriculum requirements. The supervisor nominated by the parent-controlled board of the private school must be approved by the local municipal officials, and must make a yearly report to these officials testifying that the private school is following all curriculum requirements. Teachers generally possess the same qualifications as public school teachers and are paid on the governmental salary schedule.

Even with the high level of governmental support for private schools, 90 percent of Danish children attend the public school. There is little social cachet attached to private schooling since it is highly subsidized by the government, and therefore available to all citizens. The public schools in Denmark apparently satisfy the desires of the citizenry in this small, culturally homogeneous nation. Private schools are financially supported by the government in order to ensure that parents will have meaningful choices regarding the school their children attend.

Private schools in England are known as public schools, and offer an elite education, without governmental support, to about 7 percent of the student population. In a nation where class consciousness is still prominent, these private independent schools offer the English upper classes a special enclave for the education of their children. There are also a large number of nonpublic schools, known as maintained schools, that receive state funding on the same basis as public schools. About one-third of these publicly supported maintained schools are associated with religious denominations, chiefly the Roman Catholic Church and the Church of England. These nonpublic schools must meet the same curriculum and other educational requirements as the public schools. Every nonpublic school in England must register with the Department of Education and Science and be inspected periodically by the same cadre of governmental inspectors who visit public schools. All schools in England, public or private, must provide some form of religious instruction as prescribed by the Act of Daily Worship law.

Support of nonpublic schools in Canada varies among the ten provinces. Throughout Canada, more than 40 percent of students attend church-related schools that enjoy various levels of governmental financial support. About 5 percent of Canadian students attend private schools that do not receive governmental support. As in America, these truly private schools are not closely monitored in most Canadian provinces. Generally, the degree of public support for these private schools is related to the degree of public control over their operations. Private schools in Canada are becoming more popular as Canadian citizens become disenchanted with their public schools.

Religiously oriented schools in Canada that receive full public funding are known as denominational public schools. Such schools receive public finding on an equal basis with nondenominational public schools. About 90 percent of the two million students attending these denominational public schools are Catholic. Mechanisms for establishing and maintaining these denominational public schools vary among the provinces. Some districts with an overwhelmingly Catholic or Protestant population simply elect to operate one denominational school reflecting the religious orientation of the local citizens. Other localities operate dual school systems featuring Protestant and Catholic denominational schools. Still other localities operate nondenominational public schools while providing financial support for students attending denominational schools. In some localities, taxpayers may designate the type of school that will receive their tax monies. The provincial government is the major funding source for both denominational and nondenominational public schools in most provinces. Denominational public schools are fully integrated into the public system and must satisfy all governmental requirements regarding curriculum, teacher certification, school leaving examinations, and student assessments. The Canadian solution to providing for the educational needs of its diverse population is remarkable in light of the intensity of the ethnic and religious conflicts that have been a prominent part of Canadian history.

It is ironic that the United States, with the most diverse population ethnically, culturally, and religiously, has evolved the least satisfactory mechanism for providing pluralism in education. Other nations offer a multitude of successful models for providing governmental support for nonpublic education. Every other country in this survey has found a successful mechanism to create and nurture both public and nonpublic schools. (See summary of governmental and financial comparisons in Table 9.1.)

SOCIETY, CULTURE, AND THE SCHOOLS

We have seen that the social and cultural contexts in which schools function profoundly affect the educational system in each country surveyed. Neither the successes nor the failures of an educational system can be attributed solely to the schools themselves. Instead, we must look to the history of the country, the character of its people, and the goals of its schools to develop a context for evaluating the schools in each nation. Understanding the societal factors that influence educational quality will help us to identify the cultural constraints on school improvement. Such an understanding will enable us to recommend societal practices that, together with school-specific changes, could produce significantly more effective schools in the United States.

The most basic cultural influence on the school is the attitude that the general society displays toward the rearing and education of children. Children in America have traditionally been thought of as primarily a private concern of the family, requiring only incidental and supplemental involvement by the state. The material, moral, and social welfare of the child is seen in America as almost exclusively a parental responsibility. Unfortunately, changes in American society in recent decades have seriously eroded the capacity of the family to provide these basic essentials to our children.

From health care to moral education, American children are ill-served by their society in comparison to other nations in this study. The United States consistently fares poorly among industrialized nations on measures such as infant mortality rates, availability of health care, children living in poverty, child abuse and neglect, and family dissolution and dysfunction. Only Denmark, among the countries in this study, surpasses the United States in the proportion of births to unmarried women (see Figure 9.1).[10] Surely, America's dismal record on child welfare issues significantly impacts on the quality and effectiveness of the educational program that children receive.

The basic strength of the family unit varies greatly among the nations surveyed. Fulbright Exchange teachers frequently reported that the levels of divorce and separation in the United States far exceeded the rates in their own countries. The divorce rate in the United States is significantly higher than other nations in the survey. Japan and Germany have the lowest divorce rates (see Figure 9.2).[11]

Divorce among families with young children in the United States most often creates a situation where a single mother, with limited skills and

Births to unmarried women as a percentage of all live births in selected countries: 1970 and 1986

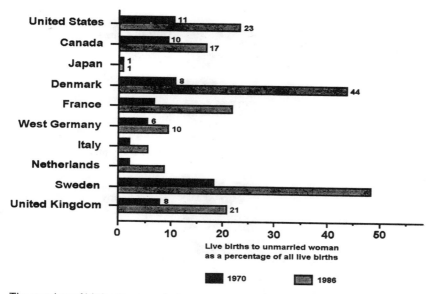

The number of births to unmarried women rose rapidly in many countries, including the United States. Although the proportion of births to unmarried women also has been rising, wide divergences in rates are evident. In Japan, only 1 percent of the 1986 births were to unmarried women compared with 48 percent in Sweden and 44 percent in Denmark. The rates in the U.S. (23 percent) are similar to those in France (22 percent) and the United Kingdom (21 percent), but are higher than those in Canada (17 percent) and West Germany (10 percent).

Figure 9.1 Births to unmarried women in selected countries. Source: U.S. Department of Education. 1991. Youth Indicators 1991: Trends in the Well-Being of American Youth. *Washington, DC: U.S. Department of Education, p. 25.*

income, must provide for her small children. The census bureau reported that by 1991, 26 percent of all American children were living in single parent families, usually with the mother.[12] Lacking the social supports of national health care or child allowances, such young mothers must join the work force to provide basic necessities for their children. Since adequate child care is often unavailable, many young children are essentially unsupervised for large portions of each day.

Every nation in this study, except the United States, has some systematic method to ensure adequate health care for its citizens, including children. England, Denmark, and Canada have national systems to ensure health care for children. Germany requires that each worker be

Divorce rates in selected countries: 1986

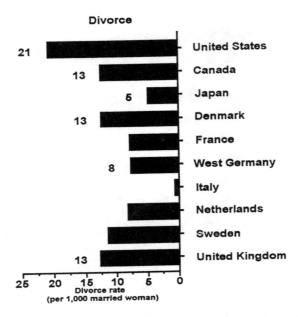

The United States has had a much higher divorce rate than these other countries. However, since 1980, divorce rates in these countries have risen, while they have declined slightly in the United States.

Figure 9.2   *Divorce rates in selected countries. Source: U.S. Department of Education. 1991. Youth Indicators 1991: Trends in the Well-Being of American Youth. Washington, DC: U.S. Department of Education, p. 19.*

covered by health insurance through his or her employer, effectively guaranteeing health care for almost all children. Japan provides universal health care through generous private company programs, supplemented by government programs where needed.

In America the children of the working poor are not covered by health insurance programs. Skilled American workers with good jobs generally receive health care coverage through their employers, while welfare recipients are eligible for health services as part of the public assistance programs financed by state and federal sources. Almost 40 million Americans, including a disproportionate number of children, have no health care coverage. Employer-provided health care coverage is often a major incentive for a single mother to enter the work force on a full-time basis, even though her young children may not be properly supervised.

There are some signs that America is moving toward reforming its health care delivery system. Minnesota is setting up a state-subsidized insurance program to help families without medical insurance. Florida is committed to providing a basic health care guarantee to all its citizens by 1995. Vermont will be selecting from one of two models to provide universal health care to its citizens by 1995.[13] Health care was also a major issue in the 1992 presidential campaign. Parents of young children are at a stage in life where their financial obligations are growing while their earning power has not yet reached its peak. Most other nations in this survey respond to this reality by granting child allowances for families with children.

In Denmark, parents receive an allowance of about $800 per year for each child under the age of eighteen. In Germany, every family receives a government monthly stipend for each child. Small grants are also given to families with children in both Canada and England. Japan does not provide direct grants to parents in the form of child allowances. Child allowances reinforce the concept that children are a natural resource that needs to be supported and nurtured by the general society. Children in America are often viewed as consumer goods or "lifestyle choices," of little concern to the general society.

The moral development of children is very much influenced by the cultural values of each nation. The United States, with its belief in the primacy of the individual and its distrust of governmental interference in moral or religious issues, traditionally relied on the family and the church to provide moral guidance to children. Teachings from the home were reinforced by a general Protestant Christian ethic that permeated the public school during the first half of this century.

In the 1990s a relatively small proportion of American children receive systematic moral instruction through their churches. In 1990 only 30 percent of high school seniors attended religious services on a weekly basis. The traditional role of the family in transmitting moral values has been weakened by the disintegration of the family unit itself. Legal challenges to the schools on issues involving religion, or any value-laden topics, have produced a totally secularized school environment where moral relativism is the only practical operating principal. Television, which occupies the typical elementary school student for thirty-five or more hours each week, has become a primary vehicle for transmitting our culture and values to children. Among American thirteen-year-old children, 42 percent watch three to four hours of television each day, while an additional 31 percent watch five or more hours per day.[14]

Other nations take a more direct approach to formally involving the schools in the moral development of youth. Religious studies are a part of the curriculum in the public schools of Germany and Denmark. In Canada, students may attend denominational public schools that provide religious instruction and receive full government funding. The Act of Worship law in England requires that every school provide some type of religious or moral lesson on a daily basis. Church-related schools, offering religious instruction in a particular faith, are also eligible for full public support in England. The national curriculum in Japan requires one hour of moral education each week during each year of public education. Such instruction does not have a specifically religious content, but does transmit the general moral tenets and values of Japanese society. Only in America is the moral education of children left entirely to chance.

American children from dysfunctional families, often without the benefits of a good income or health insurance, typically reside in economically depressed areas. Because of the American system of heavy reliance on local taxes to fund schools, such children attend the schools with the fewest resources. The prevailing educational funding mechanism thus becomes a powerful instrument to institutionalize the cycle of poverty from one generation to the next. A fair generalization about education in the United States is that school districts that need the most resources to overcome the deprivations of their students have the least resources, while those school systems serving advantaged youths with intact families, good family incomes, access to medical care, and cultural advantages have the most resources for education. Every other country in the survey does a much more effective job of equalizing educational resources than does the United States.

The educational system in the United States is very tolerant of students who perform poorly during their elementary and secondary years. There are a multitude of second chances provided to American students to accommodate late-bloomers, students who only become academically motivated late in their academic careers. Other nations have emulated the openness of our system to a greater or lesser degree. As other nations such as Denmark and Germany move toward greater educational opportunities for larger numbers, there is a corresponding concern in these nations that the traditional standards of academic excellence be maintained.

Another cultural difference between the United States and most other nations surveyed involves the importance of academic credentials within the society. Japan, Germany, and Denmark, in particular, attach great significance to academic or vocational credentials in determining the qualification of candidates for a wide range of occupations. In these cultures, formal qualifications, obtainable only through the school system, largely determine the future economic and social status of students. Academic credentials are also important in the United States, although there is still a sense among many people that success in adult life is not related to academic success in school. This difference in perceptions regarding the importance of education to future success has a positive impact on student motivation, attitude, and performance in Japan, Denmark, and Germany. In spite of liberalization in recent years, these cultures are still far less forgiving of poor academic performance than is the American system, where students are almost always afforded another chance to succeed. These harsher realities in other industrialized nations foster a more serious tone in the academic enterprise.

Each of the cultural comparisons discussed previously places the United States at a disadvantage in providing a school system featuring high academic achievement. Although there are a host of steps that can be taken within the schools to improve our educational system, significant gains will not be made unless and until these social and cultural issues are resolved satisfactorily.

REFERENCES

1. U.S. Department of Education. 1990. *The Condition of Education 1990, Volume 1.* Washington, DC: U.S. Department of Education, p. 80.
2. National Center for Education Statistics. 1991. *Digest of Education Statistics 1990.* Washington, DC: U.S. Government Printing Office, p. 156.
3. 1990. *The Philadelphia Inquirer* (July 3):A12.
4. August, R. L. 1992. "Education," in *Japan: A Country Study.* Washington, DC: Department of the Army, p. 138.
5. 1992. *The Philadelphia Inquirer* (April 8):3.
6. 1992. *The Philadelphia Inquirer* (April 8):3.
7. National Center for Education Statistics, p. 19.
8. Yamada, C. Interview with author, March 1992.
9. August, R. L., p. 156.

10. U.S. Department of Education. 1991. *Youth Indicators 1991: Trends in the Well-Being of American Youth.* Washington, DC: U.S. Department of Education, p. 25.

11. U.S. Department of Education, *Youth Indicators 1991,* p. 19.

12. 1992. *The Philadelphia Inquirer* (July 17):A2.

13. Fitzgerald, S. 1992. ''On Health Care Issue, States Take Initiative,'' *The Philadelphia Inquirer* (July 26):F1, F8.

14. U.S. Department of Education, *Youth Indicators 1991,* pp. 80, 122.

CHAPTER 10

Lessons for America's Schools

PREVIOUS CHAPTERS HIGHLIGHT numerous policies and procedures in foreign schools that differ significantly from American practice. There are, however, many practices in foreign schools which will strike an American as quite familiar. The similarities that exist between schools in the United States and the other countries surveyed often represent a direct effort by these countries to model various aspects of American schooling. For example, the American concept of relatively open access to higher education, and the commitment to provide students with second and third chances to succeed, are essentially American ideals that have been adopted, to varying degrees, by other nations.

American schools, on the other hand, make little attempt to adapt successful foreign schooling practices to American culture and society. Our long-standing economic, military, and cultural preeminence has lulled us into a sense of complacency. We tend to believe in the innate superiority of our own schooling practices, even though study after study documents inferior academic performance by American students relative to that of students in other industrialized nations. We have seen that the other survey nations have developed fairly common approaches to major educational issues. The United States meanwhile, pursues its own unique, and demonstrably less effective approaches to these same issues.

The recommendations that follow are based on successful models from abroad. They represent a comprehensive outline for promoting the academic reform of our educational system that continues to elude us after ten years of national attention and effort. Although many of the following proposals are not new, in aggregate they provide a more global approach to reforming American education than has been previously proposed. Many, in fact, have been successfully implemented in individual school districts throughout the United States.

A clear lesson from the six-nation survey is that the political, social, and cultural contexts in which schools function have a critical impact on school effectiveness. Only a society-wide commitment to better schooling will improve our educational system. The absence of this commitment during the past ten years of school reform efforts has produced only sporadic and piecemeal improvements, rather than the systematic regeneration that is so critically needed.

The recommendations are grouped under the major dimensions of schooling that have been used to survey the six nations compared in this study. While the adoption of each recommendation would be helpful in its own right, it is their cumulative effect that will lead to significant school improvement.

SCHOOL GOVERNANCE

1. Strengthen the powers of state-level educational governance and diminish the prerogatives of local school governance.

Under our political system, educational governance is one of the powers reserved to the states. This tradition is a practical necessity because of the enormous size of our nation. Our preference for local control of schools, coupled with parsimonious funding of the administrative arm of state educational agencies, generally translates into weak and ineffective statewide educational leadership. In most states, school governance involves the enforcing of rather trivial bureaucratic rules and regulations. States that do attempt to substantively influence curriculum, instruction, and student achievement, often lack sufficient personnel resources to implement and enforce strong curriculum regulations and student assessment practices.

The powerful educational role played by the German Länder and Canadian provinces should be emulated in the United States. In both countries, these regional governments provide strong curriculum leadership, set requirements for student assessments and qualifying examinations of various types, provide the major share of funding for the schools, and provide effective administrative and supervisory mechanisms to monitor individual school effectiveness. In the United States, this local administrative and supervisory function could best be performed at the county level.

2. State sources should fund as much as 75 percent of educational costs by means of broad-based state taxes. Local property taxes should play a minor role in school funding. Some federal funding should be provided to the poorest states.

Fulbright Exchange teachers visiting America are appalled that we allow a child's educational opportunities to be largely determined by the wealth of his or her local community. The reliance on local funding for schools routinely creates a situation where $6,000 per student is available in one school district, while another district in the same county may spend $12,000 per student. On a national level there are poor rural districts spending only $3,000 per pupil, while in the most affluent districts in the nation as much as $15,000 is spent on each pupil.

Critics of equalized school spending proposals are quick to claim that money is not a major influence on school performance. If such critics truly believed this assertion, they would support taking money from the affluent districts to redistribute to the poorer districts, since in their view, fewer dollars for wealthy districts should not negatively affect school quality. In reality, the suburban enclaves of affluence greet such redistribution proposals with shocked indignation. The fact is that economically and educationally advantaged parents will either reside in an area with a well-financed public school, or will send their children to expensive private schools. By voting with their feet, such parents are tacitly acknowledging their own belief that there is indeed a relationship between financial resources and school quality.

Every other country in this survey does a much better job of providing school financial equity than we do in the United States. It is ironic that the country that prides itself on being the world's leader in providing educational opportunities to its citizens, continually allows unconscionable disparities to exist in educational resources provided to different children, based on their area of residence.

As in other countries, educational financing should be either regionalized or nationalized. In our country, the best approach would be to raise about 75 percent of school funds at the state level and 25 percent at the local level. The local share of taxes should be raised at the county level, rather than by the local districts, thus further equalizing expenditures even within the local county. The federal government should also offer a subsidy, on a sliding scale, to the very poorest states so that per pupil expenditure is at least comparable to that of the wealthier states. As a goal, funding policies should seek to limit variations in expenditures between the richest and poorest areas to not more than 10 to 20 percent. State and federal funding of education would also reduce the current dependence on the local property tax, a divisive force in many communities, as a major source of school funding.

3. *The federal government should play a leading role in establishing broad educational goals, national educational standards, and coordination of critical educational policies among the states.*

The German model has much to offer in this area. There are, in Germany, federal-level commission of education ministers and others who meet periodically to coordinate broad educational goals for schools throughout Germany. Each German state references these general goals when devising curricula and setting educational regulations within its borders. In this way, Germany has national unity on major educational issues but is able to modify and adapt these goals to conditions in each state.

There already exists in America an organization known as the Education Commission of the States. In addition, there is a national organization for the chief school administrators from each state. We also have a national Department of Education, as well as frequent reports from national commissions on various aspects of education. Sufficient vehicles now exist for America to initiate a prestigious national Commission on Education, whose task it would be to establish broad policy guidelines for individual states to follow in operating their school systems. The educational goals for the year 2000, formulated by the president and the state governors in 1990, represent an initial attempt to establish national educational goals. The tremendous mobility of Americans among the fifty states provides an additional argument for more coordination and cooperation among the states on educational issues.

4. *Teacher salaries should be set and funded at the state level.*

Canada excepted, other foreign countries in this survey set teacher salaries at the national level. This approach largely eliminates the local controversy and contentiousness over teacher salaries that are so common in the United States. Local bargaining over salaries places teachers in conflict with vocal property owners who are dedicated to minimizing local taxes. Teacher strikes for higher wages create emotional scars within a community that often require years to heal. The demeaning spectacles associated with the more militant forms of collective bargaining destroy the mutual respect and sense of common purpose that should exist among teachers, students, and parents.

Establishing teacher salaries at the state level would eliminate one of the major impediments to good relations between the schools and their communities. Tens of thousands of hours of productive time could be saved by local educators who would otherwise be engaged in productive educational activity. A statewide salary schedule would eliminate wealth-based competition among adjacent districts to recruit teachers. Standard salary schedules would also eliminate the all-too-common practice of a wealthier and better paying school district recruiting excellent young teachers from a neighboring, but poorly paying school district. This single statewide salary schedule could include small supplements for designated areas where living costs are particularly high relative to the rest of the state.

5. Local school boards, as currently constituted, are dysfunctional and should be replaced by a more effective local governance mechanism.

The Twentieth Century Fund released a study indicating that American school boards devote little or no time to policy issues, but instead tend to become ensnared in relatively trivial concerns and controversies. Boards of education are often preoccupied with concerns over school budgets, teacher negotiations, student discipline, busing controversies, school construction, and community arguments over issues such as values clarification or sex education. School boards are left with little time or energy to provide proper educational leadership to the school district. School boards often include single-issue members concerned about property taxes, teacher contracts, or athletic programs. Such members can undermine school board effectiveness, producing a policymaking gridlock at the school board level.

The local school board of old—composed of respected community leaders who interviewed the teachers, fixed the boiler, and selected textbooks—is an anachronism. We persist in the myth that school boards are the agents of local control of the schools, whereas in reality they are unable to promote meaningful change in the schools. The limited executive abilities of many board members, coupled with the political infighting common to local school operations, make many local school boards a major obstacle to positive change.

A stronger state role in teacher negotiations, curriculum development, and school funding, would make a local board superfluous in these critical areas. Further, a strong regional board at the county level could effectively supervise the operation of individual schools within the county through a cadre of administrators and curriculum specialists. Current local board members with interest and skills in management issues could be elected to these regional boards to contribute their talents in these areas. Single-issue candidates with a specific axe to grind would, presumably, be less likely to win election to these countywide school board positions.

6. Create school boards consisting of parents, teachers, and the principal to operate each school.

Each local school board currently has several members who have children in the schools and who are genuinely interested in educational excellence. These people, and other like-minded parents, could serve on school boards for each school in a region. The principal would assume the role that a school superintendent now performs with a local school board. A minority of the seats on the board would be held by teachers at the school. The majority of the members would be parents of the students, elected by parents of children attending that school.

Since the curriculum would be established by the state, taxes would be raised at the state and county levels, and teacher negotiations would be done on the state level, these local school-based boards would be free to deal with the educational program within the school. This is the model of school-level governance currently operating in Denmark, Germany, England, and to a lesser extent in Japan. This model actually provides parents with more direct influence over their child's education than is found under our current system of district-level school boards.

These school-level boards would operate within the curriculum and other regulations set at the state level. They would have control over a small instructional budget to purchase textbooks, supplies, and other instructional materials. This board would establish school rules for students and be active in resolving major disciplinary issues. Teachers would be formally employed at the regional level, but the local principal and board would have appropriate involvement in the selection of teachers for their school. This board would be directly involved in selecting the principal for the school and evaluating his or her performance. Individual schools that fail to meet specified performance standards would first be placed on probation, and, if necessary, administered directly by the regional school authority. Operational authority would revert to the individual school board once all critical deficiencies were corrected.

CURRICULUM AND INSTRUCTION

1. All American children should have the opportunity to learn a standard basic curriculum.

England, Germany, Denmark, Japan, and most Canadian provinces consider the provision of a common curriculum as the primary vehicle to ensure educational equity within their countries. Only in America do we find opposition to the proposition that students in different parts of the country, or of different ability levels, should receive a similar basic education. The American fear of centralized determination of curriculum standards is simply not an issue with teachers, or the general public, in the other countries surveyed.

In reality, American schools have greater similarities in their curricula than is generally believed. In the absence of coherent and uniform curriculum policies in most states and districts, the textbooks selected by teachers become the de facto curriculum for most students. Such textbooks, with their suggested supplementary activities, unit tests, and teacher's guide, often represent the total instructional program offered by the teacher.

Competing textbooks for a given course or subject are typically produced by a few large publishers. Since several large states, including California and Texas, have statewide textbook adoptions, competing textbooks exhibit a similarity in content and blandness of style necessary to satisfy the varied requirements of these large markets. The resulting *dumbing down* of the American school textbook is viewed by many as a major contributing factor to the unchallenging nature of much of the instruction in our public schools.

The implementation of a curriculum, as defined by the textbook, varies widely from teacher to teacher. Some teachers follow the textbook slavishly, others pick and choose topics from the textbook, and still others essentially ignore the textbook. Our penchant for ability grouping students, either by achievement levels within a school, or by entire schools because of socioeconomic levels and residential patterns, creates a wide disparity in the instructional content offered to American students. The curriculum for many students consigned to lower academic groups is the equivalent of intellectual junk food. The students may possibly enjoy it, but it contains no intellectual nourishment. In other countries, virtually all elementary and lower secondary school students are exposed to the same academically challenging curriculum.

Ian Westbury, in a recent analysis of the relative achievement of

American and Japanese students on an international mathematics test, demonstrates the power of a common curriculum in promoting educational excellence. His analysis of data from the Second International Mathematics Study demonstrates that American students who were exposed to the mathematics content included on the test did about as well as the Japanese students. The problem is that far fewer American students are exposed to the algebra material at the eighth grade level, or the calculus content at the twelfth grade level, than is true in Japan with its common, and rigorous, curriculum for all students. This study supports the proposition that the performance of American students on such international tests would improve dramatically if we were to offer a more challenging curriculum to a wider range of the student population.[1]

The proposed National Education Commission should establish the broad goals for American education. Achievement standards established by the National Assessment of Educational Progress during the past twenty years should serve as the benchmarks for achievement levels in each of the basic academic subjects. Each state should adopt these goals and standards and develop curricula in each subject and grade level to implement the standards. The resulting curriculum should be mandatory in each school within a state. A cadre of state officials should regularly visit schools to monitor the delivery of the curriculum and to assist teachers in presenting the curriculum.

2. Each state should implement a student assessment program for students in grades four, eight, and twelve.

In the past decade, many states have instituted student assessment programs to provide some measure of accountability. Such tests have enforced at least a modicum of uniformity in the basic curriculum, but have not succeeded in materially improving student performance. School people generally view such tests as an intrusion in their schedule and complain that they should not be required to "teach to the test," or to concentrate on mere facts and basic skills to the exclusion of concepts and higher-level thinking skills. Many teachers prepare their students for these tests by drill and practice exercises designed to have the students achieve a correct answer on the tests. Other teachers undermine the testing programs even more blatantly by simply falsifying the test results.

We should carefully examine the English experiment of developing student assessments that go beyond multiple choice and short answer-type responses. We should develop instruments that require demonstrations, portfolios of student work, and writing samples. Such assessments would be difficult to develop and implement, and would be costly to administer. However, the time, effort , and cost would be worthwhile if we were able to implement a truly effective assessment program.

The assessment tests should be administered and evaluated by the regional level educational officials discussed under recommendation 1 of the ''School Governance'' section. Extra temporary help should be employed to facilitate the annual testing process at three grade levels. Teachers and principals at the school level should have absolutely nothing to do with test administration or evaluation. Assessment tools such as those described previously should satisfy the justifiable concerns about the limitations of our current testing programs. The objection that such testing requires too much of our limited instructional time will be addressed in a later recommendation regarding increasing the length of the school year.

The assessment at the fourth grade level should be used mainly for diagnostic purposes. Students and schools in need of extra remediation and help would be identified, and the regional educational authority would be required to provide such help. The minimal standards established for the eighth grade assessment should be considered the lowest acceptable academic achievement level for an adult in our society. A state certificate should be issued to each student who achieves the minimal standard on his or her assessment, testifying to the fact that the student has achieved basic literacy. The standard achievement level appropriate for this eighth grade assessment should approximate that now identified in many existing state assessment programs as the minimum for high school graduation.

About 70 percent of students should be able to pass this assessment on their first attempt. Students who do not meet the minimum criterion would receive remedial help until they passed the assessment. Requiring this certificate as a prerequisite for applying for a driver's license would be a strong incentive to those students most in need of motivation for academic work. Such a requirement would, in my view, result in at least 95 percent of an age cohort meeting this basic literacy standard by the age of sixteen.

The twelfth grade assessment would be modeled on the German Abitur, the English GCE A-level, the Danish Studentereksamen, and the Japanese university entrance exams. Students would be required to pass these state assessments as a prerequisite for admission to any four-year degree-granting institution in the United States. The implementation of this system would ensure that any student who enrolled in college would be academically capable of true college or university quality work. Students who do not meet this criterion would be permitted to attend two-year colleges, vocational and technical schools, and other post-secondary institutions that do not offer four-year degrees. These students would be free to retake the twelfth grade assessment at any future date and either transfer to a four-year institution, or enroll at a college or university as an adult student.

If such a system were initiated tomorrow, only about 25 percent of our current high school seniors could meet the criterion.[2] Setting such a standard, however, would create the incentive, motivation, and academic purpose among our high school students so that in short order about 40 percent of them would be able to meet the criterion. An additional 20 percent of students would achieve the criterion following remedial work and additional courses during their first few post-high school years. Within five years we would have approximately the same level of participation in higher education as we do today, but students would be much better prepared to benefit from the experience.

The curriculum and testing initiatives recommended previously could be a powerful engine for promoting educational excellence. Twenty-five years in public education convinces me that students will rise to the occasion if provided the proper challenges, incentives, and remedial supports necessary for serious academic achievement. Our young people are most certainly capable of meeting the challenges that rigorous standards imply.

3. Reconfigure the length of the school year, the distribution of vacation time, and the pace of the typical American school day.

A surprising finding in this survey was that students in other nations do not spend more time in academic classroom situations than their American counterparts. The superficial comparison of the number of school days in each country obscures the day-to-day realities of school life in other nations. We have seen, for example, that primary school children in most other nations surveyed have a shorter school day than do American children. Also, schools in many other nations schedule more field trips, cultural excursions, sports festivals, and even overnight class trips, than are common in American schools.

The most significant difference between American schools and the others surveyed relates to the pace of the school day. An American secondary school typically has a seven- or eight-period school day with only three or four minutes between classes, and thirty minutes for lunch. Other countries allow more time between class periods or schedule ten- to fifteen-minute breaks for both students and teachers every few class periods. One-hour lunch periods are common abroad, and, in some nations, the student day ends early enough for students to have a late lunch at home. In any event, the school day in foreign cultures proceeds at a more leisurely pace than is typical in American schools. Frequent breaks allow foreign teachers and students to return to their academic work refreshed and alert.

Foreign schools schedule less time each day for purely academic instruction than is common in America. These countries do, however, typically schedule ten to twenty more school days each year than is standard in the United States. Some states in Germany schedule as many as 226 days while Japanese schools schedule 240 days, including forty half-day Saturday sessions. Every other country, except Canada, has a significantly different method of scheduling vacation time within the year. Other countries schedule about six weeks of summer vacation, two weeks at Christmas, two at Easter, and one each during the fall and spring terms. This form of scheduling avoids both the tedium of long periods of schooling without a vacation break, and the regression in student achievement levels caused by a three-month summer vacation.

Along with adopting the vacation schedules of the other countries, we should also move toward a 200-day school year. This extra time could be used to adopt a more humane daily schedule for teachers and students, and to provide the necessary time to implement an effective student assessment program. Such changes in the school day and school year would also have a positive impact on student behavior and teacher and student morale. Taken together, these school calendar and daily scheduling changes would of themselves lead to improved student achievement.

4. Restrict the use of ability grouping, reduce the number of courses offered at the secondary level, and severely restrict retention in grade.

Except for the United States, no other country surveyed divides student classes by ability until the late middle school or high school years. The common American practice of grouping students for basic academic subjects by the middle elementary years ensures that a large percentage of students will be unprepared for serious academic work by the time they reach high school. Other countries surveyed allow children several more years to develop intellectually before consigning them to less challenging educational tracks.

There is some irony in Americans criticizing other nations for consigning students to less academic programs at too early an age. In the United States we often achieve the same result by grouping practices within schools that serve to stifle the intellectual development of children at a very early age. By high school age a large minority of our students have been systematically denied access to the challenging class work necessary to form the academic base for more challenging high school work. Ability grouping in American elementary schools should be eliminated.

Implementing the previous recommendations would make it possible for secondary school students to be scheduled with the same group for most of their school day. The large American high school of today, with its hundreds of courses and individualized computer schedules, while perhaps a tribute to technology and management, is often alienating to individual students. Adoption of the common curriculum and assessment program recommended previously would accelerate a movement toward more restricted course offerings and fewer ability-grouped classes. Within large American high schools there would be groups of students, pursuing identifiable course and program patterns, who would spend much of their school day together. This organizational pattern would resemble the Gesamtschule, the German version of the American comprehensive high school.

Most of the foreign schools surveyed, by circumstance or design, schedule the same group of students together for most of the day, often over a period of several years. A camaraderie develops in such an environment that can enhance the school experience for students and that closely emulates typical work groups that students will encounter in the adult world. Close association of students and teachers over a period of years can also reduce the levels of interpersonal miscommunication and alienation that often trigger student misbehavior.

Retention in grade is not employed as an instructional strategy for younger students in any of the countries surveyed. Grade retention is often proposed by America's public school critics as a way of toughening standards and promoting better student performance. Countries such as Japan, Germany, and Denmark, where student performance is very good, do not use retention in grade at the elementary level as a method to motivate achievement or punish lack of achievement. These nations believe that young children are better served by being kept with their age group and provided with appropriate remedial help to overcome academic deficiencies. In keeping with their stricter standards for older students, however, most of the survey countries do retain students in grade at the secondary level.

5. *Reintroduce daily homework assignments as an integral part of the learning process.*

Students from those countries with the best student achievement records do a significant amount of homework on a regular basis. Time spent on homework in Denmark, Germany, and Japan typically requires from thirty to sixty minutes at the elementary level and two or three hours at the secondary level. Also, a far higher proportion of foreign students are given homework assignments than is common in the United States.

The mundane strategy of assigning homework offers a potent tool for improving American educational performance. If a student were to spend an average of even one hour a night on homework throughout his or her school career, that student would gain the equivalent of two full years of additional academic instruction. This additional academic study time would occur with absolutely no cost to the taxpayer. Sadly, American teachers are not skilled in assigning proper homework assignments, and American students are currently not disposed to complete such assignments when they are given.

The virtual absence of out-of-class assignments for many students means that classroom instruction has taken on the passive character of watching a spectator sport or a television program. The student neither reflects upon nor practices what he or she has learned in today's class, nor does the student anticipate or prepare for tomorrow's lesson. This lack of an opportunity for the student to reflect on his or her learning promotes superficiality and prevents the acquisition of the information in long-term memory.

Teachers in other nations make far better use of homework as an instructional tool than do their American counterparts. Since the typical American thirteen-year-old spends thirty or more hours per week watching television, the prospect of productively using five or ten of those hours to complete homework assignments should be embraced all the more enthusiastically.

STRENGTHENING TEACHING IN AMERICA

Few differences among the six survey nations are as pronounced as the plight of the American teacher relative to his or her peers in Japan,

Germany, and Denmark. American teachers are often ill-prepared for their tasks, are assigned a crushing work load, and are accorded little respect by parents, students, or the general culture. They are too often poorly compensated relative to other occupations in their society, and they must endure the vagaries of an unstable school governance and funding system. Professionalizing the role of the American teacher is a major prerequisite to achieving educational reform.

1. Raise the academic requirements and rigor of teacher certification programs.

Raising the academic rigor of high school programs by requiring college entrance exams similar to those of other countries will improve the general academic preparation of students entering teacher training programs from high school. Currently, teaching candidates represent the academically weaker members of entering college classes, the type of student presently ill-served by undemanding coursework at the high school level. A more demanding high school program should lead to a dramatic improvement in the general knowledge and skill levels of future teachers.

Elementary teachers should continue to be educated in teacher education programs in four-year colleges and universities. The recruitment of better-prepared students from high school should make possible an increase in the rigor and extent of the academic component of these programs. A rigorous academic achievement test should be required of teacher education graduates as a part of their initial certification to teach. Certification should continue to be a state function.

Secondary teachers should be required to graduate with a major in the academic subject they will teach. Permanent certification regulations should require that a secondary teacher earn a master's degree in a field relating to his or her teaching assignment within the first five years of teaching. Secondary teachers would also be required to pass rigorous subject area tests as a condition for initial certification.

2. Teacher salaries should be established at the state level, with salary supplements paid to secondary teachers and to teachers in schools serving depressed socioeconomic areas.

Merit pay for teachers, a constantly recurring notion in the United States, was not a factor in the salary programs of any nation surveyed in this study. Instead, nations typically have either a single national or state salary schedule, or as in Japan, a national salary guideline that is closely followed by regional governments. England and Canada follow the

American practice of placing both elementary and secondary teachers on the same salary scale.

Denmark, Germany, and Japan pay somewhat higher salaries to teachers at the secondary school level. This practice should be adopted by individual American states. This differential would reflect the more difficult academic requirements proposed to obtain a secondary teaching certificate, as well as the competitive demands from industry for secondary trained persons, particularly in the fields of science and math. In countries having such differentiated salary schedules, secondary teachers earn from 10 to 20 percent more than equally experienced elementary colleagues. In Chapter 8, Table 8.2 illustrated that far fewer American secondary teachers considered themselves to be academically qualified to teach their subjects than is true of their counterparts in several other countries. Ensuring that students are provided with academically qualified teachers is a fundamental first step toward improving student achievement in academic subjects.

The law of supply and demand dictates that additional steps must be taken to recruit competent teachers to work in our inner cities and rural poverty areas. A supplement to the standard salary schedule of from 10 to 20 percent should also be provided to teachers who work in schools designated by the state as economically depressed. Failure to provide such incentives will guarantee that the existing shortage of qualified teachers for the students in most need of quality instruction will continue into the future.

Teacher salaries, in general, should be improved moderately, relative to salaries of other occupations in the United States. This should be achieved in conjunction with an extension of the school year by about twenty days. Some improvement in teacher salaries occurred in the second half of the 1980s, but these gains were eroded during the 1990–1992 recession. Teachers in many of our affluent suburbs are currently paid appropriately, while teachers in poorer localities and states continue to receive abysmal wages. Data provided in Chapter 8, Table 8.4, demonstrates that the compensation of American teachers within their own culture is the lowest among the survey countries. In countries with high-quality school systems, teachers are highly regarded and are compensated well, relative to other occupations within their nation.

3. Professionalize the responsibilities and the worklife of teachers.
Fulbright Exchange teachers working for one year in American schools are generally amazed at the heavy work load and the number of

noninstructional responsibilities required of teachers in America. Teachers in Japan, Germany, and Denmark typically devote about twelve to eighteen clock-hours per week providing direct instruction to students. Their American counterparts spend twenty to twenty-five hours providing direct instruction. In addition, American teachers spend several additional hours each week supervising students in the cafeteria, study halls, and playgrounds—activities that are not generally the responsibility of teachers in the countries cited above.

This dual burden on American teachers of more classroom instructional time, with heavier out-of-class supervisory responsibilities, ensures both high frustration and low job satisfaction. American teachers must prepare for approximately 50 percent more instructional hours within a work week, with about 50 percent less preparation time, than is common in many of the other survey countries. This unreasonably heavy work load creates a numbing exhaustion in the more conscientious teachers. It also produces a mindless superficiality in the teaching of those unwilling or unable to devote the hours and effort to excel under these draconian conditions. In the jargon of the day, the better teacher will *burn out*, while the less committed teacher will simply *chill out*. Neither response to these heavy work loads is in the best interest of the students.

Significant reductions in teacher work loads will require either more teachers, an expensive proposition, or increases in class sizes. Class sizes in most schools could be reasonably increased by three or four students, on the average, as a necessary trade-off to buy dramatic decreases in teacher work loads. Simply increasing class sizes by one student would, in most schools, provide sufficient resources to employ paraprofessionals to fully staff supervisory duties.

For example, a middle school of 800 students with forty teachers could add one student to each class, thus reducing its teaching force by two teachers, and saving $80,000—$100,000 in salary and fringe benefits costs. This amount of money could fund eight paraprofessionals, without medical benefits, at about $7.00 per hour for six hours each school day. These extra adults could provide sufficient supervision for students to cover bus duty, cafeteria duty, study hall duty, and similar responsibilities now performed by teachers. In addition, some time would still be available to provide teachers with much needed secretarial and clerical support.

A further increase in average class size of three students would allow each teacher to have an additional forty-five-minute planning period each day, with a corresponding decrease in one teaching period each day. These relatively modest changes in the size of class groups would dramatically improve the worklife and productivity of the typical secondary teacher. Consider a teacher who currently spends twenty clock-hours in direct instruction, five clock-hours on supervisory duties, and five clock-hours for lesson planning. Slightly larger class sizes would permit this teacher to devote about fifteen hours to direct classroom instruction, and fifteen hours to lesson planning, professional development, and participation in schoolwide policy development and school management. A teacher in such an environment could also be expected to be motivated to invest an additional ten to fifteen hours each week to out-of-school lesson preparation, evaluation of student work, test preparation and grading, etc.

Skeptics may argue that my recommendations for professionalizing the role of the teacher underestimates the baneful effects of increasing class sizes, even by three or four students. This proposal to marginally increase class size would be workable only if other previous recommendations relating to the elimination of some course offerings, the narrowing of the curriculum, and the more restrictive practices on ability grouping were also implemented.

Class sizes of twenty-five to thirty would not be a problem in a school environment where students were better prepared for their classes, where teachers had more time and energy to prepare for each lesson, where there were more frequent short breaks during the school day, and where students were motivated to meet rigorous academic standards needed to proceed to college or highly skilled vocational or technical careers.

In high schools particularly, the teacher resources now necessary to staff very small class sizes in the more esoteric courses, and to staff the typical small enrollments in classes at both extremes of the ability-grouping continuum, could be redeployed to maintain reasonable class sizes in the remaining class sections. The professionalization of the worklife of teachers outlined previously can be achieved with minimal impact on overall staffing costs.

4. Enhance teaching skills through regularly scheduled curriculum workshops, seminars on instructional techniques, and development of sample lessons at the school site.

The opening up of the daily schedule for teachers will provide both the time and the opportunity for collaborative staff development by teachers with their school colleagues. Strong peer coaching relationships can be fostered among teachers who teach the same subjects to similar students in a common work environment. Many such sessions could be planned and conducted by the teachers themselves, while others could be led by curriculum and instruction specialists employed by the regional branch of the state education department.

This approach would largely replace the existing practice of teachers taking a series of unrelated courses at a nearby college or university, providing neither a coherent body of knowledge and skills for the teacher, nor an opportunity for the teacher to work with his or her colleagues to resolve common problems and challenges. A large proportion of staff development funding in American public schools is devoted both to tuition reimbursement for teachers taking these graduate courses, and for salary schedule advancement based upon the accumulation of often unrelated graduate credits. Such resources should be redirected toward more productive staff development activities at the school site. This suggested model closely follows existing practice in Japanese schools.

5. Directly involve teachers in policy-level decisions by the local school's board of directors.

The recent thrust in the United States toward school site management has been a reality for some time in several of the nations included in this survey. Denmark and England, in particular, directly involve teachers in the governance of their schools. This approach provides a governance board with direct testimony regarding the challenges in the school, promotes teacher ownership of school problems and proposed solutions, and facilitates a collaborative relationship between parents and teachers.

The governing boards of individual schools might consist of five parent members elected by other parents, three teachers elected by the teaching staff, and the principal by virtue of his or her position. Assuming that teacher salaries would be set at the state levels, and that overall staffing parameters would be essentially determined by an equalized state funding system, serving on school boards would not constitute a conflict of interest on the part of teachers. Instead, teachers and parents would be in a position to collaborate closely to provide the best education possible for students, within the constraints of the state curriculum, testing programs, and financial allocations. Each school would have a large measure of freedom in selecting appropriate means to reach the goals and standards adopted at the state level.

DIVERSITY AND THE COMMON GOOD

A major finding from this survey is the surprising ease with which other countries resolved the issue of public support for religious and other private schools. Even Canada, with its traditional ethnic and religious divisions and animosities, has fashioned a satisfactory system for supporting private and religious schools. Denmark, Germany, and England also provide substantial support for nonpublic schools. Japan, the most ethnically homogeneous of the nations surveyed, provides significant public funding for the 25 percent of its students who attend private high schools.

The question of public support for nonpublic schools has long been an issue of bitter disagreement in the United States. The "establishment of religion" clause in the United States Constitution has been a barrier to direct public support for religious schools and has, through legal precedents, evolved into the concept of a wall of separation between church and state. For the purpose of this discussion, we will assume that the courts will be adopting a more accommodating attitude toward public support of religious and other private schools, and that this financial support will be found to be constitutional under certain carefully prescribed conditions.

If such public support is constitutionally permissible, the question will remain as to whether or not such assistance is socially, politically, and educationally desirable. Other nations in this study have answered that question in the affirmative. The school choice movement in the United States is clearly gaining political support. A state school voucher referendum may soon be on the ballot in California. The Wisconsin Supreme Court recently upheld the right of Milwaukee parents to choose private schools paid for with tax dollars. Legislatures in Ohio, Illinois, and Pennsylvania are seriously considering various school choice proposals.[3]

At present, the cultural wars being fought among various ethnic and religious subcultures in America are using the public schools as a battleground. The intensity of some of these battles is diverting school officials and teachers from their primary task, which is the intellectual development of their students. By attempting to satisfy an increasingly diverse clientele, while not giving offense to an increasingly strident minority, public schools are being deprived of the strong sense of mission and common purpose that is necessary to the success of any educational enterprise.

The time has come for America to "cross the Rubicon" on the issue of public support for nonpublic schools. The experience of other countries in this study indicates that such support for nonpublic schools does not destroy the public schools, but does provide an appropriate accommodation for parents to exercise their inherent rights regarding the education of their children. The successful resolution of this issue in the United States could promote a better-educated citizenry regardless of the type of school individual students choose to attend. Following are several recommendations for implementing a program of public support for nonpublic schools in the United States.

1. To receive public funds, nonpublic schools would need to comply with all substantive state requirements applicable to public schools.

Private schools receiving state aid would need to follow the state-approved curriculum, participate in state-mandated student assessments and school leaving examinations, and select textbooks from a state-approved list. Teachers and administrators would need to meet state certification requirements and would be compensated according to the state salary schedule. These schools would be periodically monitored by the same regional educational authorities performing a similar function for the public schools. Such schools would accept students on the same nondiscriminatory and nonselective basis as existing public schools.

2. State-aided nonpublic schools would be permitted to provide instruction in the areas of religious, ethical, and moral development, and would be permitted to establish school rules and operating procedures supportive of the overall mission and ethos of the school.

The nonpublic school might offer religious instruction several times each week, enforce strict discipline and dress code requirements, require public service as a graduation requirement, and impose regulations and practices that are difficult or impossible to arrange in a traditional public school setting. The public purpose would be served through the strict curriculum and monitoring requirements that such schools would need to meet.

The special interests of the parents would be accommodated through the extra religious or values classes and related school rules that the schools would require. Such schools would also have a school-level board of directors consisting of parents and teachers, as was recommended for the public schools.

3. Public funding for these nonpublic schools should be limited to 85 percent of the monies provided to operate public schools within the region.

Funding at the 85 percent level would be considered as full funding for the purely secular and public purposes that the school fulfills. The remaining 15 percent of the cost would be met by tuition or donations to support the purely private purposes of the school. The need for some tuition payments by parents would increase the commitment of people who chose to operate such schools, and would also prevent the proliferation of such private schools for frivolous or whimsical reasons. Student transportation would be the responsibility of the regional educational agency and would be provided on an equal basis to public and nonpublic students alike.

4. Private schools, receiving no public support, would continue as an educational option for parents.

A small minority of parents will not be satisfied with nonpublic schools that are required to meet the previously mentioned conditions to receive public funding. Under our Constitution, parents have the right to provide a private education to their students totally at their own expense. Schools that operate in a manner significantly different from the public school model, or which provide a level of program far beyond that available in a public setting, would continue to operate as they do today. The experience in other countries is that only from 3 to 7 percent of the students will enroll in such totally independent private schools.

The previous recommendations provide a model for accommodating the educational requirements of a diverse population, while at the same time ensuring that the public goal of an educated citizenry is achieved. The adoption of an earlier recommendation that each local public school be governed directly by parents would almost certainly increase the level of support for the public schools. Americans have a deeply ingrained commitment to, and affection for, their public schools. Empowering parents to be more directly involved in the governance of their schools would, for the great majority of parents, make the local public school their school of choice. Thus, on a national basis, perhaps 15 to 20 percent of the student body would choose to be enrolled at publicly supported nonpublic schools.

The opportunity to create such schools, however, would provide some choices to parents and would serve as a stimulus to public schools to be client oriented. Far from destroying public education, I believe that a carefully conceived program for publicly supporting different types of schools will strengthen public education in America. The experience of other countries indicates that the public sector has little to fear from offering parents some publicly funded options for educating their children.

ADMINISTRATIVE AND SUPPORT SERVICES

Only Canada, among the countries in this study, trains and utilizes building principals and district superintendents in a manner similar to the American model. Other nations could profit from an organized training program for their school principals, including training in the supervision and evaluation of teachers. The lack of periodic evaluation of teachers by their supervisors represents a weakness in the educational systems of other countries in this study. While teacher evaluation in the United States is not accorded the priority that it should have, American administrators are more active in this area than their counterparts in other nations.

Consistent with previous recommendations in this chapter, the following proposals are offered for the area of school administration.

1. The role of the school principal relative to the board of the individual school should be similar to the current role of a district superintendent relative to the district school board.

The building principal should be the chief executive officer of the board, carrying out all policy decisions and board resolutions on a day-to-day basis. The principal would also recommend policies and initiatives to the board that would advance instructional effectiveness in the school. The principal should be an employee of the regional educational authority, appointed by the regional superintendent following input from the board of the school. The principal should serve at a given school for a period of from three to five years, after which he or she may be renewed by the board, or the board could make a request of the regional superintendent that the principal be transferred.

2. Teachers should be employed by the regional educational authority and supervised and evaluated by the building principal.

The principal would have the formal responsibility to evaluate the teachers in his or her building and to resolve problems between teachers and parents. Ratings of a teacher by the principal that could lead to suspension or dismissal would be reviewable by the regional administration before any adverse action could be taken. This step would prevent a teacher's job from being jeopardized by a concerted effort of a few parents or by the principal. Subject area and instructional specialists would assist the principal in supervising the teaching staff and providing appropriate assistance as needed.

3. The role of the principal as an instructional leader should take priority over purely managerial functions.

Implementation of this recommendation will require that sufficient clerical and other support be made available to the principal so that he or she may function in a true executive capacity. The principal should be held accountable for the educational achievement of his or her students in a manner similar to the level of accountability expected of a CEO in a business organization.

4. The sharp role differentiation in American schools should be de-emphasized so that professional educators can perform several related functions.

American principals should be involved in classroom instruction for at least a few periods each week. Counseling functions can be performed by appropriately trained teachers on a part-time rather than a full-time basis. A school might employ two half-time assistant principals who each have a half-time teaching load, rather than one assistant principal with no teaching responsibilities. Uncertified individuals could be employed to manage the routine functions of the school that do not have a purely educational component.

The previous suggestions will eliminate many of the current barriers between teachers and other building professionals such as principals, assistant principals, and counselors. Also, a small cadre of part-time assistants will free the principal to exert the executive leadership duties necessary to promote a high-quality school program.

5. As the instructional leader of the school, the principal will have a pivotal role in allocating the instructional budget, developing teacher schedule assignments, and establishing goals for the school.

Each of these functions should be achieved through a collaborative working relationship with the teaching staff and the school board. The instructional budget will be developed through input from subject departments and the entire faculty. The teaching schedule for teachers will be devised by the principal after receiving recommendations from appropriate teacher committees and departments. Goals for the school should be collaboratively developed by the total faculty or by appropriate committees. The product of each of these processes should be presented to the board for comment, possible modification, and ultimate approval. This suggested process allows for greater involvement by parents and teachers than is currently the case in American schools. All of the previously mentioned activities should take place within the broad parameters established by the required curriculum and associated tests of student achievement.

BOLSTERING STUDENT MOTIVATION AND ACHIEVEMENT

The following recommendations represent positive steps that the schools can take to improve student motivation and achievement. The active cooperation of the students in bringing these recommendations to fruition is assumed. American rhetoric on school reform emphasizes the accountability of schools and of teachers. Rarely do we hear of the need for students and parents to be accountable.

In Japan, Germany, Denmark, and England the school leaving examinations emphasize the accountability of individual students for their own academic success. In America we often speak as though students were passive recipients of education, rather than active participants in the process. While teacher and school accountability are certainly worthy objectives, we need to accord students themselves a more central role in the quality equation.

1. More closely monitor student school attendance with appropriate sanctions and incentives.

Epidemic levels of student absenteeism are a critical problem in many American schools. Visiting Fulbright Exchange teachers expressed surprise at the number of student absences considered acceptable by American educators. Schools in the inner cities have daily absentee rates approaching 40 percent, a number that translates into an appalling total of seventy-two absences per year for the average student. A quality education under these circumstances is impossible.

Even suburban high schools in good neighborhoods may have a daily absentee rate of 10 percent, at least twice the number that can be reasonably attributed to student illness. Such an absentee rate represents eighteen days absence each year for the average student. Since highly academic students contribute little to this average, many other students miss between one and two full months of school each year. Continuity of instruction is difficult, if not impossible, under these conditions. It is axiomatic that a student is more likely to learn if he or she is physically present at school. Many students graduate from high school with an attendance record that would quickly get them fired in the real world.

Social workers and even truant officers need to be reinstated in school districts that have discontinued them because of budget constraints. A much closer alliance needs to be struck between the schools and the employers of students. By law, the number of hours of work for teenagers should be tightly governed, and should vary according to the academic and attendance records of the student.

Society needs to send a clear message that school attendance is a top priority. The establishment of rigorous achievement standards for high school graduation should help to induce better attendance patterns for many students. The dropout rate will undoubtedly increase under such a program for at least a time, but restoring some integrity to the meaning of a high school diploma will produce a long-term positive effect.

2. Student involvement with other students as a class or group should be emphasized and reinforced.

The individualistic course and scheduling patterns of American secondary school students serve to isolate, and even alienate them from the rest of the student body. Grading systems often pit one student against another in seeking the best grades, and in the absence of external student assessments, the teacher is viewed as the sole judge of the student's academic achievement.

Other nations, especially Japan, promote a collaborative learning effort among both elementary and secondary students. Students often are assigned to the same group of peers throughout the school day, often over a period of several years. Teachers and students work together to prepare students to pass the external exams or meet other goals common to all class members. The students perceive the teacher, at least partially, as a mentor or coach to help them prepare for the external evaluation. Students in such an environment feel a sense of group identity that serves to motivate them to attend school and contribute to the academic achievements of the group.

3. Dramatically expand after-school clubs, activities, and sports programs to involve the majority of students on a regular basis.

Foreign exchange teachers comment favorably on the extent of extracurricular activities sponsored by many secondary schools in the United States. Some other nations in this study, notably Denmark and Germany, have fewer such programs and rely on municipal organizations and private clubs to sponsor these activities. Other countries, such as Canada and England, follow the American practice of school-sponsored activities. Japanese secondary schools consider student participation in at least one after-school activity as an important part of the student's academic credentials.

American schools are rightly criticized for an overemphasis on major sports involving only a few students, with the majority of students being reduced to the role of spectators. A sports mania sometimes develops in individual schools that can overshadow the academic mission of the school. Aggressive steps should be taken to diminish the dominant role played by interscholastic sports in daily life of American secondary schools. This recommendation will be among the most difficult to implement because of the extent to which high school athletics are enshrined in the American culture.

Participation in intramural sports and other activities, on the other hand, should be emphasized and even required of all students, at least in the late elementary and early secondary years. Such programs should be operated by the schools and supervised by interested community members, on a paid basis, and managed by a few school staff members. The cost of such extensive programs would be minuscule in relation to the benefits derived for the students, their parents, and the general society.

A small fee could be charged to parents, on a sliding scale, reflecting ability to pay. Such comprehensive after-school programs would partially resolve the latchkey child problem, provide the students with wholesome physical and mental activities, and promote positive student attitudes toward the school and fellow students.

4. Seriously disruptive students should be removed from the regular school setting and assigned to regionally operated alternative schools.

Disruptive and even violent behavior by students is a greater problem in the United States than in the other countries surveyed. Fulbright teachers from several countries testified that the schools in their countries had few major discipline problems and seldom suspended or expelled students. The Fulbright teachers from abroad did not present their students as paragons of virtue. Rather, the importance placed on education, the stricter standards of achievement required of students, and the option to leave full-time schooling at an earlier age, may all contribute to a more ordered and purposeful atmosphere in these foreign schools than is the case in many American schools.

Restructuring American education according to the recommendations in this chapter would dramatically improve student discipline in American schools. There will always be a small number of students, however, whose uncontrollable behavior represents a serious disruption to the academic environment. There needs to be an absolute standard in every school which requires that no student will be permitted to interfere with his or her classmate's basic right to an education. It is these students who need to be temporarily or permanently removed from the regular school environment.

The principal of a school should be able to suspend a student for misbehavior for a period of up to ten days. Very serious infractions should be referred to the individual school's board of directors, composed of parents and teachers, to determine appropriate sanctions. Available sanctions should include the option of reassigning the student to a regional alternative school for up to one full school year. Such schools would have available the personnel and other resources required to ensure a high success rate in salvaging the education, and even the lives, of their troubled students. Individual schools that appear to rely too frequently on this option would be advised by the regional authorities regarding the establishment of a more successful disciplinary system.

School boards composed of parents and teachers would be likely to better balance the right of the entire student body to an education, against the right of the individual student to continue to attend the school. Currently, superintendents and district school board members, who are more removed from the actual problems, are more susceptible to political pressure from parents and pressure groups to minimize or ignore serious discipline problems.

The existence of various schools of choice within a region would also act as an incentive for schools to develop and implement effective models for maintaining effective school discipline. The existing monolithic public school system provides most parents with no alternatives if they are displeased with student discipline in the school their child attends.

5. *Training in morals, ethics, and civic responsibility should be a part of every child's school experience.*

The consensus on values that once made moral education a part of the public school experience no longer exists. Court challenges have not only removed prayer from the schools, but have made school teachers and officials wary of making firm statements on any moral issue, for fear that they will be accused of manipulating the minds of their students. Nevertheless, educators see a critical need for moral instruction, a need that they attempt to meet through values clarification activities that satisfy no one, but anger and offend a vocal minority.

The type of public support for nonpublic schools suggested earlier will allow individual school boards of parents and teachers to develop programs of moral training for students. Such programs will be a factor for parents to consider in choosing a school for their children. In most places the public schools will find that they have greater latitude in this area than previously, since parents will have a viable option to send their child to another school if they so choose. Depending on the desires of a school, this moral instruction could be provided in religion classes or in classes on moral education without a specifically religious content. The specific values of the school would be further expressed through school rules, activities, and traditions.

Schools in the other nations surveyed consider the moral development of students as an educational priority. The Japanese concept of ningen, referring to the development of full human beings, forms the basis for their one hour per week of required moral education at every grade level. The English act of daily worship and the provision for religious instruction in the school of Germany and Denmark, also speak to this commitment to moral instruction. Canada also has developed strategies for including moral and religious instruction in the educational experiences of its students.

A minority of American children still receive solid moral training from their family and church. Most children, however, do not have this advantage. Formal attention to the moral dimension will encourage these children to accept responsibility for themselves and others, and enable them to place a higher value on their own human dignity and on their potential to contribute positively to their world.

SOCIAL AND CULTURAL INFLUENCES ON SCHOOLS

A consistent theme in this book is that the social and cultural context in which schools function has a significant impact on school effectiveness. Although knowledgeable and detailed social and cultural commentary is clearly beyond the scope of this book, some general comments and recommendations seem appropriate. While the adoption of many of the previous recommendations will produce positive results, our nation will never educate its students properly until the related social and cultural issues are addressed.

A review of social and cultural supports for families and children provided in other countries in this survey leads to the following recommendations.

1. Modify the tax and social services systems to provide greater economic security for families with children.

American children are the most likely segment of our society to live in poverty conditions.[4] This sorry situation has many causes, including (1) the reality that parents of young children have not reached their peak earning years, (2) the burden of taxation to support social security falls heavily upon wage earners, (3) many children live in single parent households because of the number of children born out of wedlock and the high rates of divorce, (4) the scourge of drug and alcohol abuse among parents of many young children, and (5) high unemployment because of the low educational level of many young parents.

Other nations use their tax systems to provide greater tax deductions for families with children, or even child allowances to provide cash to parents to meet the physical needs of their children. This policy should be adopted in the United States. The National Commission on Children recommends that the current system of tax exemptions for children be replaced by a refundable tax credit, or children's allowance of $1,000 per child. The current value of a tax exemption for lower income families is only about $330 per year.[5] Children are our most valuable natural resource, and parents should be financially supported for the contribution to society that the rearing of children represents. The care and nurturing of children should not be purely a private family matter, but should be of concern to the entire society.

2. Health care should be available to every child, regardless of the employment or economic status of the parent.

Health care is provided to children in the United States if their parents are covered by a company health plan, or if the family is eligible for public assistance and Medicaid. Children of the working poor typically have no health care coverage. Many single mothers of young children take full-time jobs, not only for the dollar income, but to provide health care coverage for their children. This incentive to full-time employment has contributed to the problem of latchkey children and diverts the energies of the young parent away from his or her child to the workplace.

All other countries in this study have a health care system that is available to all of their citizens. Fulbright Exchange teachers in America are amazed at our apparent indifference to the fact that millions of our children do not have access to the most elementary health care services. The lack of basic health care for these children has a definite negative effect on their educational achievement.

3. Greater social stigma should be attached to antisocial and irresponsible behaviors such as sexual promiscuity, family desertion, and drug and alcohol abuse.

The impact of these behaviors on families and children needs to be emphasized by opinion leaders and the media. We must come to a national recognition that these individual lifestyle choices have devastating effects on innocent children. Furthermore, the damage done to these children will reflect itself in the dissolution and dysfunction of the larger society as these children reach adulthood. Educational, church, political, media, and other opinion leaders need to be far more outspoken on these issues than has been the case in recent years.

THE PUBLIC PULSE ON EDUCATIONAL REFORM

Is the American public ready to embrace some of the types of fundamental reforms recommended in this chapter? The annual Gallup Poll of the Public's Attitudes toward the Public Schools provides some surprisingly strong support for many of the changes recommended previously. A summary of this poll is published each September in *Phi Delta Kappan*. Although only a sample of the issues discussed in this book are addressed by this poll, the opinions expressed on these specific issues are instructive.

One question dealt with the sources of America's strength, and asked respondents to rate the importance of each listed item. Eighty-nine percent felt that having the best educational system in the world was very important, 59 percent considered it very important to have the most efficient industrial system in the world, while 41 percent considered building the strongest military force as very important.

The concept of public school report cards, to show the progress of schools toward meeting the national goals, was favored by 76 percent of the respondents. For the first time, a proposal to extend the school year by thirty days was approved by a slim majority (51 percent) of those polled. Support for this proposal has risen gradually over the years. Fifty-five percent of respondents favored tax-supported preschool programs for three- and four-year-olds operated by the public schools.

A national curriculum required for the local public schools was favored by 68 percent of those polled. Eighty-one percent favored requiring public schools to conform to national achievement standards and goals. Nationally standardized tests to measure academic achievement of students were favored by 77 percent of those polled. A voucher system, a government grant of money for each child's education to be used at any public or private school, was endorsed by 50 percent of those polled. Allowing parents and students to select which public school they would like to attend, regardless of where they live, was favored by 62 percent of respondents.

Sixty-two percent of those participating in the poll favored revoking driver's licenses from students under eighteen who drop out of school. Shifting decision-making power in local districts from the superintendent and school board to principals and teachers was favored by 76 percent of the respondents. The concept of a council of parents, teachers, and the principal as a decision-making mechanism was favored by 79 percent of those polled. Eighty percent of those polled favored equal funding for all students within a state, whether they reside in a wealthy or a poor district.[6] These opinions indicate clearly that the general public is far ahead of its political and educational leaders in its willingness to support fundamental change in its public school system.

EPILOGUE

Ten years of reform following the publication of *A Nation at Risk* in 1983 have produced little real improvement in our schools. In some respects our schools have continued to deteriorate. The theme of this book is that successful school reform will require nothing less than a cultural revolution. The educational and other needs of our children, an increasing percentage of whom are poor and from minority groups, must become our primary national concern in the post-Cold War era.

Many of the comments made by Fulbright Exchange teachers, as well as the educational practices that I found in the countries surveyed, seemed surprisingly familiar to me. This sense of familiarity was reinforced by a comment made by an American teacher present at the spring meeting of the Fulbright Exchange teachers held in Annapolis, Maryland. After listening to the foreign teachers comment on their experiences in the United States, the American teacher remarked that there was nothing said by the Fulbright Exchange teachers that he had not heard repeatedly over the years in the faculty room of his suburban Washington D.C. high school. Most of the comments of foreign teachers and the reports on successful practices from abroad cited in this book are not startling revelations. Many have already been recommended by educational theorists and practitioners and other interested Americans.

Every other country surveyed in this book acknowledges the importance of children and education by establishing national or regional performance standards, and by developing funding mechanisms that provide for a reasonably equitable distribution of available educational resources. The United States persists in following its nineteenth-century model of operating the schools as 15,000 separate fiefdoms. With the exception of initiatives in a few states, we do not have effective mechanisms for implementing and assessing meaningful performance standards, or for closing the growing gap in financial resources between our richest and poorest school districts.

By shortchanging its children, America is devouring its seed corn. Our educational practices belie our stated belief in educational equality and equity. Our failure to provide our poorest citizens with the educational means to rise above their impoverished state is a repudiation of our Judeo-Christian traditions. Finally, we imperil our social and economic self-interest by acquiescing to an undereducated and undermotivated work force in an increasingly competitive world economy. Our response to the needs of our children will prove to be the determining factor in the fate of our nation as we enter the twenty-first century.

REFERENCES

1. Westbury, I. 1992. "Comparing American and Japanese Achievement: Is the United States Really a Low Achiever?" *Educational Researcher,* 21(5):18−24.
2. Tucker, M. 1992. "Many U.S. Colleges Are Really Inefficient High Priced Secondary Schools," *The Chronicle of Higher Education* (June 5):A36.
3. Brown, M. C. 1992. "School Choice Is Gaining Momentum," *The Philadelphia Inquirer* (July 22):A15.
4. National Center for Education Statistics. 1991. *Digest of Education Statistics 1990.* Washington, DC: U.S. Government Printing Office, p. 27.

5. Binzen, P. 1992. "Low Wages Create Much of U.S. Poverty," *The Philadelphia Inquirer* (April 18): A9.

6. Elam, S. M., L. C. Rose, and A. M. Gallup. 1991. "The 23rd Annual Gallup Poll of the Public's Attitudes toward the Public Schools," *Phi Delta Kappan,* 73(1):41−56.

Anderson, R. S. 1981. "Japanese Education," *Comparative Educational Systems,* Itasca, IL: F.E. Peacock, Publishers, pp. 233 – 284.

Archer, E. G. and B. T. Peck. 1992. *The Teaching Profession in Europe.* Glasgow: Jordanhill College of Education.

August, R. L. 1992. "Education," in *Japan: A Country Study,* Washington, DC: Department of the Army.

Ball, S. A. 1987. *The Micro-Politics of the School.* London: Methuen and Co. Ltd.

Baron, G., ed. 1981. *The Politics of School Government.* Oxford: Pergamon Press Ltd.

Barro, S. M. and L. Suter. 1988. *International Comparisons of Teachers' Salaries: An Exploratory Study.* Washington, DC: National Center for Education Statistics.

Benjamin, G. R. and E. James. 1989. "Public and Private Schools and Educational Opportunity in Japan," *Japanese Schooling,* J. J. Shields, Jr., ed., University Park, PA: The Pennsylvania State University Press, pp. 152 – 162.

Binzen, P. 1992. "Low Wages Create Much of U.S. Poverty," *The Philadelphia Inquirer* (April 18):A9.

Bjerg, J. 1991. "Reflections on Danish Comprehensive Education, 1903 – 1990," *European Journal of Education,* 26(2):133 – 141.

Bolman, L. J. and T. E. Deal. 1984. *Modern Approaches to Understanding and Managing Organizations.* San Francisco, CA: Jossey-Bass, Inc.

Bracey, G. W. 1991. "Why Can't They Be Like We Were?" *Phi Delta Kappan,* 73(2):104 – 117.

Campbell, R. F., L. L. Cunningham, R. O. Nystrand, and M. D. Usdan. 1985. *The Organization and Control of American Schools.* Columbus, OH: Charles E. Merrill Publishing Co.

Cannell, J. 1987. *Nationally Normed Elementary Achievement Testing in America's Public Schools: How All Fifty States Are above the National Average.* Daniels, WV: Friends of Education.

Central Office of Information. 1992. *Britain 1992, an Official Handbook.* London: Central Office of Information.

Cremin, L. A. 1964. *The Transformation of the Schools.* New York, NY: Vintage Books.

Cusick, P. A. 1973. *Inside High School.* New York, NY: Holt, Rinehart and Winston, Inc.

Department of Education and Science. 1989. *Education in Denmark: Aspects of the Work of the Folkeskole.* London: Department of Education and Science.

Duke, B. C. 1989. "Variations on Democratic Education: Divergent Patterns in Japan and the United States," *Japanese Schooling,* J. J. Shields, Jr., ed., University Park, PA: The Pennsylvania State University Press, pp. 260−269.

Elam, S. M., L. C. Rose, and A. M. Gallup. 1991. "The 23rd Annual Gallup Poll of the Public's Attitudes toward the Public Schools," *Phi Delta Kappan,* 73(1): 41−56.

Elvin, L., ed. 1984. *The Educational Systems in the European Community: A Guide.* Brussels: The NFER-Nelson Publishing Company.

Feiler, B. S. 1991. *Learning To Bow.* New York, NY: Ticknor and Fields.

Department of Education and Science. 1982. *Federal Republic of Germany.* London: Department of Education and Science.

Filson, G. 1988. "Ontario Teachers' Deprofessionalism and Proletarianization," *Comparative Education Review,* 32(3):298−317.

Finn, C. E., Jr. 1991. *We Must Take Charge: Our Schools and Our Future.* New York, NY: The Free Press.

Fitzgerald, S. 1992. "On Health Care Issue, States Take Initiative," *The Philadelphia Inquirer,* July 26.

Fujita, H. 1989. "A Crisis of Legitimacy in Japanese Education," *Japanese Schooling,* J. J. Shields, Jr., ed., University Park, PA: The Pennsylvania State University Press, pp. 124−138.

Gammage, P. 1991. "Changing Ideologies and Provision in Western Canadian Primary Education," *Comparative Education,* 27(3):311−322.

Glenn, C. L. 1989. *Choice of Schools in Six Nations.* Washington, DC: U.S. Department of Education.

Halpin, D., S. Power, and J. Fitz. 1991. "Grant-Maintained Schools: Making a Difference without Being Really Different," *British Journal of Educational Studies,* 39(4):409−423.

Henderson, N. 1992. "Budget Blues in Canada's Health Care System," *Kiplinger's Personal Finance Magazine,* 46(3):102.

Hidenori, F. 1989. "A Crisis in Legitimacy in Japanese Education," *Japanese Schooling,* J. J. Shields, Jr., ed., University Park, PA: The Pennsylvania State University Press, pp. 124−138.

Hill, D., B. O. Smith, and J. Spinks. 1990. *Local Management of Schools.* London: Paul Chapman Publishing Ltd.

Hirsch, E. D., Jr. 1987. *Cultural Literacy.* Boston, MA: Houghton Mifflin Co.

Holmes, B., ed. 1983. *International Handbook of Education Systems.* Chichester: John Wiley & Sons.

Ignas, E. and R. J. Corsini, eds. 1981. *Comparative Educational Systems.* Itasca, IL: F.E. Peacock Publishers, Inc.

Imamura, A. E. 1989. "Interdependence of Family and Education: Reactions of Foreign Wives of Japanese to the School System," *Japanese Schooling,* J. J. Shields, Jr., ed., University Park, PA: The Pennsylvania State University Press, pp. 16−27.

Iwama, H. F. 1989. "Japan's Group Orientation in Secondary Schools," *Japanese Schooling,* J. J. Shields, Jr., ed., University Park, PA: The Pennsylvania State University Press, pp. 73−84.

Judge, H. G. 1988. "Cross-National Perceptions of Teachers," *Comparative Education Review,* 32(2):143−158.

Kidder, T. 1990. *Among Schoolchildren.* New York, NY: Avon Books.

Kobayashi, V. N. 1988. "Japan," *World Education Encyclopedia, Vol. 2*, G. Kurian, ed., New York, NY: Facts on File Publications, pp. 696−714.

Kurian, G. 1988. "Denmark," *World Education Encyclopedia, Vol. 1*, G. Kurian, ed., New York, NY: Facts on File Publications, pp. 310−320.

Kramer, R. 1991. *Ed School Follies*. New York, NY: The Free Press.

Langlois, D. E. and R. P. McAdams. 1992. *Performance Appraisal of School Management: Evaluating the Administrative Team*. Lancaster, PA: Technomic Publishing Company, Inc.

Leo, J. 1992. "The Sorry State of Teachers," *U. S. News and World Report* (April 27):28.

Lewis, C. C. 1989. "Cooperation and Control in Japanese Nursery Schools," *Japanese Schooling*, J. J. Shields, Jr., ed., University Park, PA: The Pennsylvania State University Press, pp. 28−44.

1992. *London Times Education Supplement* (May 29):12.

Maeroff, G. 1992. "Focusing on Urban Education in Britain," *Phi Delta Kappan*, 73(5):352−358.

McKormick, K. 1988. "Vocationalism and the Japanese Educational System," *Comparative Education*, 24(1):37−50.

Ministry of Education. 1988. *The Folkeskole*. Copenhagen, Denmark.

Ministry of Education. 1991. *Danish Secondary Education*. Copenhagen, Denmark.

Ministry of Education. 1991. *The Main Flows through the Education System*. Copenhagen, Denmark.

Ministry of Education. 1992. *General Upper Secondary Education in Denmark*. Copenhagen, Denmark.

Mitter, W. 1991. "Comprehensive Schools in Germany: Concepts, Developments, and Issues," *European Journal of Education*, 26(2):156−165.

Monikes, W. 1991. "The School System in the Federal Republic of Germany," *Education and Science*, 3/4(e).

Mullins, I. V. S., E. H. Owens, and G. W. Phillips. 1990. *America's Challenge: Accelerating Academic Achievement*. Princeton, NJ: Educational Testing Service.

Murname, R, J., J. D. Singer, J. B. Willet, J. J. Kample, and R. J. Olsen. 1991. *Who Will Teach?* Cambridge, MA: Harvard University Press.

Myers, D. 1992. "A Social Recession Grips the Nation," *The Philadelphia Inquirer*, May 22.

National Center for Education Statistics. 1991. *The Condition of Education, Vol. 1*. Washington, DC: U.S. Department of Education.

National Center for Education Statistics. 1991. *Digest of Education Statistics 1990*. Washington, DC: U.S. Government Printing Office.

Nelson, F. H. 1991. *International Comparisons of Public Spending on Education*. Washington, DC: American Federation of Teachers, AFL-CIO.

1992. "A National Curriculum: Seeking Fairness for All," *New York Times* (January 8): A1, B7.

Ota, H. 1989. "Political Teacher Unionism in Japan," *Japanese Schooling*, J. J. Shields, Jr., ed., University Park, PA: The Pennsylvania State University Press, pp. 243−259.

Pearce, J. 1986. "School Oversight in England and Wales," *European Journal of Education*, 21(4):331−344.

1992. *The Philadelphia Inquirer* (April 8):A3.

1992. *The Philadelphia Inquirer* (July 3):A12.

Poppleton, P. 1990. "The Survey Data," *Comparative Education*, 26(2/3):183−208.

Postlethwaite, T. N., ed. 1985. *The International Encyclopedia of Education, Vol. 5.* Oxford: Pergamon Press.

Postlethwaite, T. N., ed. 1988. *Encyclopedia of Comparative Education and National Systems of Education.* Oxford: Pergamon Press.

Purves, A. C., ed. 1989. *International Comparisons and Educational Reform.* Washington, DC: Association for Supervision and Curriculum Development.

Rasell, M. E. and L. Mishel. 1990. *Shortchanging Education: How U.S. Spending on Grades K−12 Lags behind Other Industrial Nations.* Washington, DC: Economic Policy Institute.

Roffel, J. A. and L. R. Groff. 1990. "Shedding Light on the Dark Side of Teacher Moonlighting," *Educational Evaluation and Policy Analysis*, 12(4):403−414.

Rubinger, R. 1989. "Continuity and Change in Mid-Nineteenth Century Japanese Education," *Japanese Schooling*, J. J. Shields, Jr., ed., University Park, PA: The Pennsylvania State University Press, pp. 224−233.

Rust, V. D. 1988. "West Germany," *World Education Encyclopedia, Vol. 1.* New York, NY: Facts on File Publications.

Sato, N. and M. W. McLaughlin. 1992. "Context Matters: Teaching in Japan and the United States," *Phi Delta Kappan*, 73(5):359−366.

Schieser, H. 1981. "West German Education," *Comparative Education Systems*, E. Ignas and R. Corsini, eds., Itasca, IL: F.E. Peacock Publishers, Inc., pp. 384−426.

Sergiovanni, T. J., M. Burlingame, F. S. Coombs, and P. W. Thurston. 1987. *Educational Governance and Administration.* Englewood Cliffs, NJ: Prentice-Hall Inc.

Shields, J. J., Jr., ed. 1989. *Japanese Schooling: Patterns of Socialization, Equality, and Political Control.* University Park, PA: The Pennsylvania State University Press.

Shimahara, N. K. 1989. "Japanese Education Reforms in the 1980s: A Political Commitment," *Japanese Schooling*, J. J. Shields, Jr., ed., University Park, PA: The Pennsylvania University Press, pp. 270−281.

Singleton, J. 1989. "Gambaru: A Japanese Cultural Theory of Learning," *Japanese Schooling*, J. J. Shields, Jr., ed., University Park, PA: The Pennsylvania State University Press, pp. 8−15.

Sizer, T. R. 1984. *Horace's Compromise: The Dilemma of the American High School.* Boston, MA: Houghton Mifflin Co.

Stevenson, H. A. and J. D. Wilson. 1988. *Quality in Canadian Education: A Critical Assessment.* London: The Falmer Press.

Stevenson, H. W. 1989. "The Asian Advantage: The Case of Mathematics," *Japanese Schooling*, J. J. Shields, Jr., ed., University Park, PA: The Pennsylvania State University Press, pp. 85−95.

Stigler, J. W. and H. W. Stevenson. 1991. "How Asian Teachers Polish Each Lesson to Perfection," *American Educator*, 15(1):12−20, 43−47.

Taylor, P. H. and R. Lowe. 1981. "English Education," *Comparative Education Systems*, E. Ignas and R. Corsini, eds., Itasca, IL: F.E. Peacock Publishers, Inc., pp. 135−184.

Tucker, M. 1992. "Many U.S. Colleges Are Really Inefficient High-Priced Secondary Schools," *The Chronicle of Higher Education* (June 5):A36.

United States Bureau of the Census. 1991. *Statistical Abstract of the United States, 111th Edition.* Washington, DC: U.S. Government Printing Office.

United States Department of Education. 1990. *Digest of Education Statistics.* Washington, DC: United States Department of Education.

United States Information Agency. 1989, 1990 and 1991. Reports submitted by American Fulbright Exchange Teachers in England (individual identities protected by Freedom of Information Act). Washington, DC: United States Information Agency.

United States Information Agency. 1991. *Your Year in Denmark.* Washington, DC: United States Information Agency.

United States Information Agency. 1991. *Your Year in Germany.* Washington, DC: United States Information Agency.

United States Information Agency. 1991. *Your Year in the United Kingdom.* Washington, DC: United States Information Agency.

1992. "Schools for Scandal," *U.S. News and World Report* (April 27):66−72.

Welsh, P. 1986. *Tales Out of School.* New York, NY: Viking Penguin Inc.

Westbury, I. 1992. "Comparing American and Japanese Achievement: Is the United States Really a Low Achiever?" *Educational Researcher,* 21(5):18−24.

White, M. 1987. *The Japanese Educational Challenge.* New York, NY: The Free Press.

1991. *Youth Indicators 1991: Trends in the Well-Being of American Youth.* Washington, DC: U.S. Department of Education.

RICHARD P. McADAMS spent twenty-five years actively involved in public education as a science teacher, high school principal, and fifteen years as superintendent of a local school district. He is coauthor of a book on administrative evaluation titled *Performance Appraisal of School Management*. He currently serves as the CEO for a health care provider company in Lancaster, Pennsylvania and also remains active as a freelance writer. He and his wife have three adult children, as well as their youngest child, a son, who resides with them in Kennett Square, Pennsylvania.